LEARN, TEACH...

SUCCEED...

With **REA's PRAXIS II® Middle School Mathematics (0069)** test prep, you'll be in a class all your own.

WE'D LIKE TO HEAR FROM YOU!

Visit **www.rea.com** to send us your comments
or email us at **info@rea.com**

PRAXIS II® MIDDLE SCHOOL MATHEMATICS (0069)

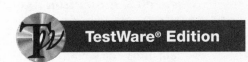

TestWare® Edition

Mel Friedman, M.S.

Lead Mathematics Editor

Research & Education Association

Research & Education Association

Visit our Educator Support Center: www.rea.com/teacher

Updates to the test and this book: www.rea.com/PRAXIS/math0069.htm

Research & Education Association
61 Ethel Road West
Piscataway, New Jersey 08854
E-mail: info@rea.com

PRAXIS II Middle School Mathematics (0069)
with TestWare® on CD-ROM, 2nd Edition

Copyright © 2012 by Research & Education Association, Inc.

Previous editions copyright © 2008, 2007 by Research & Education Association, Inc. All rights reserved. No part of this book may be reproduced in any form without permission of the publisher.

Printed in the United States of America

Library of Congress Control Number 2011929894

ISBN-13: 978-0-7386-0960-7
ISBN-10: 0-7386-0960-9

The competencies presented in this book were created and implemented by Educational Testing Service. For individual state requirements, consult your state education agency. For further information visit the PRAXIS website at www.ets. org. PRAXIS II® is a registered trademark of Educational Testing Service (ETS), and PRAXIS™ and The Praxis Series™ are trademarks of ETS, which does not endorse this product. All other trademarks cited in this publication are the property of their respective owners.

About Our Editor

Mel H. Friedman, M.S., is REA's Lead Mathematics Editor. He has a diversified background in mathematics and has developed test items for Educational Testing Service. His teaching experience is at both the high school and college levels.

About Research & Education Association

Founded in 1959, Research & Education Association is dedicated to publishing the finest and most effective educational materials—including software, study guides, and test preps—for students in middle school, high school, college, graduate school, and beyond.

REA's Test Preparation series includes books and software for all academic levels in almost all disciplines. Research & Education Association publishes test preps for students who have not yet entered high school, as well as for high school students preparing to enter college. Students from countries around the world seeking to attend college in the United States will find the assistance they need in REA's publications. For college students seeking advanced degrees, REA publishes test preps for many major graduate school admission examinations in a wide variety of disciplines, including engineering, law, and medicine. Students at every level, in every field, with every ambition can find what they are looking for among REA's publications.

REA's practice tests are always based upon the most recently administered exams and include every type of question that you can expect on the actual exams.

Today, REA's wide-ranging catalog is a leading resource for teachers, students, and professionals.

We invite you to visit us at *www.rea.com* to find out how "REA is making the world smarter."

Acknowledgments

We would like to thank Pam Weston, Vice President, Publishing, for setting the quality standards for production integrity and managing the publication to completion; Larry Kling, Vice President, Editorial, for his editorial direction; John Cording, Vice President, Technology, for coordinating the design development of REA's TestWare®; Kathleen Casey, Senior Editor, for project management and preflight editorial review; Christine Saul, Senior Graphic Artist, for cover design; Heena Patel, Technology Project Manager, for software testing and development; and Maureen Mulligan, Graphic Artist, for post-production file mapping.

We also gratefully acknowledge the team at Transcend Creative Services (TCS) for typesetting the manuscript.

CONTENTS

CHAPTER 7
MATHEMATICAL REASONING, PROOF, CONNECTIONS   183

PRACTICE TEST 1   195

PRACTICE TEST 2   217

PRACTICE TEST 3   241

ANSWER SHEETS   265

INSTALLING REA's TestWare®   280

Introduction: Passing the Test

About This Book and TestWare®

REA's *Praxis II Middle School Mathematics (0069)* test is a comprehensive guide designed to assist you in preparing for this required test for teachers of middle school mathematics. To enhance your chances of success in this important step toward your career as a mathematics teacher, this test guide:

- presents an accurate and complete overview of the Praxis II

- identifies all of the important information and its representation on the test

- provides a comprehensive review of every content category on the test

- provides three full-length practice tests

- suggests tips and strategies for successfully completing standardized tests

- replicates the format of the official test, including levels of difficulty

- supplies the correct answer and detailed explanations for each question on the practice tests, which enable you to identify correct answers and understand why they are correct and, just as important, why the other answers are incorrect.

This guide is the result of studying many resources. The editors considered the most recent test administrations and professional standards. They also researched information from the Educational Testing Service, professional journals, textbooks, and educators. This guide includes the best test preparation materials based on the latest information available.

Practice Tests 1 and 2 are included in two formats: in printed form in this book and in TestWare® format on the enclosed CD. We recommend that you begin your preparation by first taking the computerized version of your test. The software provides the added benefits of enforced time conditions and instantaneous, accurate scoring, making it easier to pinpoint your strengths and weaknesses.

About the Test

The Praxis II Middle School Mathematics test is designed to assess the mathematical knowledge and competencies for a beginning middle school teacher. Below are the content and process categories used as the basis for this test, as well as the approximate percentage of the total test that each category occupies. These categories represent the knowledge that teams of teachers, subject area specialists, and district-level educators have determined to be important for begin-

Praxis II: Middle School Mathematics (0069)			
	Content Categories	**Approx # questions**	**Percentage**
	PART A		
I.	Arithmetic and Basic Algebra	12	20%
II.	Geometry and Measurement	10	17%
III.	Functions and the Graphs	8	13%
IV.	Data, Probability, and Statistical Concepts; Discrete Mathematics	10	17%
	PART B		
	Constructed Response		
V.	Problem-Solving Exercises	3	33%
	Process Categories	**Distributed Across Content Categories**	
	Mathematical Problem Solving Mathematical Reasoning and Proof Mathematical Connections Mathematical Representation Use of Technology	Distributed across all of the Content Categories	

ning teachers. This book contains a thorough review of all these categories, as well as the specific skills that demonstrate each area.

Who Administers the Test?

All the Praxis II tests are administered by the Educational Testing Service (www.ets.org/Praxis).

Can I Retake the Test?

Most states and institutions allow candidates who do not pass the Praxis II to retake it as often as necessary until a passing score is achieved. In these cases, candidates must reregister each time they take a test. However, please check with your state or testing institution for their specific requirements. Candidates who have passed a Praxis II test have met that part of the testing requirement for certification and, therefore, are not eligible to retake the test again.

When Should the Praxis II Be Taken?

Individual states, institutions, and associations set their own requirements and passing scores for the Praxis. Some states specify the passing of additional or different tests. Check with your state agency for details.

ETS offers the Praxis II Middle School Mathematics (0069) test six times a year at a number of locations across the nation. The usual testing day is Saturday, but examinees may request an administration on an alternate day if there is a conflict, such as a religious obligation.

To receive information on upcoming administrations of the Praxis II, consult the Praxis II Information Bulletin (found at www.ets.org/Media/Tests/PRAXIS/pdf/01361. pdf), or contact the ETS at:

Educational Testing Service
Teaching and Learning Division
P.O. Box 6051
Princeton, NJ 08541-6051
Phone: (609) 771-7395
Website: www.ets.org/praxis
E-mail: www.ets.org./praxis/contact/email_praxis

Is There a Registration Fee?

To take the Praxis II Middle School Mathematics test there is a fee. A complete summary of the registration fees can be found at the website or phone number listed above.

Calculators

Examinees are allowed to use a four-function, scientific, or graphing calculator during the Praxis II Middle School Mathematics examination, although a calculator is not required. On test day, bring your calculator to the testing site as one will not be provided. Please see the ETS website (www.ets.org/Praxis/prxcalc.html) for further details on the types of calculating devices that are prohibited.

How to Use This Book and TestWare®

How Do I Begin Studying?

Take a moment to review the organization of this test preparation guide.

1. To best utilize your study time, follow our Praxis II Independent Study Schedule. The schedule is based on a eight-week program, but can be condensed to four weeks if necessary.

2. Take the first practice test on CD-ROM, score it according to the directions, then review the explanations to your answers carefully, studying the areas that your scores indicate need further review.

3. Review the format of the Praxis II.

4. Review the test-taking advice and suggestions presented later in this section.

5. Pay attention to the information about content and the objectives of the test.

6. Spend time reviewing topics that stand out as needing more study.

7. Take the second practice test on CD-ROM and follow the same procedure as #2 above.

8. Take the third practice test in this book.

9. Follow the suggestions at the end of this section for the day before and the day of the test.

Note: Graphic calculators can be brought for the test. See the ETS website for details on what to bring to the test site, including which brands and models of calculators are acceptable.

When Should I Start Studying?

It is never too early to start studying for the Praxis II. The earlier you begin, the more time you will have to sharpen your skills. Do not procrastinate!

An eight-week study schedule is provided at the end of this section to assist you in preparing for the test. This schedule can be adjusted to meet your unique needs. If your test date is only four weeks away, you can halve the time allotted to each section, but keep in mind that this is not the most effective way to study. If you have several months before your test date, you may wish to extend the time allotted to each section. Remember, the more time you spend studying, the better your chances of achieving your aim—a passing score on the Praxis II.

Studying for the Test

It is very important for you to choose the time and place for studying that works best for you. Some students set aside a certain number of hours every morning to study, while some choose the night time, before going to sleep, and others study during the day, while waiting in line, or even while eating lunch. Choose a time when you can concentrate and your study will be most effective. Be consistent and use your time wisely. Work out a study routine and stick to it.

When you take the practice tests, simulate the conditions of the actual test as closely as possible. Turn your television and radio off and sit down at a quiet table with your calculator, if you will be using one. As you complete each practice test, score it and thoroughly review the explanations to the questions you answered incorrectly. Do not, however, review too much at any one time. Concentrate on one problem area at a time by examining the question and explanation, and by studying our review until you are confident that you have mastered the material. Keep track of your scores to discover general weaknesses in particular sections and to gauge your progress. Give extra attention to the review sections that cover your areas of difficulty, as this will build your skills in those areas.

Format of the Praxis II

The Praxis II Middle School Mathematics test is composed of five main content categories with both multiple-choice and constructed-response questions. The test utilizes five process categories as charted on page two.

Part A of the content categories contains 40 multiple-choice questions, and each contains four response options, A through D. Part B of the content categories is composed of three problem-solving exercises. These are three equally weighted constructed-response questions whose focus is distributed across the four content categories. The content categories were designed to measure the ability to integrate knowledge of mathematics and may involve more than one competency, as well as competencies from more than one content area.

Entry-level middle school mathematics teachers must demonstrate that they have an understanding of the various ways in which math content knowledge is acquired and used. The process categories assess this ability and one or more may be applied to any of the content topics in the test.

You are given two hours to complete the test, so be aware of the amount of time you are spending on each question. Using the practice tests will help you prepare to pace your time evenly, efficiently, and productively.

About the Review Sections

The reviews in this book are designed to help you sharpen the basic skills needed to approach the Praxis II, as well as provide strategies for attacking the questions.

Each teaching category is examined in a separate chapter. The skills required for all categories are extensively discussed to optimize your understanding of what this Praxis II test covers.

Your schooling has taught you most of what you need to succeed on the test. Our review is designed to help you fit the information you have acquired into specific content and process categories. Reviewing your class notes and textbooks together with our reviews will give you an excellent springboard for passing the Praxis II.

Scoring the Test

On the multiple-choice questions, examinees are not penalized for wrong answers. A question answered correctly is worth one raw point, and your total raw score is the number of questions answered correctly on the full test.

How many correctly answered questions equal a passing grade? According to ETS, there is no way to predict this. There are several editions of each Praxis test. and each edition contains different questions. The questions on one edition may be slightly more difficult (or easier) than those on another edition. To make all editions of a test comparable, the conversion tables adjust for difficulty among editions. There is no way to predict which edition of the test you will take next.

Constructed-response questions are scored by educational professionals in the appropriate content area. The Praxis Series constructed-response tests do not all use the same scoring procedure. There are two scoring models used. One requires that two scorers rate your response to each question independently. If they disagree by more than a specified amount, a third scorer rates your response. The second scoring model requires that each constructed-response item be rated independently by a different scorer. Under no circumstances does your total score depend entirely on one individual scorer.

Also, on some constructed-response tests, the ratings assigned by the scorers are simply added together to determine your total raw score. On others, the ratings are first multiplied by scoring weights, which can be different for different questions, and the weighted ratings are added to determine your total raw score. The raw point score is then converted to a scaled score that adjusts for the difficulty of that particular edition of the test.

Passing scores vary from state to state, and test-takers should check with their state board of education for their state's requirements.

To gage how well you do on our practice tests, if you score 70% or above, you have passed.

Score Results

Your test scores will be mailed approximately four weeks after test day to those who you designated to receive them. There is a fee for each additional score report requested.

Test-Taking Tips

Although you may not be familiar with tests like the Praxis II, this book will help acquaint you with this type of test and help alleviate your test-taking anxieties. Listed below are ways to help you become accustomed to the Praxis II, some of which may be applied to other tests as well.

Tip 1. Become comfortable with the format of the Praxis II. When you are practicing, stay calm and pace yourself. After simulating the test only once, you will boost your chances of doing well, and you will be able to sit down for the actual test with much more confidence.

Tip 2. Read all of the possible answers. Just because you think you have found the correct response, do not automatically assume that it is the best answer. Read through each choice to be sure that you are not making a mistake by jumping to conclusions.

Tip 3. Use the process of elimination. Go through each answer to a question and eliminate as many of the answer choices as possible. By eliminating two answer choices, you have given yourself a better chance of getting the item correct since there will only be two choices left from which to make your guess. Answer all questions you can; you are not penalized for wrong answers, but you are rewarded for correct ones.

Tip 4. Place a question mark in your answer booklet next to answers you guessed, then recheck them later if you have time.

Tip 5. Work quickly and steadily. You will have two hours to complete the test, so work quickly and steadily to avoid focusing on any one problem too long. Taking the practice tests in this book will help you learn to budget your precious time.

Tip 6. Learn the directions and format of the test. This will not only save time, but will also help you avoid anxiety (and the mistakes caused by getting anxious).

Tip 7. Be sure that the answer circle you are marking corresponds to the number of the question in the test booklet. Since the test is multiple-choice, it is graded by machine, and marking one answer in the wrong circle can throw off your answer key and your score. Be extremely careful.

The Day of the Test

Before the Test

On the day of the test, make sure to dress comfortably, so that you are not distracted by being too hot or too cold while taking the test. Plan to arrive at the test center early. This will allow you to collect your thoughts and relax before the test, and will also spare you the anguish that comes with being late.

You should check your Praxis II information bulletin or registration information to find out what time to arrive at the testing center.

Before you leave for the test center, make sure that you have your admission ticket and two forms of identification, one of which must contain a recent photograph, your name, and signature (i.e., driver's license). You will not be admitted to the test center if you do not have proper identification.

You must bring several sharpened No. 2 pencils with erasers and an approved graphic calculator (see above) as none will be provided at the test center.

If you would like, you may wear a watch to the test center. However, you may not wear one that makes noise, because it may disturb the other test takers. Dictionaries, textbooks, notebooks, briefcases, laptop computers, or packages will not be permitted. Drinking, smoking, and eating are prohibited.

During the Test

The Praxis II is given in one sitting with no breaks. Procedures will be followed to maintain test security. Once you enter the test center, follow all of the rules and instructions given by the test supervisor. If you do not, you risk being dismissed from the test and having your scores cancelled.

When all of the materials have been distributed, the test instructor will give you directions for filling out your answer sheet. Fill out this sheet carefully since this information will be printed on your score report.

Once the test begins, mark only one answer per question, completely erase unwanted answers and marks, and fill in answers darkly and neatly.

After the Test

When you finish your test, hand in your materials and you will be dismissed. Then, go home and relax—you deserve it!

Study Schedule

The following study schedule allows for thorough preparation for the Praxis II Middle School Mathematics test. The course of study is eight weeks, but you can condense or expand the timeline to suit your personal schedule. It is vital that you adhere to a structured plan and set aside ample time each day to study. The more time you devote to studying, the more prepared and confident you will be on the day of the test.

Week	Activity
Week 1	Take the first practice test on CD-ROM as a diagnostic test. The score will indicate your strengths and weaknesses. Carefully review the explanations for the items you answered incorrectly.
Week 2	Study REA's review material and answer the drill questions. Highlight key terms and information. Take notes as you review the book's sections, putting new terms and information on note cards. Taking these notes will aid retention.
Weeks 3 and 4	Review your references, reread all your notes, refresh your understanding of the test's content and skills, review your college textbooks, and read over class notes you've previously taken. This is also the time to consider any other supplementary materials that your education instructor or the ETS provide. See "Test at a Glance" (TAAG) on the ETS website at *www.ets.org/praxis* under the Praxis II Download tab.
Week 5	Condense your notes and findings. You should have a structured outline with specific facts. You may want to use more index cards to help you memorize important information. Test yourself using the index cards.
Week 6	Take the second practice test on CD-ROM. Review the explanations for the items you answered incorrectly.
Week 7	Study any areas you consider to be your weaknesses by using your test results, study materials, references, and notes.
Week 8	Take your third practice test in this book. Review the explanations for the items you answered incorrectly. Review REA's advice, tips, and strategies for approaching test-day and taking the official test. If time allows, retake Practice Tests 1 and 2 in this book.

Arithmetic and Basic Algebra

Integers and Real Numbers

Most of the numbers used in algebra belong to a set called the **real numbers** or **reals**. This set can be represented graphically by the real number line.

Given the number line below, we arbitrarily fix a point and label it with the number 0. In a similar manner, we can label any point on the line with one of the real numbers, depending on its position relative to 0. Numbers to the right of zero are positive, while those to the left are negative. Value increases from left to right, so that if a is to the right of b, it is said to be greater than b.

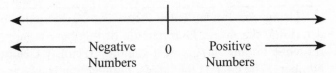

If we now divide the number line into equal segments, we can label the points on this line with real numbers. For example, the point 2 lengths to the left of zero is -2, while the point 3 lengths to the right of zero

is $+3$ (the $+$ sign is usually assumed, so $+3$ is written simply as 3). The number line now looks like this:

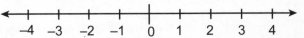

These boundary points represent the subset of the reals known as the **integers**. The set of integers is made up of both the positive and negative whole numbers: $\{\ldots -4, -3, -2, -1, 0, 1, 2, 3, 4, \ldots\}$. Some subsets of integers are:

Natural Numbers or Positive Numbers—the set of integers starting with 1 and increasing: $N = \{1, 2, 3, 4, \ldots\}$.

Whole Numbers—the set of integers starting with 0 and increasing: $W = \{0, 1, 2, 3, \ldots\}$.

Negative Numbers—the set of integers starting with -1 and decreasing: $Z = \{-1, -2, -3\ldots\}$.

Prime Numbers—the set of positive integers greater than 1 that are divisible only by 1 and themselves: $\{2, 3, 5, 7, 11, \ldots\}$,

Even Integers—the set of integers divisible by 2: $\{\ldots, -4, -2, 0, 2, 4, 6, \ldots\}$.

Odd Integers—the set of integers not divisible by 2: $\{\ldots, -3, -1, 1, 3, 5, 7, \ldots\}$.

Prime and Composite Numbers

A prime number is a whole number that has exactly two factors, 1 and itself. The numbers 7, 11, 17, and 23 are examples of prime numbers. The number 2 is the only even prime.

Composite numbers are whole numbers that have more than two different factors.

The number 6 is a composite number because its factors are 1, 2, 3, and 6. The number 20 is also a composite number because its factors are 1, 2, 4, 5, 10, and 20.

The number 1 is neither prime nor composite.

The Fundamental Theorem of Arithmetic

The fundamental theorem of arithmetic states that any number can be subdivided uniquely (except for order) into a product of prime numbers. The following examples illustrate a method by which this prime factorization can be done.

PROBLEM

Write the prime factorization of 24.

SOLUTION

We begin with two numbers whose product is 24, such as 4 and 6. So, $24 = 4 \times 6$. Then, because $4 = 2 \times 2$ and $6 = 2 \times 3$, we can write $24 = 2 \times 2 \times 2 \times 3$. The answer is more commonly written as $2^3 \times 3$.

PROBLEM

Write the prime factorization of 60.

SOLUTION

Select two numbers whose product is 60. Let's choose 6 and 10. Then $60 = 6 \times 10$. Because $6 = 2 \times 3$ and $10 = 2 \times 5$, we can express 60 as $2 \times 3 \times 2 \times 5$, which is equivalent to $2^2 \times 3 \times 5$.

We usually write the prime factorization in ascending order of the bases with the associated exponents. Also, there is usually more than one way to write a number as a product of two factors. The final prime factorization is always unique. We could have written $60 = 15 \times 4 = 3 \times 5 \times 2 \times 2$. The final answer is still $2^2 \times 3 \times 5$.

PROBLEM

Write the prime factorization of 45.

SOLUTION

$45 = 5 \times 9 = 5 \times 3 \times 3 = 3^2 \times 5$.

PROBLEM

Write the prime factorization of 100.

SOLUTION

$100 = 10 \times 10 = 2 \times 5 \times 2 \times 5 = 2^2 \times 5^2$.

Greatest Common Factor

Using the fundamental theorem of arithmetic to determine the prime factorization of numbers is helpful when finding the greatest common factor (GCF) of numbers. The GCF is the largest number that is a factor of two or more whole numbers.

PROBLEM

Find the greatest common factor for 16 and 40.

SOLUTION

First, write each number in prime factorization form: $16 = 2 \times 8 = 2 \times 2 \times 2 \times 2 = 2^4$ and $40 = 4 \times 10 = 2 \times 2 \times 2 \times 5 = 2^3 \times 5$. Our next step is to determine the largest factor in both numbers. This is done by identifying common bases and using the lowest exponent present for each base. The only common base for 16 and 40 is 2, for which the lowest exponent is 3. So the GCF is $2^3 = 8$.

PROBLEM

Find the greatest common factor for 90 and 72.

SOLUTION

$90 = 2 \times 3 \times 3 \times 5 = 2 \times 3^2 \times 5$ and $72 = 2 \times 2 \times 2 \times 3 \times 3 = 2^3 \times 3^2$. The common bases are 2 and 3. For the base 2, the lowest exponent is 1. For the base 3, both numbers contain 3^2, so the lowest exponent is 2. Therefore, the GCF is $2 \times 3^2 = 18$.

NOTE:

> If there is no common base for the given numbers, the GCF becomes 1. As an example, $9 = 3^2$ and $35 = 5 \times 7$. So the GCF of 9 and 35 must be 1.

Least Common Multiple

Sometimes it is necessary to find the least common multiple (LCM) of numbers.

The LCM is the smallest number that is a multiple of a given set of numbers. There are three steps involved in finding the LCM of two numbers.

PROBLEM

Find the least common multiple for 18 and 20.

SOLUTION

First, find the prime factorization of each number: $18 = 2 \times 3^2$ and $20 = 2^2 \times 5$.

Second, identify each different base in these numbers, including bases that appear in both numbers. The bases are 2, 3, and 5.

Third, use each base with the highest exponent found in either number. For both bases 2 and 3, the highest exponent present is 2. For the base 5, the highest exponent is 1. Therefore, the LCM is $2^2 \times 3^2 \times 5 = 180$.

PROBLEM

Find the least common multiple of 12 and 105.

SOLUTION

$12 = 2^2 \times 3$ and $105 = 3 \times 5 \times 7$. The four different bases are 2, 3, 5, and 7. For each of 3, 5, and 7, the highest exponent is 1. For the base 2, the highest (and only) exponent is 2. Therefore, the LCM is $2^2 \times 3 \times 5 \times 7 = 420$.

PROBLEM

Find the LCM of 11, 28, and 80.

SOLUTION

The number 11 is already in prime factorization form; $28 = 2^2 \times 7$ and $80 = 2^4 \times 5$. The four different bases are 2, 5, 7, and 11. Each of the bases 5, 7, and 11 occurs only once. The highest exponent for the base 2 is 4. Therefore, the LCM $= 2^4 \times 5 \times 7 \times 11 = 6160$.

NOTE:

> If there is no common base for the given numbers, the LCM is simply the product of the numbers. As an example, the LCM for the numbers 20 and 21 is $(20)(21) = 420$.

Divisibility Rules

In many types of problems, such as finding the prime factorization of a number, it is helpful to know whether some numbers are divisible by other numbers. The following are basic divisibility rules:

1. A number is divisible by 2 if the last digit is even.
2. A number is divisible by 3 if the sum of the digits in the number is divisible by 3.
3. A number is divisible by 4 if the number made by the last two digits is divisible by 4.
4. A number is divisible by 5 if the number ends in 0 or 5.
5. A number is divisible by 6 if the number is divisible by 2 and 3.
6. A number is divisible by 9 if the sum of the digits in the number is divisible by 9.
7. A number is divisible by 10 if the last digit is 0.

PROBLEM

Given the five-digit number 43,10_, how many different units digits are possible in order for this number to be divisible by 3?

SOLUTION

The sum of the digits shown is 8. We can add any digit, as long as the final sum is divisible by 3. There are three acceptable digits, namely, 1, 4, and 7. Each of the numbers 43,101, and 43,104, and 43,107 are divisible by 3.

PROBLEM

If the six-digit number 112,_86 is divisible by both 6 and 9, what digit(s) is(are) possible for the hundreds place?

SOLUTION

Divisibility by 6 implies divisibility by 2 and by 3. Because the divisibility rule for 9 already includes the divisibility rule for 3, we need an even number for which the sum of its digits is 9. The given number is already even, and the sum of the digits shown is 18. If we replace the placeholder for the hundreds digit by either a 0 or 9, the sum of the digits will be either 18 or 27. Note that the numbers 112,086 and 112,986 are divisible by both 6 and 9.

PROBLEM

Given the five-digit number 32,5_0, how many different tens digits are possible for this number to be divisible by 8?

SOLUTION

Because the rightmost three digits must represent a number that is divisible by 8, there are only two choices for the tens digit, namely, 2 or 6. Note that 32,520 and 32,560 are each divisible by 8.

Rational and Irrational Numbers

A rational number is any number that can be written in the form $\frac{a}{b}$ where a is any integer and b is any integer except zero. An irrational number is a number that cannot be written as a simple fraction. It is an infinite and non-repeating decimal.

The tree diagram below shows you the relationships between the different types of numbers.

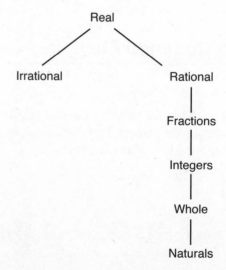

EXAMPLE

Here are some examples of some rational numbers.

2   3   5   10   32   −2   −4   −18   −25

$\frac{1}{4}$ $\frac{1}{2}$ $\frac{2}{3}$ $-\frac{1}{4}$ $\frac{4}{7}$ $-\frac{10}{55}$ $\frac{21}{9}$ $\frac{101}{635}$

EXAMPLE

Here are some examples of irrational numbers.

π — approximately equal to 3.14159

e — approximately equal to 2.71828

$\sqrt{2}$ — approximately equal to 1.41421

$\sqrt{3}$ — approximately equal to 1.73205

$\sqrt{5}$ — approximately equal to 2.23607

PROBLEM

List the numbers shown below from least to greatest.

$\frac{1}{3}$, $\sqrt{3}$,   3,   0.3

SOLUTION

$\frac{1}{3} \approx 0.33333$

$\sqrt{3} \approx 1.73205$

Therefore, the numbers from least to greatest are:

$0.3, \frac{1}{3}, \sqrt{3}, 3$

Absolute Value

The **absolute value** of a number is represented by two vertical lines around the number, and is equal to the given number, regardless of sign.

The absolute value of a real number A is defined as follows:

$$|A| = \begin{cases} A \text{ if } A \geq 0 \\ -A \text{ if } A < 0 \end{cases}$$

EXAMPLE

$|5| = 5, |-8| = -(-8) = 8.$

Absolute values follow the given rules:

(A) $|-A| = |A|$

(B) $|A| \geq 0$, equality holding only if $A = 0$

(C) $\left|\dfrac{A}{B}\right| = \dfrac{|A|}{|B|}, B \neq 0$

(D) $|AB| = |A| \times |B|$

(E) $|A|^2 = A^2$

Absolute value can also be expressed on the real number line as the distance of the point represented by the real number from the point labeled 0.

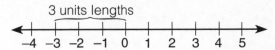

So $|-3| = 3$ because - 3 is 3 units to the left of 0.

PROBLEM

Classify each of the following statements as true or false. If it is false, explain why.

(1) $|-120| > 1$

(2) $|4 - 12| = |4| - |12|$

(3) $|4 - 9| = 9 - 4$

(4) $|12 - 3| = 12 - 3$

(5) $|-12a| = 12|a|$

SOLUTION

(1) True

(2) False, $|4 - 12| = |4| - |12|$

$|-8| = 4 - 12$

$8 \neq -8$

In general, $|a + b| \neq |a| + |b|$

(3) True

(4) True

(5) True

PROBLEM

Calculate the value of each if the following expressions:

(1) $||2 - 5| + 6 - 14|$

(2) $\dfrac{11}{6} + \left| -\dfrac{5}{16} \right|$

SOLUTION

Before solving this problem, one must remember the order of operations: parenthesis, multiplication and division, addition and subtraction.

(1) $||-3| + 6 - 14| = |3 + 6 - 14| = |9 - 14|$

$= |-5| = 5$

(2) $\dfrac{11}{6} + \left| -\dfrac{5}{16} \right| = \dfrac{11}{6} + \dfrac{5}{16} = \dfrac{88}{48} + \dfrac{15}{48} = \dfrac{103}{48}$

PROBLEM

Using the number line below, graph the solution to $-5 - (-3)$.

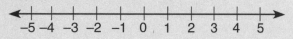

SOLUTION

Step 1 is to graph point -5 on the number line.

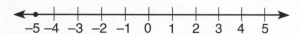

Step 2 is to move 3 units to the *right* of -5. In this problem we move to the right of -5 because a negative number is being subtracted. Since -2 is 3 units to the right of -5, graph -2 on the number line.

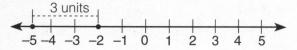

Order of Operations

When a series of operations involving addition, subtraction, multiplication, or division is indicated, first resolve any operations in parentheses, then resolve exponents, then resolve multiplication and/or division, and finally perform addition and/or subtraction. One way to remember this is to recite "Please excuse my dear Aunt Sally." The **P** stands for parentheses, the **E** for exponents, the **M** for multiplication, the **D** for division, the **A** for addition and the **S** for subtraction.

Consider

$60 - 25 \div 5 + 15 - 100 + 4 \times 10$

$= 60 - 25 \div 5 + 15 - 100 + 40$

$= 60 - 5 + 15 - 100 + 40$

$= 115 - 105$

$= 10$

Notice that $25 \div 5$ could be evaluated at the same time that 4×10 is evaluated, since they are both part of the multiplication/division step.

Decimals

When we divide the denominator of a fraction into its numerator, the result is a **decimal**. The decimal is based upon a fraction with a denominator of 10, 100, 1,000, ... and is written with a **decimal point**. Whole numbers are placed to the left of the decimal point where the first place to the left is the units place; the second to the left is the tens; the third to the left is the hundreds, etc. The fractions are placed on the right where the first place to the right is the tenths; the second to the right is the hundredths, etc.

EXAMPLE

$12\dfrac{3}{10} = 12.3 \qquad 4\dfrac{17}{100} = 4.17 \qquad \dfrac{3}{100} = .03$

Since a **rational number** is of the form $\dfrac{a}{b}$, $b \neq 0$, then all rational numbers can be expressed as decimals by dividing b into a. The result is either a **terminating decimal**, meaning that b divides a with a remainder of 0 after a certain point; or **repeating decimal**, meaning that b continues to divide a so that the decimal has a repeating pattern of integers.

EXAMPLE

(A) $\dfrac{1}{2} = .5$

(B) $\dfrac{1}{3} = .333...$

(C) $\dfrac{11}{16} = .6875$

(D) $\dfrac{2}{7} = .285714285714...$

(A) and (C) are terminating decimals; (B) and (D) are repeating decimals. This explanation allows us to define **irrational numbers** as numbers whose decimal form is non-terminating and non-repeating, e.g.,

$$\sqrt{2} = 1.414...$$
$$\sqrt{3} = 1.732...$$

Operations With Decimals

A) **To add numbers containing decimals**, write the numbers in a column, making sure the decimal points are lined up, one beneath the other. Add the numbers as usual, placing the decimal point in the sum so that it is still in line with the others. It is important not to mix the digits in the tenths place with the digits in the hundredths place, and so on.

EXAMPLES

$2.558 + 6.391$ $57.51 + 6.2$

$$\begin{array}{r} 2.558 \\ +6.391 \\ \hline 8.949 \end{array} \qquad \begin{array}{r} 57.51 \\ +\ 6.20 \\ \hline 63.71 \end{array}$$

Similarly with subtraction,

$78.54 - 21.33$ $7.11 - 4.2$

$$\begin{array}{r} 78.54 \\ -21.33 \\ \hline 57.21 \end{array} \qquad \begin{array}{r} 7.11 \\ -4.20 \\ \hline 2.91 \end{array}$$

Note that if two numbers differ according to the amount of digits to the right of the decimal point, zeros must be added.

$.63 - .214$ $15.224 - 3.6891$

$$\begin{array}{r} .630 \\ -.214 \\ \hline .416 \end{array} \qquad \begin{array}{r} 15.2240 \\ -\ 3.6891 \\ \hline 11.5349 \end{array}$$

B) **To multiply numbers with decimals**, simply multiply as usual. Then, to figure out the number of decimal places that belong in the product, find the total number of decimal places in the numbers being multiplied.

EXAMPLES

$$\begin{array}{r} 6.555 \quad \text{(3 decimal places)} \\ \times\ \ 4.5 \quad \text{(1 decimal place)} \\ \hline 32775 \\ 26220 \\ \hline 294975 \\ 29.4975 \quad \text{(4 decimal places)} \end{array}$$

$$\begin{array}{r} 5.32 \quad \text{(2 decimal places)} \\ \times\ .04 \quad \text{(2 decimal places)} \\ \hline 2128 \\ 000 \\ \hline 2128 \\ .2128 \quad \text{(4 decimal places)} \end{array}$$

C) **To divide numbers with decimals**, you must first make the divisor a whole number by moving the decimal point the appropriate number of places to the right. The decimal point of the dividend should also be moved the same number of places. Place a decimal point in the quotient, directly in line with the decimal point in the dividend.

EXAMPLES

$12.92 \div 3.4$ $40.376 \div 7.21$

$$\begin{array}{r} 3.8 \\ 3.4.\overline{)12.9.2} \\ -102 \\ \hline 272 \\ -272 \\ \hline 0 \end{array} \qquad \begin{array}{r} 5.6 \\ 7.21.\overline{)40.37.6} \\ -3605 \\ \hline 4326 \\ -4326 \\ \hline 0 \end{array}$$

D) When comparing two numbers with decimals to see which is the larger, first look at the tenths place. The larger digit in this place represents the larger number. If the two digits are the same, however, take a look at the digits in the hundredths place, and so on.

EXAMPLES

.518 and .216

5 is larger than 2, therefore

.518 is larger than .216

.723 and .726

6 is larger than 3, therefore

.726 is larger than .723

PROBLEM

> Round the following decimal to the nearest thousandth: 0.9196.

SOLUTION

Step 1 is to determine the digit that will be rounded.

0.9196

Since the digit "9" is in the thousandths' place, it will be rounded.

Step 2 is to locate the digit to the right of "9."

0.9196

The digit "6" is to the right of "9." In this case, there are no digits to the right of "6" to set equal to "0."

0.9196

Step 3 is to determine if the decimal will be rounded up or down. Since "6" is greater than or equal to 5, the decimal will be rounded up. To do this, set "6" equal to "0," and increase "9" by one. Since "9" increased by one is ten, carry the addition over to the remaining decimal places.

0.9200

The correct answer is 0.920.

Percentages

A **percent** is a way of expressing the relationship between part and whole, where whole is defined as 100%. A percent can be defined by a fraction with a denominator of 100. Decimals can also represent a percent. For instance,

$$56\% = 0.56 = \frac{56}{100}$$

PROBLEM

> Compute the value of
>
> (1)   90% of 400   (3)   50% of 500
>
> (2)   180% of 400   (4)   200% of 4

SOLUTION

The symbol % means per hundred, therefore $5\% = \frac{5}{100}$

(1) 90% of $400 = \frac{90}{100} \times 400 = 90 \times 4 = 360$

(2) 180% of $400 = \frac{180}{100} \times 400 = 180 \times 4$
$= 720$

(3) 50% of $500 = \frac{50}{100} \times 500 = 50 \times 5 = 250$

(4) 200% of $4 = \frac{200}{100} \times 4 = 2 \times 4 = 8$

PROBLEM

> What percent of
>
> (1)   100 is 99.5   (2)   200 is 4

SOLUTION

(1) $99.5 = x \times 100$
$99.5 = 100x$
$.995 = x$; but this is the value of x per
          hundred. Therefore,
$x = 99.5\%$

(2) $4 = x \times 200$
$4 = 200x$
$.02 = x$. Again this must be changed to
          percent, so
$x = 2\%$

Equivalent Forms of a Number

Some problems may call for converting numbers into an equivalent or simplified form in order to make the solution more convenient.

1. Converting a fraction to a decimal:
$$\frac{1}{2} = 0.50$$

Divide the numerator by the denominator:

$$2\overline{)1.00} \quad \begin{array}{r} .50 \\ \hline -10 \\ \hline 00 \end{array}$$

2. Converting a number to a percent:
$$0.50 = 50\%$$

Multiply by 100:

$$0.50 = (0.50 \times 100)\% = 50\%$$

3. Converting a percent to a decimal:

$$30\% = 0.30$$

Divide by 100:

$$30\% = \frac{30}{100} = 0.30$$

4. Converting a decimal to a fraction:

$$0.500 = \frac{1}{2}$$

Convert .500 to $\frac{500}{1000}$ and then simplify the fraction by dividing the numerator and denominator by common factors:

$$\frac{2 \times 2 \times 5 \times 5 \times 5}{2 \times 2 \times 2 \times 5 \times 5 \times 5}$$

and then cancel out the common numbers to get $\frac{1}{2}$.

PROBLEM

> Express
> (1) $1\frac{1}{10}$ as a percent
> (2) 0.7 as a fraction
> (3) $-\frac{10}{20}$ as a decimal
> (4) $\frac{4}{2}$ as an integer

SOLUTION

(1) $\left(1\frac{1}{10}\right)(100) = \left(\frac{11}{10}\right)\left(\frac{100}{1}\right) = 110\%$

(2) $0.7 = \frac{7}{10}$

(3) $-\frac{10}{20} = -0.5$

(4) $\frac{4}{2} = 2$

PROBLEM

> Convert the following fraction to a percent: $\frac{17}{20}$.

SOLUTION

Step 1 is to write the problem as a proportion.
$$\frac{17}{20} = \frac{?}{100}$$

Step 2 is to rewrite the proportion in the following format:

$$AD = BC \qquad 17(100) = ?(20)$$

Step 3 is to solve the left side of the proportion.

$$17(100) = 1,700$$

Step 4 is to rewrite the proportion.

$$1,700 = ?(20)$$

Step 5 is to find the missing integer that solves the proportion. To do this, divide both sides by the known mean, 20.

$$\frac{1,700}{20} = 85 \qquad \frac{?(20)}{20} = ?$$

Step 6 is to rewrite the proportion.

$$85 = ?$$

The new fraction is $\frac{85}{100}$.

Step 7 is to change the numerator to a percent.

$$85 = 85\%$$

The answer is 85%.

PROBLEM

> Convert the following decimal to percent: 12.69

SOLUTION

Step 1 is to multiply the decimal by 100.

$12.69 \times 100 = 1,269.00$

Step 2 is to write the decimal as a percent.

$1,269.00 = 1,269\%$

The correct answer is 1,269%.

PROBLEM

> Convert the following percent to decimal: 0.009%.

SOLUTION

Step 1 is to write the percent as a real number.

$0.009\% = 0.009$

Step 2 is to divide the real number by 100.

$0.009 \div 100 = 0.00009$

The correct answer is 0.00009.

PROBLEM

> Which of the following statements is true?
>
> a) $0.002\% = 0.200$ c) $-0.95 > -93\%$
>
> b) $1.967 = 196.7\%$ d) $1.00 < 100\%$

SOLUTION

Statement a is incorrect because 0.200 is equivalent to 20%. Since 20% does not equal 0.002%, this statement cannot be true.

Statement b is correct. 1.967 is equivalent to 196.7%.

Statement c is incorrect because -0.95 is equivalent to –95%. Since –95% is not greater than –93%, this statement is not true.

Statement d is incorrect because 1.00 is equivalent to 100%, not less than 100%.

The only correct statement is statement b.

Estimation

EXAMPLE

Jim is hosting a pizza party for 11 of his close friends. He wants to serve each guest a mini-pizza. Mini-pizzas cost $6.79 each. Estimate the total cost.

Round 11 to 10. Round $6.79 to $7.00. Now, multiply $7 times 10. The estimated cost is $70.00.

NOTE:

> The exact cost is $74.69.

EXAMPLE

The chart below shows the number of fishing lures a factory produced over a 6-year period.

Year	Fishing Lures
2000	6,257
2001	10,374
2002	5,890
2003	12,125
2004	9,642
2005	13,092

Estimate the total number of fishing lures produced from 2000 through 2005.

First, round each number to the thousands. Then, add the rounded numbers in order to find the estimate.

$6,000 + 10,000 + 6,000 + 12,000 + 10,000 + 13,000 = 57,000$ lures

NOTE:

| The actual number of lures is 57,380. |

PROBLEM

A rectangular duck pond (43 feet by 47 feet) is on a lot that measures 108 feet by 96 feet. The rest of the lot is a flower garden. Estimate the size of the flower garden in square feet.

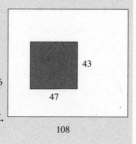

SOLUTION

First, estimate the area of the duck pond. Round 47 to 50, and round 43 to 40. Now, multiply: $50 \times 40 = 2,000$. The area of the duck pond is about 2,000 square feet. Now, calculate the area of the lot. Round 96 to 100, and 108 to 100. Multiply: $100 \times 100 = 10,000$. In order to find the approximate area of the flower garden, subtract the area of the duck pond from the area of the lot. $10,000 - 2,000 = 8,000$. The flower garden is about 8,000 square feet.

NOTE:

| The actual area of the flower garden is 8,347 square feet. |

PROBLEM

Mr. Taylor drove his car to the gas station to fill it up. By the time he got there, the gas tank was empty. The total cost to fill up his gas tank was $31.45. Gasoline costs $1.46 per gallon. Estimate how many gallons Mr. Taylor's gas tank holds.

SOLUTION

Round $31.45 to $30.00 and $1.46 to $1.50. Divide: $30 \div 1.5 = 20$ gallons.

NOTE:

| The actual number of gallons that the tank holds is 21.54. |

PROBLEM

A rancher owns 26,450 acres of land. According to the results from a recent geological survey and soil analysis, 38% of the land is farmable. Estimate the number of farmable acres.

SOLUTION

Round 26,450 to 25,000. Round 38% to 40%, which is 0.4 in decimal form. Then, multiply $25,000 \times 0.4 = 10,000$ acres.

NOTE:

| The actual number is 10,051 acres. |

Radicals

The **square root** of a number is a number that when multiplied by itself results in the original number. So, the square root of 81 is 9 since $9 \times 9 = 81$. However, –9 is also a root of 81 since $(-9)(-9) = 81$. Every positive number will have two roots. Yet, the principal root is the positive one. Zero has only one square root, while negative numbers do not have real numbers as their roots.

A **radical sign** indicates that the root of a number or expression will be taken. The **radicand** is the number of which the root will be taken. The **index** tells how many times the root needs to be multiplied by itself to equal the radicand. e.g.,

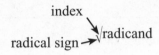

(1) $\sqrt[3]{64}$;

3 is the index and 64 is the radicand.
Since $4 \times 4 \times 4 = 64$, $\sqrt[3]{64} = 4$.

(2) $\sqrt[5]{32}$;

5 is the index and 32 is the radicand.
Since $2 \times 2 \times 2 \times 2 \times 2 = 32$, $\sqrt[5]{32} = 2$.

Operations With Radicals

A) **To multiply two or more radicals**, we utilize the law that states,

$$\sqrt{a} \times \sqrt{b} = \sqrt{ab}.$$

Simply multiply the whole numbers as usual. Then, multiply the radicands and put the product under the radical sign and simplify. e.g.,

(1) $\sqrt{12} \times \sqrt{5} = \sqrt{60} = 2\sqrt{15}$

(2) $3\sqrt{2} \times 4\sqrt{8} = 12\sqrt{16} = 48$

(3) $2\sqrt{10} \times 6\sqrt{5} = 12\sqrt{50} = 60\sqrt{2}$

B) **To divide radicals**, simplify both the numerator and the denominator. By multiplying the radical in the denominator by itself, you can make the denominator a rational number. The numerator, however, must also be multiplied by this radical so that the value of the expression does not change. You must choose as many factors as necessary to rationalize the denominator.
e.g.,

(1) $\dfrac{\sqrt{128}}{\sqrt{2}} = \dfrac{\sqrt{128} \times \sqrt{2}}{\sqrt{2} \times \sqrt{2}} = \dfrac{\sqrt{256}}{2} = \dfrac{16}{2} = 8$

(2) $\dfrac{\sqrt{10}}{\sqrt{3}} = \dfrac{\sqrt{10} \times \sqrt{3}}{\sqrt{3} \times \sqrt{3}} = \dfrac{\sqrt{30}}{3}$

(3) $\dfrac{\sqrt{8}}{2\sqrt{3}} = \dfrac{\sqrt{8} \times \sqrt{3}}{2\sqrt{3} \times \sqrt{3}} = \dfrac{\sqrt{24}}{2 \times 3} = \dfrac{2\sqrt{6}}{6} = \dfrac{\sqrt{6}}{3}$

C) **To add two or more radicals**, the radicals must have the same index and the same radicand. Only where the radicals are simplified can these similarities be determined.

EXAMPLE

(1) $6\sqrt{2} + 2\sqrt{2} = (6 + 2)\sqrt{2} = 8\sqrt{2}$

(2) $\sqrt{27} + 5\sqrt{3} = \sqrt{9}\sqrt{3} + 5\sqrt{3} = 3\sqrt{3} + 5\sqrt{3} = 8\sqrt{3}$

(3) $7\sqrt{3} + 8\sqrt{2} + 5\sqrt{3} = 12\sqrt{3} + 8\sqrt{2}$

Similarly to subtract,

(1) $12\sqrt{3} - 7\sqrt{3} = (12 - 7)\sqrt{3} = 5\sqrt{3}$

(2) $\sqrt{80} - \sqrt{20} = \sqrt{16}\sqrt{5} - \sqrt{4}\sqrt{5}$
$\qquad\qquad = 4\sqrt{5} - 2\sqrt{5} = 2\sqrt{5}$

(3) $\sqrt{50} - \sqrt{3} = 5\sqrt{2} - \sqrt{3}$

PROBLEM

Find the solutions to the following problem:
$\sqrt[3]{-1}$.

SOLUTION

Step 1 is to determine what the base would be if you raise a number to the power of "3" to get -1.

Base $= -1$

Step 2 is to raise the base "-1" to the exponent "3" to verify the solution,

$-1 \times -1 \times -1 = -1$

The correct answer is -1.

PROBLEM

Find the solution to the following problem:
$4\dfrac{1}{2}$.

SOLUTION

Any time a base is raised to a fractional exponent, the problem should be rewritten as a root.

Step 1 is to rewrite the problem as a root. The denominator will determine what the n root will be. Since the denominator is 2, take the 2nd root (or square root).

$$4^{\frac{1}{2}} = \sqrt{4}$$

Step 2 is to determine what the base would be if you raise a number to the power of "2" to get 4.

Base = 2

Step 3 is to raise the base "2" to the exponent "2" to verify the solution.

$2 \times 2 = 4$

The correct answer is 2.

PROBLEM

Find the solutions to the following problem:
$\sqrt{50}$

SOLUTION

Some square roots can be expressed as a product of two or more square roots.

Step 1 is to determine if $\sqrt{50}$ can be expressed as a product of two or more square roots.

$$\sqrt{50} = \sqrt{(2 \times 25)} = \sqrt{2}\sqrt{25}$$

Step 2 is to solve the square root that will not be an irrational number.

$$\sqrt{25} = 5$$

Step 3 is to rewrite the problem.

$$\sqrt{50} = 5\left(\sqrt{2}\right)$$

Step 4 is to determine if the problem is irrational. If so, then stop.

$5\left(\sqrt{2}\right)$ is irrational.

The correct answer is $5\left(\sqrt{2}\right)$.

Exponents

When a number is multiplied by itself a specific number of times, it is said to be **raised to a power**. The way this is written is $a^n = a$ where a is the number or **base**, n is the **exponent** or **power** that indicates the number of times the base is to be multiplied by itself, and b is the product of this multiplication.

In the expression 3^2, 3 is the base and 2 is the exponent. This means that 3 is multiplied by itself 2 times and the product is 9.

An exponent can be either positive or negative. A negative exponent implies a fraction. Such that, if n is a positive integer.

$$a^{-n} = \frac{1}{a^n}, a \neq 0. \text{ So, } 2^{-4} = \frac{1}{2^4} = \frac{1}{16}.$$

An exponent that is zero gives a result of 1, assuming that the base is not equal to zero.

$$a^0 = 1, a \neq 0.$$

An exponent can also be a fraction. If m and n are positive integers.

$$a^{\frac{m}{n}} = \sqrt[n]{a^m}.$$

The numerator remains the exponent of a, but the denominator tells what root to take. For example,

(1) $4^{\frac{3}{2}} = \sqrt[2]{4^3} = \sqrt{64} = 8$

(2) $3^{\frac{4}{2}} = \sqrt[2]{3^4} = \sqrt{81} = 9$

If a fractional exponent were negative, the same operation would take place, but the result would be a fraction. For example,

$$27^{-\frac{2}{3}} = \frac{1}{27^{\frac{2}{3}}} = \frac{1}{\sqrt[3]{27^2}} = \frac{1}{\sqrt[3]{729}} = \frac{1}{9}$$

PROBLEM

Simplify the following expressions

(1) -3^{-2} (3) $\dfrac{-3}{4^{-1}}$

(2) $(-3)^{-2}$

SOLUTION

(1) Here the exponent applies only to 3. Since

$$x^{-y} = \frac{1}{x^y}, -3^{-2} = -(3)^{-2} = -\frac{1}{3^2} = -\frac{1}{9}$$

(2) In this case the exponent applies to the negative base. Thus,

$$(-3)^{-2} = \frac{1}{(-3)^2} = \frac{1}{(-3)(-3)} = \frac{1}{9}$$

(3) $\dfrac{-3}{4^{-1}} = \dfrac{-3}{\left(\frac{1}{4}\right)^1} = \dfrac{-3}{\frac{1^1}{4^1}} = \dfrac{-3}{\frac{1}{4}}$

Division by a fraction is equivalent to multiplication by that fraction's reciprocal, thus

$$\dfrac{-3}{\frac{1}{4}} = -3 \times \dfrac{4}{1} = -12 \text{ and } \dfrac{-3}{4^{-1}} = -12$$

General Laws of Exponents

A) $a^p a^q = a^{p+q}$

$4^2 4^3 = 4^{2+3} = 1{,}024$

B) $(a^p)^q = a^{pq}$

$(2^3)^2 = 2^6 = 64$

C) $\dfrac{a^p}{a^q} = a^{p-q}$

$\dfrac{3^6}{3^2} = 3^4 = 81$

D) $(ab)^p = a^p b^p$

$(3 \times 2)^2 = 3^2 \times 2^2 = (9)(4) = 36$

E) $\left(\dfrac{a}{b}\right)^p = \dfrac{a^p}{b^p}, b \neq 0$

$\left(\dfrac{4}{5}\right)^2 = \dfrac{4^2}{5^2} = \dfrac{16}{25}$

PROBLEM

Find the solution to the following problem: $(-3^1)^2$.

SOLUTION

Step 1 is to identify the base and the exponents. In this problem, "−3" is the base, "1" and "2" are the exponents.

Step 2, since this problem raises an exponent to an exponent, multiply the exponents.

$1 \times 2 = 2$

Step 3 is to rewrite the problem.

-3^2

Step 4 is to set up the multiplication. Multiply the base, "−3," with itself.

-3×-3

Step 5 is to perform the operation.

$-3 \times -3 = 9$

The correct answer is 9.

PROBLEM

Find the solution to the following problem:
$$\left(\dfrac{6^6}{6^4}\right)$$

SOLUTION

Step 1 is to identify the base and the exponents. In this problem, "6" is the common base. "6" and "4" are the exponents.

Step 2, since the problem contains a common base, the exponents can be subtracted.

$6 - 4 = 2$

Step 3 is to rewrite the problem using the new exponent.

6^2

Step 4 is to perform the operation.

$6 \times 6 = 36$

The correct answer is 36.

Power to a Power

Consider the example $(3^2)^4$. Remembering that an exponent shows the number of times the base is to be taken as a factor and noting in this case that 3^2 is considered the base, we have

$(3^2)^4 = 3^2 \times 3^2 \times 3^2 \times 3^2$

Also in multiplication we add exponents. Thus,

$3^2 \times 3^2 \times 3^2 \times 3^2 = 3^{(2+2+2+2)} = 3^8$

Therefore,

$(3^2)^4 = 3^{(4 \times 2)}$

$= 3^8$

The laws of exponents for the power of a power may be stated as follows: To find the power of a power, multiply the exponents. It should be noted that this case is the only one in which multiplication of exponents is performed.

Real Numbers and Their Components

Real Number Properties of Equality

The standard properties of equality involving real numbers are:

Reflexive Property of Equality

For each real number a,

$$a = a$$

Symmetric Property of Equality

For each real number a, for each real number b,

if $a = b$, then $b = a$

Transitive Property of Equality

For each real number a, for each real number b, for each real number c,

if $a = b$ and $b = c$, then $a = c$

Real Number Operations and Their Properties

The operations of addition and multiplication are of particular importance. As a result, many properties concerning those operations have been determined and named. Here is a list of the most important of these properties.

Closure Property of Addition

For every real number a, for every real number b,

$$a + b$$

is a real number.

Closure Property of Multiplication

For every real number a, for every real number b,

$$ab$$

is a real number.

Commutative Property of Addition

For every real number a, for every real number b,
$$a + b = b + a.$$

Commutative Property of Multiplication

For every real number a, for every real number b,
$$ab = ba.$$

Associative Property of Addition

For every real number a, for every real number b, for every real number c,

$$(a + b) + c = a + (b + c).$$

Associative Property of Multiplication

For every real number a, for every real number b, for every real number c,

$$(ab)c = a(bc).$$

Identity Property of Addition

For every real number a,
$$a + 0 = 0 + a = a.$$

Identity Property of Multiplication

For every real number a,
$$a \times 1 = 1 \times a = a.$$

Inverse Property of Addition

For every real number a, there is a real number $-a$ such that

$$a + -a = -a + a = 0.$$

Inverse Property of Multiplication

For every real number a, $a \neq 0$, there is a real number a^{-1} such that

$$a \times a^{-1} = a^{-1} \times a = 1.$$

Distributive Property

For every real number a, for every real number b, for every real number c,

$$a(b + c) = ab + ac.$$

The operations of subtraction and division are also important, but less important than addition and multiplication. Here are the definitions for these operations.

For every real number a, for every real number b, for every real number c,

$$a - b = c \text{ if and only if } b + c = a.$$

For every real number a, for every real number b, for every real number c,

$$a \div b = c \text{ if and only if } c \text{ is the unique real number such that } bc = a.$$

The definition of division eliminates division *by* 0. Thus, for example, $4 \div 0$ is undefined, $0 \div 0$ is undefined, but $0 \div 4 = 0$.

In many instances, it is possible to perform subtraction by first converting a subtraction statement to an addition statement. This is illustrated below.

For every real number a, for every real number b,

$$\boxed{a - b = a + (-b).}$$

In a similar way, every division statement can be converted to a multiplication statement. Use the following model:

For every real number a, for every real number b, $b \neq 0$,

$$\boxed{a \div b = a \times b^{-1}}$$

We can define a new operation on a number system and check to see if the properties of closure, associativity, commutativity, and distributivity hold.

PROBLEM

Given the set of integers, let the symbol * be defined as follows: For any two integers a, b, $a * b = a + b^2$. Determine if the properties of closure, associativity, commutativity, and distributivity hold.

SOLUTION

Closure: For any two integers, $a * b = a + b^2$ is an integer, so this property holds.

Associativity: We want to check if $a * (b * c) = (a * b) * c$ for any integers a, b, c. $a * (b * c) = a * (b + c)^2 = a + (b + c^2)^2 = a^2 + b^2 + 2bc^2 + c^4$, and $(a * b) * c = (a + b^2) * c = a + b^2 + c^2$. Since these two expressions are different, associativity does not hold.

Commutativity: We want to check if $a * b = b * a$. Note that $a * b = a + b^2$, but $b * a = b + a^2$. These two expressions are different, so commutativity does not hold.

Distributivity: We want to check if $a * (b + c) = a * b + a * c$.

$a * (b + c) = a + (b + c)^2 = a + b^2 + 2bc + c^2$, whereas $a * b + a * c = a + b^2 + a + c^2 = 2a + b^2 + c^2$. This means that distributivity does not hold.

PROBLEM

Given the set of all real numbers except zero, let the symbol Δ be defined as follows:

For any two real numbers except zero, a, b,
$$a\Delta b = \frac{a}{b} + \frac{b}{a}.$$
Closure is evident because each fraction represents a nonzero real number.

SOLUTION

Associativity: We need to check if $a\Delta(b\Delta c) = (a\Delta b)\Delta c$.

$$a\Delta(b\Delta c) = \frac{a}{b\Delta c} + \frac{b\Delta c}{a}$$

$$= \frac{a}{\frac{b}{c} + \frac{c}{b}} + \frac{\frac{b}{c} + \frac{c}{b}}{a}.$$

$$= \frac{abc}{b^2 + c^2} + \frac{b^2 + c^2}{abc}$$

$$(a\Delta b)\Delta c = (\frac{a}{b} + \frac{b}{a})\Delta c = \frac{\frac{a}{b} + \frac{b}{a}}{c}$$

$$+ \frac{c}{\frac{a}{b} + \frac{b}{a}} = \frac{a^2 + b^2}{abc}$$

$$+ \frac{abc}{a^2 + b^2}$$

These expressions are different, so associativity does not hold.

Commutativity: Let's check if $a\Delta b = b\Delta a$.
$a\Delta b = \frac{a}{b} + \frac{b}{a}$ and $b\Delta a = \frac{b}{a} + \frac{a}{b}$. These expressions are identical, so this property holds.

Distributivity: Finally, we will check if $a\Delta(b + c) = (a\Delta b) + (a\Delta c)$.

$a\Delta(b + c)$

$$= \frac{a}{b+c} + \frac{b+c}{a} = \frac{a^2 + (b+c)^2}{a(b+c)} \text{ and } (a\Delta b)$$

$$+(a\Delta c) = (\frac{a}{b} + \frac{b}{a}) + (\frac{a}{c} + \frac{c}{a}) = \frac{a^2 + b^2}{ab}$$

$$+ \frac{a^2 + c^2}{ac} = \frac{c(a^2 + b^2) + b(a^2 + c^2)}{abc}.$$

Since these expressions are different, distributivity does not hold.

Complex Numbers

A **complex number** is a number that can be written in the form $a + bi$, where a and b are real numbers and $i = \sqrt{-1}$. The number a is the **real part,** and the number b is the **imaginary part** of the complex number.

Returning momentarily to real numbers, the square of a real number cannot be negative. More specifically, the square of a positive real number is positive, the square of a negative real number is positive, and the square of 0 is 0. Then i is defined to be a number with a property that

$$i^2 = -1.$$

Obviously i is not a real number. C is then used to represent the set of all complex numbers and

$$C = \{a + bi \mid a \text{ and } b \text{ are real numbers}\}.$$

Here are the definitions of addition, subtraction, and multiplication of complex numbers.

Suppose $x + yi$ and $z + wi$ are complex numbers. Then

$$(x + yi) + (z + wi) = (x + z) + (y + w)i$$
$$(x + yi) - (z + wi) = (x - z) + (y - w)i$$
$$(x + yi) \times (z + wi) = (xz - wy) +$$
$$(xw + yz)i.$$

To add, subtract, or multiply complex numbers, compute in the usual way, replace i^2 with -1, and simplify.

$$(a + bi) + (c + di) = (a + c) + (b + d)i$$
$$(a + bi) - (c + di) = (a - c) + (b - d)i$$
$$(a + bi)(c + di) = ac + adi + bci + bdi^2$$
$$= ac - bd + (ad + bc)i$$

PROBLEM

Simplify the following: $(3 + i)(2 + i)$.

SOLUTION

$$(3 + i)(2 + i) = 3(2 + i) + i(2 + i)$$
$$= 6 + 3i + 2i + i^2$$
$$= 6 + (3 + 2)i + (-1)$$
$$= 5 + 5i$$

Complex numbers, $a + bi$, may be obtained when using the quadratic formula to solve quadratic equations.

PROBLEM

Solve the equation $x^2 - x + 1 = 0$.

SOLUTION

In this equation, $a = 1$, $b = -1$ and $c = 1$. Substitute into the quadratic formula.

$$x = \frac{-(-1) \pm \sqrt{(-1)^2 - 4(1)(1)}}{2(1)}$$

$$= \frac{1 \pm \sqrt{1 - 4}}{2}$$

$$= \frac{1 \pm \sqrt{-3}}{2}$$

$$= \frac{1 \pm \sqrt{3}i}{2}$$

$$x = \frac{1 + \sqrt{3}i}{2} \text{ or } x = \frac{1 - \sqrt{3}i}{2}$$

Division of two complex numbers is usually accomplished with a special procedure that involves the conjugate of a complex number. The conjugate of $a + bi$ is denoted by

$$\overline{a + bi} \text{ and } \overline{a + bi} = a - bi.$$

Also, $(a + bi)(a - bi) = a^2 + b^2$.

The usual procedure for division is illustrated below.

$$\frac{x + yi}{z + wi} = \frac{x + yi}{z + wi} \times \frac{z - wi}{z - wi}$$

$$= \frac{(xz + yw) + (-xw + yz)i}{z^2 + w^2}$$

$$= \frac{xz + yw}{z^2 + w^2} + \frac{-xw + yz}{z^2 + w^2}i$$

All the properties of real numbers described in the previous section carry over to complex numbers, however, those properties will not be stated again.

If a is a real number, then a can be expressed in the form $a = a + 0i$. Hence, every real number is a complex number and $R \subseteq C$.

Drill: Real and Complex Numbers

DIRECTIONS: For #1–7, simplify the expressions. For #8–10, solve the equations.

1. $3i^3 =$

    (A) $-3i$ (C) $9i$

    (B) $3i$ (D) $-i$

2. $2i^7 =$

    (A) $-128i$ (C) $14i$

    (B) $2i$ (D) $-2i$

3. $-4i^4 =$

    (A) 4 (C) $4i$

    (B) -4 (D) $-4i$

4. $-5i^6 =$

    (A) -5 (C) $-i$

    (B) $-5i$ (D) 5

5. $(3 + 2i)(2 + 3i) =$

    (A) $12 + 13i$ (C) $13i$

    (B) $-12 - 13i$ (D) $-13i$

6. $(2 - i)(2 + i) =$

    (A) -5 (C) $-5i$

    (B) $5i$ (D) 5

7. $(5 - 4i)^2 =$

    (A) $9 - 40i$ (C) $41 - 40i$

    (B) $-9 - 40i$ (D) $9 + 40i$

8. $x^2 + 16 = 0$

   (A) ± 4 (C) $4 \pm i$

   (B) $\pm 4i$ (D) $-4 \pm i$

9. $4y^2 + 1 = 0$

   (A) $\pm \dfrac{1}{2}$ (C) $-i \pm \dfrac{1}{2}$

   (B) $i \pm \dfrac{1}{2}$ (D) $\pm \dfrac{1}{2} i$

10. $x^2 - 4x + 13 = 0$

    (A) $3 \pm 2i$ (C) $\pm 5i$

    (B) $\pm 6i$ (D) $2 \pm 3i$

11. How many prime numbers are greater than 20 but less than 40?

    (A) 3   (C) 5

    (B) 4   (D) 6

12. What is the least common multiple of 36 and 135?

    (A) 540   (C) 432

    (B) 500   (D) 270

13. For which of the following pairs of numbers is the greatest common factor equal to 1?

    (A) 12 and 20   (C) 26 and 78

    (B) 33 and 57   (D) 25 and 81

14. What is the prime factorization of the number 624?

    (A) $2^3 \times 3 \times 13$ (C) $2^4 \times 3 \times 13$

    (B) $2^4 \times 3^2 \times 13$ (D) $2^3 \times 3^2 \times 13$

15. Which of the following is the *smallest* number that has a remainder of 1 when it is divided by each of 2, 3, 5, and 7?

    (A) 421   (C) 106

    (B) 211   (D) 18

ANSWER KEY

1. (A)
2. (D)
3. (B)
4. (D)
5. (C)
6. (D)
7. (A)
8. (B)

9. (D)
10. (D)
11. (B)
12. (A)
13. (D)
14. (C)
15. (B)

Detailed Explanations of Answers

Drill: Real and Complex Numbers

1. (A)

$$3i^3 = 3i(i)^2 = 3i(-1) = -3i$$

2. (D)

$$2i^7 = 2i(i^2)(i^2)(i^2) = 2i(-1)(-1)(-1) = -2i$$

3. (B)

$$-4i^4 = -4(i^2)(i^2) = -4(-1)(-1) = -4$$

4. (D)

$$-5i^6 = -5(i^2)(i^2)(i^2) = -5(-1)(-1)(-1) = 5$$

5. (C)

$$
\begin{aligned}
(3+2i)(2+3i) &= 6 + \underline{9i + 4i} + 6i^2 \\
&= 6 + \quad 13i \quad -6 \\
&= 13i
\end{aligned}
$$

6. (D)

$$
\begin{aligned}
(2-i)(2+i) &= 4 + 2i - 2i - i^2 \\
&= 4 + 0 - (-1) \\
&= 5
\end{aligned}
$$

7. (A)

$$
\begin{aligned}
(5-4i)^2 &= (5-4i)(5-4i) \\
&= (25 - 20i - 20i + 16i^2) \\
&= 25 - 40i + 16(-1) \\
&= 9 - 40i
\end{aligned}
$$

8. (B)

$$
\begin{aligned}
x^2 + 16 &= 0 \\
x^2 &= -16 \\
x^2 &= (16)(-1) \\
x &= \pm 4i
\end{aligned}
$$

9. (D)

$$4y^2 + 1 = 0$$
$$4y^2 = -1 \Rightarrow y^2 = -\frac{1}{4} \quad y = \pm\frac{1}{2}i$$

10. (D)

$$x^2 - 4x + 13 = 0$$

by the quadratic formula

$$
\begin{aligned}
\frac{-b \pm \sqrt{b^2 - 4ac}}{2a} &= \frac{4 \pm \sqrt{16 - 4(1)(13)}}{2} \\
&= \frac{4 \pm \sqrt{16 - 52}}{2} \\
&= \frac{4 \pm \sqrt{-36}}{2} \\
&= \frac{4 \pm 6i}{2} \\
&= 2 \pm 3i
\end{aligned}
$$

11. (B)

The four prime numbers between 20 and 40 are 23, 29, 31, and 37.

12. (A)

$36 = 2^2 \times 3^2$ and $135 = 3^3 \times 5$. Then the least common multiple is $2^2 \times 3^3 \times 5 = 540$.

13. (D)

Since $25 = 5^2$ and $81 = 3^4$, their greatest common factor is 1. The greatest common factor for the pairs of numbers in answer choices A, B, and C are 4, 3, and 26, respectively.

14. (C)

$624 = 2 \times 312 = 2 \times 2 \times 156 = 2 \times 2 \times 2 \times 78 = 2 \times 2 \times 2 \times 2 \times 39 = 2 \times 2 \times 2 \times 2 \times 3 \times 13$. In exponential form, the answer becomes $2^4 \times 3 \times 13$.

15. (B)

The least common multiple of 2, 3, 5, and 7 is $2 \times 3 \times 5 \times 7 = 210$. Therefore, the smallest number that has a remainder of 1 when divided by each of 2, 3, 5, and 7 is $210 + 1 = 211$.

Algebra Terms

In algebra, letters or variables are used to represent numbers. A **variable** is defined as a placeholder, which can take on any of several values at a given time. A **constant**, on the other hand, is a symbol which takes on only one value at a given time. A **term** is a constant, a variable, or a combination of constants and variables. For example: 7.76, $3x$, xyz, $\dfrac{5z}{x}$, $(0.99)x^2$ are terms. If a term is a combination of constants and variables, the constant part of the term is referred to as the **coefficient** of the variable. If a variable is written without a coefficient, the coefficient is assumed to be 1.

EXAMPLES

$3x^2$	y^3
coefficient: 3	coefficient: 1
variable: x	variable: y

An **expression** is a collection of one or more terms. If the number of terms is greater than 1, the expression is said to be the sum of the terms.

EXAMPLES

$$9, 9xy, 6x + \frac{x}{3}, 8yz - 2x$$

An algebraic expression consisting of only one term is called a **monomial**; of two terms is called a **binomial**; of three terms is called a **trinomial**. In general, an algebraic expression consisting of two or more terms is called a **polynomial**.

As we know, the answer in **addition** is the **sum**. Other words that indicate addition are **plus, more, more than, increase**, and **increased by**. You can write all sums in any order since addition is commutative.

The answer in **multiplication** is the product. Another word that is used is **times**. Sometimes the word **of** indicates multiplication, as we shall see shortly. **Double** means to multiply by two, and **triple** means to multiply by three. Since multiplication is also commutative, we can write any product in any order.

Division's answer is called the **quotient**. Another phrase that is used is **divided by**.

The answer in **subtraction** is called the **difference**. Subtraction can present a reading problem because $4 - 6 \neq 6 - 4$, so we must be careful to subtract in the correct order.

Example shows how some subtraction phrases are translated into algebraic expressions.

EXAMPLE

Phrases	Expressions
a. The difference between 9 and 5	$9 - 5$
The difference between m and n	$m - n$
b. Five minus two	$5 - 2$
m minus n	$m - n$
c. Seven decreased by three	$7 - 3$
m decreased by n	$m - n$
d. Nine diminished by four	$9 - 4$
m diminished by n	$m - n$
e. Three from five	$5 - 3$
m from n	$n - m$
f. Ten less two	$10 - 2$
m less n	$m - n$
g. Ten less than two;	$2 - 10$
m less than n	$n - m$

Notice in parts f and g of Example 1 how one word makes a difference: a less b means $a - b$; a less than b means $b - a$. a is less than b means $a < b$. You must read carefully!!

The following words usually indicate an equal sign: *is, am, are, was, were, the same as, equal to*.

You also must know the following phrases for inequalities: at least ($\geq$), not more than ($\leq$), over ($>$), and under ($<$).

EXAMPLE

Phrases	Expressions
a. m times the sum of q and r	$m(q + r)$
b. Six less the product of x and y	$6 - xy$
c. The difference between c and d divided by f	$\dfrac{c - d}{f}$
d. b less than the quotient of r divided by s	$\dfrac{r}{s} - b$
e. The sum of d and g is the same as the product of h and r	$d + g = hr$

EXAMPLE

Phrases	Expressions
a. x is at least y	$x \geq y$
b. Zeb's age n is not more than 21	$n \leq 21$
c. Let I = my age, I am over 30 years old	$I > 30$
d. Let p = most people, most people are under seven feet tall	$p < 7$

Warning: The word "number" does not necessarily mean an integer or even necessarily a positive number.

Operations with Polynomials

A) **Addition of polynomials** is achieved by combining like terms, terms which differ only in their numerical coefficients, e.g.,

$$P(x) = (x^2 - 3x + 5) + (4x^2 + 6x - 3)$$

Note that the parentheses are used to distinguish the polynomials.

By using the commutative and associative laws, we can rewrite $P(x)$ as:

$$P(x) = (x^2 + 4x^2) + (6x - 3x) + (5 - 3)$$

Using the distributive law, $ab + ac = a(b + c)$, yields:

$$(1 + 4)x^2 + (6 - 3)x + (5 - 3) = 5x^2 + 3x + 2$$

B) **Subtraction of two polynomials** is achieved by first changing the sign of all terms in the expression which are being subtracted and then adding this result to the other expression, e.g.,

$$(5x^2 + 4y^2 + 3z^2) - (4xy + 7y^2 - 3z^2 + 1)$$
$$= 5x^2 + 4y^2 + 3z^2 - 4xy - 7y^2 + 3z^2 - 1$$
$$= 5x^2 + (4y^2 - 7y^2) + (3z^2 + 3z^2) - 4xy - 1$$
$$= 5x^2 + (-3y^2) + 6z^2 - 4xy - 1$$

C) **Multiplication of two or more polynomials** is achieved by using the laws of exponents, the rules of signs, and the commutative and associative laws of multiplication. Begin by multiplying the coefficients and then multiply the variables according to the laws of exponents, e.g.,

$$(y^2)\,(5)\,(6y^2)\,(yz)\,(2z^2)$$
$$= (1)\,(5)\,(6)\,(1)\,(2)\,(y^2)\,(y^2)\,(yz)\,(z^2)$$
$$= 60[(y^2)\,(y^2)\,(y)]\,[(z)\,(z^2)]$$
$$= 60(y^5)\,(z^3)$$
$$= 60y^5z^3$$

D) **Multiplication of a polynomial by a monomial** is achieved by multiplying each term of the polynomial by the monomial and combining the results, e.g.,

$$(4x^2 + 3y)\,(6xz^2)$$
$$= (4x^2)\,(6xz^2) + (3y)\,(6xz^2)$$
$$= 24x^3z^2 + 18xyz^2$$

E) **Multiplication of a polynomial by a polynomial** is achieved by multiplying each of the terms of one polynomial by each of the terms of the other polynomial and combining the results, e.g.,

$$(5y + z + 1)\,(y^2 + 2y)$$
$$[(5y)\,(y^2) + (5y)\,(2y)] + [(z)\,(y^2) + (z)\,(2y)] +$$
$$[(1)\,(y^2) + (1)\,(2y)]$$
$$= (5y^3 + 10y^2) + (y^2z + 2yz) + (y^2 + 2y)$$

$$= (5y^3) + (10y^2 + y^2) + (y^2z) + (2yz) + (2y)$$
$$= 5y^3 + 11y^2 + y^2z + 2yz + 2y$$

F) **Division of a monomial by a monomial** is achieved by first dividing the constant coefficients and the variable factors separately, and then multiplying these quotients, e.g.,

$6xyz^2 \div 2y^2z$

$$= \left(\frac{6}{2}\right)\left(\frac{x}{1}\right)\left(\frac{y}{y^2}\right)\left(\frac{z^2}{z}\right)$$
$$= 3xy^{-1}z$$
$$= \frac{3xz}{y}$$

G) **Division of a polynomial by a polynomial** is achieved by following the given procedure, called long division.

Step 1: The terms of both the polynomials are arranged in order of ascending or descending powers of one variable.

Step 2: The first term of the dividend is divided by the first term of the divisor which gives the first term of the quotient.

Step 3: This first term of the quotient is multiplied by the entire divisor and the result is subtracted from the dividend.

Step 4: Using the remainder obtained from Step 3 as the new dividend, Steps 2 and 3 are repeated until the remainder is zero or the degree of the remainder is less than the degree of the divisor.

Step 5: The result is written as follows:

$$\frac{\text{dividend}}{\text{divisor}} = \text{quotient} + \frac{\text{remainder}}{\text{divisor}}$$

divisor $\neq 0$

e.g., $(2x^2 + x + 6) \div (x + 1)$

$$
\begin{array}{r}
2x - 1 \\
(x+1)\overline{\smash{)}2x^2 + x + 6} \\
\underline{-(2x^2 + 2x)} \\
-x + 6 \\
\underline{-(-x - 1)} \\
7
\end{array}
$$

The result is $(2x^2 + x + 6) \div (x + 1) = 2x - 1 + \dfrac{7}{x + 1}$

Drill: Algebraic Terms

1. Which of the following algebraic expressions represents the phrase "x less than the quotient of 5 and z"?

   (A) $x - \dfrac{5}{z}$ (C) $\dfrac{x - 5}{z}$

   (B) $\dfrac{5}{z} - x$ (D) $\dfrac{5 - x}{z}$

2. Which of the following algebraic expressions represents the phrase "The sum of p and q is nine more than the product of w and t"?

   (A) $w + t = p + q + 9$ (C) $p + q = wt + 9$

   (B) $p + q = \dfrac{w}{t} + 9$ (D) $w + t = 9pq$

3. Which of the following is a correct translation of $x - 5 > 2y$?

   (A) Five less x is more than twice y.

   (B) Five less x is at least twice y.

   (C) Five less than x is more than twice y.

   (D) Five less than x is at least twice y.

4. Which of the following is a correct translation of $6(c + d) \le 10$?

   (A) Six multiplied by the sum of c and d is at most 10.

   (B) d added to six multiplied by c is at most 10.

   (C) Six multiplied by the sum of c and d is less than 10.

   (D) d added to six multiplied by c is less than 10.

Drill: Operations with Polynomials

Addition

DIRECTIONS: Add the following polynomials.

1. $9a^2b + 3c + 2a^2b + 5c =$

   (A) $19a^2bc$ (C) $11a^4b^2 + 8c^2$

   (B) $11a^2b + 8c$ (D) $19a^4b^2c^2$

2. $14m^2n^3 + 6m^2n^3 + 3m^2n^3 =$

   (A) $20m^2n^3$ (C) $23m^2n^3$

   (B) $23m^6n^9$ (D) $32m^6n^9$

3. $3x + 2y + 16x + 3z + 6y =$

   (A) $19x + 8y$ (C) $19x + 8y + 3z$

   (B) $19x + 11yz$ (D) $11xy + 19xz$

4. $(4d^2 + 7e^3 + 12f) + (3d^2 + 6e^3 + 2f) =$

   (A) $23d^2e^3f$ (C) $33d^4e^6f^2$

   (B) $33d^2e^2f$ (D) $7d^2 + 13e^3 + 14f$

5. $3ac^2 + 2b^2c + 7ac^2 + 2ac^2 + b^2c =$

   (A) $12ac^2 + 3b^2c$ (C) $11ac^2 + 4ab^2c$

   (B) $14ab^2c^2$ (D) $15ab^2c^2$

Subtraction

DIRECTIONS: Subtract the following polynomials.

6. $14m^2n - 6m^2n =$

   (A) $20m^2n$ (C) $8m$

   (B) $8m^2n$ (D) 8

7. $3x^3y^2 - 4xz - 6x^3y^2 =$

   (A) $-7x^2y^2z$ (C) $-3x^3y^2 - 4xz$

   (B) $3x^3y^2 - 10x^4y^2z$ (D) $-x^2y^2z - 6x^3y^2$

8. $9g^2 + 6h - 2g^2 - 5h =$

   (A) $15g^2h - 7g^2h$ (C) $11g^2 + 7h$

   (B) $7g^4h^2$ (D) $7g^2 + h$

9. $7b^3 - 4c^2 - 6b^3 + 3c^2 =$

   (A) $b^3 - c^2$ (C) $13b^3 - c$

   (B) $-11b^2 - 3c^2$ (D) $7b - c$

10. $11q^2r - 4q^2r - 8q^2r =$

    (A) $22q^2r$ (C) $-2q^2r$

    (B) q^2r (D) $-q^2r$

Multiplication

DIRECTIONS: Multiply the following polynomials.

11. $5p^2t \times 3p^2t =$

    (A) $15p^2t$ (C) $15p^4t^2$

    (B) $15p^4t$ (D) $8p^2t$

12. $(2r + s)\,14r =$

    (A) $28rs$ (C) $16r^2 + 14rs$

    (B) $28r^2 + 14sr$ (D) $28r + 14sr$

13. $(4m + p)(3m - 2p) =$

    (A) $12m^2 + 5mp + 2p^2$

    (B) $12m^2 - 2mp + 2p^2$

    (C) $7m - p$

    (D) $12m^2 - 5mp - 2p^2$

14. $(2a + b)(3a^2 + ab + b^2) =$

    (A) $6a^3 + 5a^2b + 3ab^2 + b^3$

    (B) $5a^3 + 3ab + b^3$

    (C) $6a^3 + 2a^2b + 2ab^2$

    (D) $3a^2 + 2a + ab + b + b^2$

15. $(6t^2 + 2t + 1)\,3t =$

    (A) $9t^2 + 5t + 3$ (C) $9t^3 + 6t^2 + 3t$

    (B) $18t^2 + 6t + 3$ (D) $18t^3 + 6t^2 + 3t$

Division

DIRECTIONS: Divide the following polynomials.

16. $(x^2 + x - 6) \div (x - 2) =$

    (A) $x - 3$ (C) $x + 3$

    (B) $x + 2$ (D) $x - 2$

17. $24b^4c^3 \div 6b^2c =$

    (A) $3b^2c^2$ (C) $4b^3c^2$

    (B) $4b^4c^3$ (D) $4b^2c^2$

18. $(3p^2 + pq - 2q^2) \div (p + q) =$

    (A) $3p + 2q$ (C) $3p - q$

    (B) $2q - 3p$ (D) $3p - 2q$

19. $(y^3 - 2y^2 - y + 2) \div (y - 2)$

    (A) $(y - 1)^2$

    (B) $y^2 - 1$

    (C) $(y + 2)(y - 1)$

    (D) $(y + 1)^2$

20. $(m^2 + m - 14) \div (m + 4) =$

    (A) $m - 2$ (C) $m - 3 + \dfrac{4}{m + 4}$

    (B) $m - 3 + \dfrac{-2}{m + 4}$ (D) $m - 3$

Simplifying Algebraic Expressions

To factor a polynomial completely is to find the prime factors of the polynomial with respect to a specified set of numbers.

The following concepts are important while factoring or simplifying expressions.

A) The factors of an algebraic expression consist of two or more algebraic expressions which, when multiplied together, produce the given algebraic expression.

B) A **prime factor** is a polynomial with no factors other than itself and 1. The **least common multiple (LCM)** for a set of numbers is the smallest quantity divisible by every number of the set. For algebraic expressions, the least common numerical coefficients for each of the given expressions will be a factor.

C) The **greatest common factor (GCF)** for a set of numbers is the largest factor that is common to all members of the set.

D) For algebraic expressions, the greatest common factor is the polynomial of highest degree and the largest numerical coefficient which is a factor of all the given expressions.

Some important formulas, useful for the factoring of polynomials, are listed below.

$$a(c + d) = ac + ad$$
$$(a + b)(a - b) = a^2 - b^2$$
$$(a + b)(a + b) = (a + b)^2 = a^2 + 2ab + b^2$$
$$(a - b)(a - b) = (a - b)^2 = a^2 - 2ab + b^2$$
$$(x + a)(x + b) = x^2 + (a + b)x + ab$$
$$(ax + b)(cx + d) = acx^2 + (ad + bc)x + bd$$
$$(a + b)(c + d) = ac + bc + ad + bd$$
$$(a + b)(a + b)(a + b) = (a + b)^3 = a^3 + 3a^2b + 3ab^2 + b^3$$
$$(a - b)(a - b)(a - b) = (a - b)^3 = a^3 - 3a^2b + 3ab^2 - b^3$$
$$(a - b)(a^2 + ab + b^2) = a^3 - b^3$$
$$(a + b)(a^2 - ab + b^2) = a^3 + b^3$$
$$(a + b + c)^2 = a^2 + b^2 + c^2 + 2ab + 2ac + 2bc$$
$$(a - b)(a^3 + a^2b + ab^2 + b^3) = a^4 - b^4$$
$$(a - b)(a^4 + a^3b + a^2b^2 + ab^3 + b^4) = a^5 - b^5$$
$$(a - b)(a^5 + a^4b + a^3b^2 + a^2b^3 + ab^4 + b^5) = a^6 - b^6$$
$$(a - b)(a^{n-1} + a^{n-2}b + a^{n-3}b^2 + \ldots + ab^{n-2} + b^{n-1}) = a^n - b^n$$

where n is any positive integer (1, 2, 3, 4, …).

$$(a + b)(a^{n-1} - a^{n-2}b + a^{n-3}b^2 - \ldots - ab^{n-2} + b^{n-1}) = a^n + b^n$$

where n is any positive odd integer (1, 3, 5, 7, …).

The procedure for factoring an algebraic expression completely is as follows:

Step 1: First find the greatest common factor, if there is any. Then examine each factor remaining for greatest common factors.

Step 2: Continue factoring the factors obtained in Step 1 until all factors other than monomial factors are prime.

EXAMPLE

Factoring $4 - 16x^2$,

$$4 - 16x^2 = 4(1 - 4x^2) = 4(1 + 2x)(1 - 2x)$$

PROBLEM

Express each of the following as a single term.

(1) $3x^2 + 2x^2 - 4x^2$

(2) $5axy^2 - 7axy^2 - 3xy^2$

SOLUTION

(1) Factor x^2 in the expression.

$$3x^2 + 2x^2 - 4x^2 = (3 + 2 - 4)x^2 = 1x^2 = x^2$$

(2) Factor xy^2 in the expression and then factor a.

$$5axy^2 - 7axy^2 - 3xy^2 = (5a - 7a - 3)xy^2$$
$$= [(5 - 7)a - 3]xy^2$$
$$= (-2a - 3)xy^2$$

PROBLEM

Simplify $\dfrac{\frac{1}{x-1} - \frac{1}{x-2}}{\frac{1}{x-2} - \frac{1}{x-3}}$.

SOLUTION

Simplify the expression in the numerator by using the addition rule:

$$\frac{a}{b} + \frac{c}{d} = \frac{ad + bc}{bd}$$

Notice bd is the Least Common Denominator, LCD. We obtain

$$\frac{x - 2 - (x - 1)}{(x - 1)(x - 2)} = \frac{-1}{(x - 1)(x - 2)}$$

in the numerator.

Repeat this procedure for the expression in the denominator:

$$\frac{x - 3 - (x - 2)}{(x - 2)(x - 3)} = \frac{-1}{(x - 2)(x - 3)}$$

We now have

$$\frac{\dfrac{-1}{(x - 1)(x - 2)}}{\dfrac{-1}{(x - 2)(x - 3)}}$$

which is simplified by inverting the fraction in the denominator and multiplying it by the numerator and cancelling like terms

$$\frac{-1}{(x - 1)(x - 2)} \times \frac{(x - 2)(x - 3)}{-1} = \frac{x - 3}{x - 1}$$

Drill: Simplifying Algebraic Expressions

DIRECTIONS: Simplify the following expressions.

1. $16b^2 - 25z^2 =$

   (A) $(4b - 5z)^2$ (C) $(4b - 5z)(4b + 5z)$

   (B) $(4b + 5z)^2$ (D) $(16b - 25z)^2$

2. $x^2 - 2x - 8 =$

   (A) $(x - 4)^2$ (C) $(x + 4)(x - 2)$

   (B) $(x - 6)(x - 2)$ (D) $(x - 4)(x + 2)$

3. $2c^2 + 5cd - 3d^2 =$

   (A) $(c - 3d)(c + 2d)$

   (B) $(2c - d)(c + 3d)$

   (C) $(c - d)(2c + 3d)$

   (D) $(2c + d)(c + 3d)$

4. $4t^3 - 20t =$

   (A) $4t(t^2 - 5)$ (C) $4t(t + 4)(t - 5)$

   (B) $4t^2(t - 20)$ (D) $2t(2t^2 - 10)$

5. $x^2 + xy - 2y^2 =$

   (A) $(x - 2y)(x + y)$ (C) $(x + 2y)(x + y)$

   (B) $(x - 2y)(x - y)$ (D) $(x + 2y)(x - y)$

Linear Equations

A linear equation with one unknown is one that can be put into the form $ax + b = 0$, where a and b are constants, $a \neq 0$.

To solve a linear equation means to transform it in the form $x = \dfrac{-b}{a}$.

A) If the equation has unknowns on both sides of the equality, it is convenient to put similar terms on the same sides. Refer to the following example.

$$4x + 3 = 2x + 9$$
$$4x + 3 - 2x = 2x + 9 - 2x$$
$$(4x - 2x) + 3 = (2x - 2x) + 9$$
$$2x + 3 = 0 + 9$$
$$2x + 3 - 3 = 0 + 9 - 3$$
$$2x = 6$$
$$\frac{2x}{2} = \frac{6}{2}$$
$$x = 3$$

B) If the equation appears in fractional form, it is necessary to transform it, using cross-multiplication, and then repeat the same procedure as in A. Suppose we are given:

$$\frac{3x + 4}{3} = \frac{7x + 2}{5}$$

By using cross-multiplication we would obtain:

$3(7x + 2) = 5(3x + 4)$.

This is equivalent to:

$21x + 6 = 15x + 20$,

which can be solved as in A.
$$21x + 6 = 15x + 20$$
$$21x - 15x + 6 = 15x - 15x + 20$$
$$6x + 6 - 6 = 20 - 6$$
$$6x = 14$$
$$x = \frac{14}{6}$$
$$x = \frac{7}{3}$$

C) If there are radicals in the equation, it is necessary to square both sides and then apply A.

$$\sqrt{3x + 1} = 5$$
$$(\sqrt{3x + 1})^2 = 5^2$$
$$3x + 1 = 25$$
$$3x + 1 - 1 = 25 - 1$$
$$3x = 24$$
$$x = \frac{24}{3}$$
$$x = 8$$

An algebraic formula is a special type of equation of two or more variables in which one variable is isolated on one side (usually the left side). Most formulas have direct real-life applications.

PROBLEM

The formula $F = \dfrac{9}{5}C + 32$ is used to convert temperatures in degrees from Centigrade to Fahrenheit and vice versa. If $F = 50°$, what is the value of C?

SOLUTION

$50 = \frac{9}{5}C + 32$. Subtract 32 from each side to get

$18 = \frac{9}{5}C$. Thus, $C = 18 \div \frac{9}{5} = 10°$.

PROBLEM

> The formula $A = P + PRT$ is used to find a dollar amount when money grows at a simple interest rate. What is the value of P if $A = \$1200$, $R = 0.05$, and $T = 4$?

SOLUTION

$1200 = P + (P)(0.05)(4) = P + 0.20P$. Then $1200 = 1.20P$, which means that $P = \$1000$.

PROBLEM

> The formula $V = \frac{4}{3}\pi r^3$ is used to find the volume of a sphere, given the radius. If the radius of a sphere is doubled, by what factor is the volume changed?

SOLUTION

When the radius is doubled, the new volume is given as $V = \frac{4}{3}\pi(2r)^3 = (\frac{4}{3}\pi)(8r^3) = \frac{32}{3}\pi r^3$. This means that the new volume is 8 times as large as the original volume.

Drill: Formulas

1. The formula $A = \frac{1}{3}\pi r^2 h$ is used to find the volume of a cone, given the radius and the height. What is the value of h if $A = 297\pi$ and $r = 9$?

    (A) 9   (C) 11

    (B) 10   (D) 12

2. The formula $D = \frac{(n)(n-3)}{2}$ is used to find the number of diagonals of a polygon, given the number of sides. What is the value of D if $n = 30$?

    (A) 360   (C) 810

    (B) 405   (D) 900

3. In the formula $z = \frac{12x^2}{y}$, z varies directly as the square of x and inversely as y. What is the value of x if $z = 24$ and $y = \frac{1}{8}$?

    (A) $\frac{1}{2}$ (C) $\frac{1}{4}$

    (B) $\frac{3}{8}$ (D) $\frac{1}{5}$

Slope of the Line

The slope of the line containing two points (x_1, y_1) and (x_2, y_2) is given by:

$$\text{Slope} = m = \frac{y_2 - y_1}{x_2 - x_1}$$

Horizontal lines have a slope of zero, and the slope of vertical lines is undefined. Parallel lines have equal slopes and perpendicular lines have slopes that are negative reciprocals of each other.

The equation of a line with slope m passing through a point $Q(x_0, y_0)$ is of the form:

$$y - y_0 = m(x - x_0)$$

This is called the *point-slope form* of a linear equation.

The equation of a line passing through $Q(x_1, y_1)$ and $P(x_2, y_2)$ is given by:

$$\frac{y - y_1}{x - x_1} = \frac{y_2 - y_1}{x_2 - x_1}$$

This is the *two-point form* of a linear equation.

The equation of a line intersecting the x-axis at $(x_0, 0)$ and the y-axis at $(0, y_0)$ is given by:

$$\frac{x}{x_0} + \frac{y}{y_0} = 1$$

This is the *intercept form* of a linear equation.

The equation of a line with slope m intersecting the y-axis at $(0, b)$ is given by:

$$y = mx + b$$

This is the *slope-intercept* form of a linear equation.

PROBLEMS ON LINEAR EQUATIONS:

A) Find the slope, the y-intercept, and the x-intercept of the equation $2x - 3y - 18 = 0$.

Solution: The equation $2x - 3y - 18 = 0$ can be written in the form of the general linear equation, $ax + by = c$.

$$2x - 3y - 18 = 0$$
$$2x - 3y = 18$$

To find the slope and y-intercept, we derive them from the formula of the general linear equation $ax + by = c$. Dividing by b and solving for y, we obtain:

$$\frac{a}{b}x + y = \frac{c}{b}$$
$$y = \frac{c}{b} - \frac{a}{b}x$$

where $\frac{-a}{b}$ = slope and $\frac{c}{b}$ = y-intercept

To find the x-intercept, solve for x and let $y = 0$:

$$x = \frac{c}{a} - \frac{b}{a}y$$
$$x = \frac{c}{a}$$

In this form we have $a = 2$, $b = -3$, and $c = 18$. Thus,

$$\text{slope} = -\frac{a}{b} = -\frac{2}{-3} = \frac{2}{3}$$
$$y\text{-intercept} = \frac{c}{b} = \frac{18}{-3} = -6$$
$$x\text{-intercept} = \frac{c}{a} = \frac{18}{2} = 9$$

B) Find the equation for the line passing through $(3, 5)$ and $(-1, 2)$.

Solution A): We use the two-point form with $(x_1, y_1) = (3, 5)$ and $(x_2, y_2) = (-1, 2)$. Then

$$\frac{y - y_1}{x - x_1} = \frac{y_2 - y_1}{x_2 - x_1}$$
$$\frac{y_2 - y_1}{x_2 - x_1} = \frac{2 - 5}{-1 - 3} \quad \text{thus} \quad \frac{y - 5}{x - 3} = \frac{-3}{-4}$$

Cross multiply, $\qquad -4(y - 5) = -3(x - 3)$.

Distribute, $\qquad -4y + 20 = -3x + 9$

Place in general form, $3x - 4y = -11$.

Solution B): Does the same equation result if we let $(x_1, y_1) = (-1, 2)$ and $(x_2, y_2) = (3, 5)$?

$$\frac{y_2 - y_1}{x_2 - x_1} = \frac{5 - 2}{3 - (-1)} \quad \text{thus} \quad \frac{y - 2}{x + 1} = \frac{3}{4}$$

Cross multiply, $4(y - 2) = 3(x + 1)$

Distribute $3x - 4y = -11$

Place in general form, $3x - 4y = -11$.

Hence, either replacement results in the same equation. Keep in mind that the coefficient of the x-term should always be positive.

C) (a) Find the equation of the line passing through $(2, 5)$ with slope 3.

(b) Suppose a line passes through the y-axis at $(0, b)$. How can we write the equation if the point-slope form is used?

Solution C): (a) In the point-slope form, let $x_1 = 2$, $y_1 = 5$, $m = 3$.

The point-slope form of a line is:

$$y - y_1 = m(x - x_1)$$
$$y - 5 = 3(x - 2)$$
$$y - 5 = 3x - 6 \qquad \text{Distributive property}$$
$$y = 3x - 1 \qquad \text{Transposition}$$

(b) $y - b = m(x - 0)$
$$y = mx + b.$$

Notice that this is the slope-intercept form for the equation of a line.

PROBLEM

> Construct the graph of the function defined by $y = 3x - 9$.

SOLUTION

This linear equation is in the slope-intercept form, $y = mx + b$.

A line can be determined by two points. Let us choose the intercepts. The x-intercept lies on the x-axis and the y-intercept is on the y-axis.

We can find the y-intercept by assigning 0 to x in the given equation and then find the x-intercept by assigning 0 to y. It is helpful to have a third point. We find a third point by assigning 4 to x and solving for y. Thus, we get the following table of corresponding numbers:

x	$y = 3x - 9$	y
0	$y = 3(0) - 9$	-9
3	$0 = 3x - 9, x = \dfrac{9}{3} = 3$	0
4	$y = 3(4) - 9$	3

The three points are $(0, -9)$, $(3, 0)$, and $(4, 3)$. Draw a line through them as in Figure below.

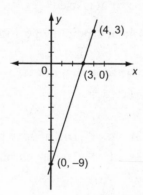

PROBLEM

> Graph the function defined by $3x - 4y = 12$.

SOLUTION

Solve for y:
$$3x - 4y = 12$$
$$-4y = 12 - 3x$$
$$y = -3 + \frac{3}{4}x$$
$$y = \frac{3}{4}x - 3$$

The graph of this function is a straight line since it is of the form $y = mx + b$. The y-intercept crosses (intersects) the y-axis at the point $(0, -3)$ since for $x = 0$, $y = b = -3$. The x-intercept crosses (intersects) the x-axis at the point $(4, 0)$ since for $y = 0$, $x = (y + 3) \times \dfrac{4}{3} = (0 + 3) \times \dfrac{4}{3} = 4$.

These two points, $(0, -3)$ and $(4, 0)$ are sufficient to determine the graph (see Figure below). A third point, $(8, 3)$, satisfying the equation of the function is plotted as a partial check of the intercepts. Note that the slope of the line is $m = \dfrac{3}{4}$. This means that y increases three units as x increases four units anywhere along the line.

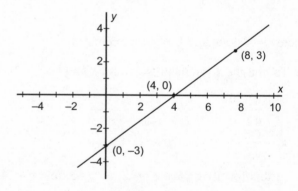

Two Linear Equations

Equations of the form $ax + by = c$, where a, b, c are constants and a, $b \neq 0$ are called **linear equations** with two unknown variables.

There are several ways to solve systems of linear equations with two variables.

Method 1: **Addition or subtraction**—If necessary, multiply the equations by numbers that will make the coefficients of one unknown in the resulting equations numerically equal. If the signs of equal coefficients are the same, subtract the equation; otherwise, add.

The result is one equation with one unknown; we solve it and substitute the value into the other equations to find the unknown that we first eliminated.

Method 2: **Substitution**—Find the value of one unknown in terms of the other. Substitute this value in the other equation and solve.

Method 3: **Graph**—Graph both equations. The point of intersection of the drawn lines is a simultaneous solution for the equations, and its coordinates correspond to the answer that would be found analytically.

If the lines are parallel they have no simultaneous solution.

Dependent equations are equations that represent the same line; therefore, every point on the line of a dependent equation represents a solution. Since there is an infinite number of points on a line, there is an infinite number of simultaneous solutions. For example,

$$\begin{cases} 2x + y = 8 \\ 4x + 2y = 16 \end{cases}$$

These equations are dependent. Since they represent the same line, all points that satisfy either of the equations are solutions of the system.

A system of linear equations is consistent if there is only one solution for the system.

A system of linear equations is inconsistent if it does not have any solutions.

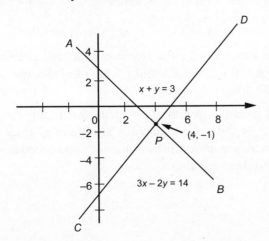

EXAMPLE

Find the point of intersection of the graphs of the equations as shown in the previous figure.

$$x + y = 3$$
$$3x - 2y = 14$$

To solve these linear equations, solve for y in terms of x. The equations will be in the form $y = mx + b$, where m is the slope and b is the intercept on the y-axis.

$$x + y = 3$$

Subtract x from both sides: $y = 3 - x$

Subtract $3x$ from both sides: $3x - 2y = 14$

Divide by -2: $\quad\quad\quad -2y = 14 - 3x$

$$y = -7 + \frac{3}{2}x$$

The graphs of the linear functions, $y = 3 - x$ and $y = 7 + \frac{3}{2}x$ can be determined by plotting only two points. For example, for $y = 3 - x$, let $x = 0$, then $y = 3$. Let $x = 1$, then $y = 2$. The two points on this first line are $(0, 3)$ and $(1, 2)$. For $y = -7 + \frac{3}{2}x$ let $x = 0$, then $y = -7$. Let $x = 1$, then $y = -5\frac{1}{2}$. The two points on this second line are $(0, -7)$ and $(1, -5\frac{1}{2})$.

To find the point of intersection P of

$$x + y = 3 \text{ and } 3x - 2y = 14,$$

solve them algebraically. Multiply the first equation by 2. Add these two equations to eliminate the variable y.

$$\begin{array}{r} 2x + 2y = 6 \\ 3x - 2y = 14 \\ \hline 5x \quad\quad = 20 \end{array}$$

Solve for x to obtain $x = 4$. Substitute this into $y = 3 - x$ to get $y = 3 - 4 = -1$. P is $(4, -1)$. AB is the graph of the first equation, and CD is the graph of the second equation. The point of intersection P of the two graphs is the only point on both lines. The coordinates of P satisfy both equations and represent the desired solution of the problem. From the graph, P seems to be the point $(4, -1)$. These coordinates satisfy both equations, and hence are the exact coordinates of the point of intersection of the two lines.

To show that $(4, -1)$ satisfies both equations, substitute this point into both equations.

$$x + y = 3 \qquad\qquad 3x - 2y = 14$$
$$4 + (-1) = 3 \qquad 3(4) - 2(-1) = 14$$
$$4 - 1 = 3 \qquad\qquad 12 + 2 = 14$$
$$3 = 3 \qquad\qquad\qquad 14 = 14$$

EXAMPLE

Solve the equations $2x + 3y = 6$ and $4x + 6y = 7$ simultaneously.

We have two equations and two unknowns,

$$2x + 3y = 6 \qquad\qquad (1)$$

and

$$4x + 6y = 7 \qquad\qquad (2)$$

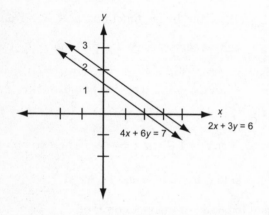

There are several methods to solve this problem. We have chosen to multiply each equation by a different number so that when the two equations are added, one of the variables drops out. Thus,

Multiply equation (1) by 2: $4x + 6y = 12$ (3)

Multiply equation (2) by -1: $\underline{-4x - 6y = -7}$ (4)

Add equations (3) and (4): $\qquad 0 = 5$

We obtain a peculiar result!

Actually, what we have shown in this case is that if there were a simultaneous solution to the given equations, then 0 would equal 5. But the conclusion is impossible; therefore, there can be no simultaneous solution to these two equations, hence no point satisfying both.

The straight lines which are the graphs of these equations must be parallel if they never intersect, but not identical, which can be seen from the graph of these equations (see the figure).

EXAMPLE

Solve the equations $2x + 3y = 6$ and $y = -\left(\dfrac{2x}{3}\right) + 2$ simultaneously.

We have two equations and two unknowns.

$$2x + 3y = 6 \qquad\qquad (1)$$

and

$$y = -\left(\frac{2x}{3}\right) + 2 \qquad\qquad (2)$$

There are several methods of solution for this problem. Since equation (2) already gives us an expression for y, we use the method of substitution.

Substitute $-\left(\dfrac{2x}{3}\right) + 2$ for y in the first equation:

$$2x + 3(-\frac{2x}{3} + 2) = 6$$

Distribute: $\qquad 2x - 2x + 6 = 6$
$$6 = 6$$

The result $6 = 6$ is true, but indicates no solution. Actually, our work shows that no matter what real number x is, if y is determined by the second equation, then the first equation will always be satisfied.

The reason for this peculiarity may be seen if we take a closer look at the equation $y = -\left(\dfrac{2x}{3}\right) + 2$. It is equivalent to $3y = -2x + 6$, or $2x + 3y = 6$.

In other words, the two equations are equivalent. Any pair of values of x and y which satisfies one satisfies the other.

It is hardly necessary to verify that in this case the graphs of the given equations are identical lines, and that there are an infinite number of simultaneous solutions to these equations.

A system of three linear equations in three unknowns is solved by eliminating one unknown from any two of the three equations and solving them. After finding two unknowns, substitute them in any of the equations to find the third unknown.

PROBLEM

Solve the system

$$2x + 3y - 4z = -8 \qquad (1)$$
$$x + y - 2z = -5 \qquad (2)$$
$$7x - 2y + 5z = 4 \qquad (3)$$

SOLUTION

We cannot eliminate any variable from two pairs of equations by a single multiplication. However, both x and z may be eliminated from equations (1) and (2) by multiplying equation (2) by -2. Then

$$2x + 3y - 4z = -8 \qquad (1)$$
$$-2x - 2y + 4z = 10 \qquad (4)$$

By addition, we have $y = 2$. Although we may now eliminate either x or z from another pair of equations, we can more conveniently substitute $y = 2$ in equations (2) and (3) to get two equations in two variables. Thus, making the substitution $y = 2$ in equations (2) and (3), we have

$$x - 2z = -7 \qquad (5)$$
$$7x + 5z = 8 \qquad (6)$$

Multiply equation (5) by 5 and multiply (6) by 2. Then add the two new equations. Then $x = -1$. Substitute x in either equation (5) or (6) to find z.

The solution of the system is $x = -1, y = 2,$ and $z = 3$. Check by substitution.

A system of equations, as shown below, that has all constant terms $b_1, b_2, \ldots, b_n$ equal to zero is said to be a homogeneous system.

$$\begin{cases} a_{11}x_1 + a_{12}x_2 + \ldots + a_{1n}x_m = b_1 \\ a_{21}x_1 + a_{22}x_2 + \ldots + a_{2n}x_m = b_2 \\ \vdots \qquad \vdots \qquad \qquad \vdots \\ a_{n1}x_1 + a_{n2}x_2 + \ldots + a_{nn}x_m = b_n \end{cases}$$

A homogeneous system (one in which each variable can be replaced by a constant and the constant can be factored out) always has at least one solution which is called the trivial solution that is $x_1 = 0, x_2 = 0, \ldots, x_m = 0$.

For any given homogeneous system of equations, in which the number of variables is greater than or equal to the number of equations, there are non-trivial solutions.

Two systems of linear equations are said to be equivalent if and only if they have the same solution set.

Drill: Two Linear Equations

DIRECTIONS: Find the solution set for each pair of equations.

1. $3x + 4y = -2$
   $x - 6y = -8$
   (A) $(2, -1)$ (C) $(-2, -1)$
   (B) $(1, -2)$ (D) $(-2, 1)$

2. $2x + y = -10$
   $-2x - 4y = 4$
   (A) $(6, -2)$ (C) $(-2, 6)$
   (B) $(-6, 2)$ (D) $(2, 6)$

3. $6x + 5y = -4$
   $3x - 3y = 9$
   (A) $(1, -2)$ (C) $(2, -1)$
   (B) $(1, 2)$ (D) $(-2, 1)$

4. $4x + 3y = 9$
   $2x - 2y = 8$
   (A) $(-3, 1)$ (C) $(3, 1)$
   (B) $(1, -3)$ (D) $(3, -1)$

5. $x + y = 7$
   $x = y - 3$
   (A) $(5, 2)$ (C) $(2, 5)$
   (B) $(-5, 2)$ (D) $(-2, 5)$

Quadratic Equations

A second-degree equation in x of the type $ax^2 + bx + c = 0$, $a \neq 0$, a, b, and c are real numbers, is called a quadratic equation.

To solve a quadratic equation is to find values of x which satisfy $ax^2 + bx + c = 0$. These values of x are called solutions, or roots, of the equation.

A quadratic equation has a maximum of two roots. Methods of solving quadratic equations:

A) Direct solution: Given $x^2 - 9 = 0$.

We can solve directly by isolating the variable x:

$x^2 = 9$

$x = \pm 3$

B) Factoring: Given a quadratic equation $ax^2 + bx + c = 0$, a, b, $c \neq 0$, to factor means to express it as the product $a(x - r_1)(x - r_2) = 0$, where r_1 and r_2 are the two roots.

Some helpful hints to remember are:

(a) $r_1 \cdot r_2 = \dfrac{c}{a}$.

(b) $r_1 + r_2 = \dfrac{-b}{a}$.

Given $x^2 - 5x + 4 = 0$.

Since $r_1 + r_2 = \dfrac{-b}{a} = \dfrac{-(-5)}{1} = 5$, the possible solutions are $(3, 2)$, $(4, 1)$, and $(5, 0)$.

Also $r_1 r_2 = \dfrac{c}{a} = \dfrac{4}{1} = 4$; this equation is satisfied only by the second pair, so $r_1 = 4$, $r_2 = 1$ and the factored form is $(x - 4)(x - 1) = 0$.

If the coefficient of x^2 is not 1, it is necessary to divide the equation by this coefficient and then factor.

Given $2x^2 - 12x + 16 = 0$.

Dividing by 2, we obtain:

$x^2 - 6x + 8 = 0$

Since $r_1 + r_2 = \dfrac{-b}{a} = 6$, the possible solutions are $(6, 0)$, $(5, 1)$, $(4, 2)$, $(3, 3)$. Also $r_1 r_2 = 8$, so the only possible answer is $(4, 2)$ and the expression $x^2 - 6x + 8 = 0$ can be factored as $(x - 4)(x - 2)$.

C) Completing the square: If it is difficult to factor the quadratic equation using the previous method, we can complete the square.

Given $x^2 - 12x + 8 = 0$.

We know that the two roots added up should be 12 because $r_1 + r_2 = \dfrac{-b}{a} = \dfrac{-(-12)}{1} = 12$. The possible roots are $(12, 0)$, $(11, 1)$, $(10, 2)$, $(9, 3)$, $(8, 4)$, $(7, 5)$, $(6, 6)$.

But none of these satisfy $r_1\, r_2 = 8$, so we cannot use (B).

To complete the square it is necessary to isolate the constant term,

$x^2 - 12x = -8$.

Then take $\dfrac{1}{2}$ coefficient of the x term, square it and add to both sides

$$x^2 - 12x + \left(\dfrac{-12}{2}\right)^2 = -8 + \left(\dfrac{-12}{2}\right)^2$$
$$x^2 - 12x + 36 = -8 + 36 = 28$$

Now we can use the previous method to factor the left side: $r_1 + r_2 = 12$, $r_1 r_2 = 36$ is satisfied by the pair $(6, 6)$, so we have:

$(x - 6)(x - 6) = (x - 6)^2 = 28$.

Now take the square root of both sides and solve for x. Remember when taking a square root that the solution can be positive or negative.

$(x - 6) = \pm\sqrt{28} = \pm 2\sqrt{7}$

$x = \pm 2\sqrt{7} + 6$

So the roots are: $x = 2\sqrt{7} + 6$, $x = -2\sqrt{7} + 6$

PROBLEM

Solve $2x^2 + 8x + 4 = 0$ by completing the square.

SOLUTION

Divide both members by 2, the coefficient of x^2.

$x^2 + 4x + 2 = 0$

Subtract the constant term, 2, from both members.

$x^2 + 4x = -2$

Add to each member the square of one-half the coefficient of the x-term.

$x^2 + 4x + 4 = -2 + 4$

Factor

$(x + 2)(x + 2) = (x + 2)^2 = 2$

Set the square root of the left member (a perfect square) equal to ± the square root of the right member and solve for x.

$x + 2 = \sqrt{2}$ or $x + 2 = -\sqrt{2}$

The roots are $\sqrt{2} - 2$ and $-\sqrt{2} - 2$. Check each solution.

$2\left(\sqrt{2} - 2\right)^2 + 8\left(\sqrt{2} - 2\right) + 4$

$\qquad = 2\left(2 - 4\sqrt{2} + 4\right) + 8\sqrt{2} - 16 + 4$

$\qquad = 4 - 8\sqrt{2} + 8 + 8\sqrt{2} - 16 + 4$

$\qquad = 0$

$2\left(-\sqrt{2} - 2\right)^2 + 8\left(-\sqrt{2} - 2\right) + 4$

$\qquad = 2\left(2 + 4\sqrt{2} + 4\right) - 8\sqrt{2} - 16 + 4$

$\qquad = 4 + 8\sqrt{2} + 8 - 8\sqrt{2} - 16 + 4$

$\qquad = 0$

Quadratic Formula

Consider the polynomial:

$ax^2 + bx + c = 0$, where $a \neq 0$.

The roots of this equation can be determined in terms of the coefficients a, b, and c as shown below:

$$x = \frac{-b \pm \sqrt{b^2 - 4ac}}{2a}$$

where $(b^2 - 4ac)$ is called the discriminant of the quadratic equation.

Note that if the discriminant is less than zero $(b^2 - 4ac < 0)$, the roots are complex numbers, since the discriminant appears under a radical and square roots of negatives are complex numbers, and a real number added to an imaginary number yields a complex number.

If the discriminant is equal to zero $(b^2 - 4ac = 0)$, the result is one real root.

If the discriminant is greater than zero $(b^2 - 4ac > 0)$, then the roots are real and unequal. Further, the roots are rational if and only if a and b are rational and $(b^2 - 4ac)$ is a perfect square, otherwise the roots are irrational.

Example: Compute the value of the discriminant and then determine the nature of the roots of each of the following four equations:

A) $4x^2 - 12x + 9 = 0$

B) $3x^2 - 7x - 6 = 0$

C) $5x^2 + 2x - 9 = 0$

D) $x^2 + 3x + 5 = 0$

A) $4x^2 - 12x + 9 = 0$,

Here a, b, and c are integers,

$\qquad a = 4$, $b = -12$, and $c = 9$.

Therefore,

$\qquad b^2 - 4ac = (-12)^2 - 4(4)(9) = 144 - 144 = 0.$

Since the discriminant is 0, the roots are rational and equal.

B) $3x^2 - 7x - 6 = 0$

Here a, b, and c are integers,

$\qquad a = 3$, $b = -7$, and $c = -6$.

Therefore,

$b^2 - 4ac = (-7)^2 - 4(3)(-6) = 49 + 72 = 121 = 11^2.$

Since the discriminant is a perfect square, the roots are rational and unequal.

C) $5x^2 + 2x - 9 = 0$

Here a, b, and c are integers,

$a = 5$, $b = 2$, and $c = -9$.

Therefore,

$b^2 - 4ac = 2^2 - 4(5)(-9) = 4 + 180 = 184$.

Since the discriminant is greater than zero, but not a perfect square, the roots are irrational and unequal.

D) $x^2 + 3x + 5 = 0$

Here a, b, and c are integers,

$a = 1$, $b = 3$, and $c = 5$.

Therefore,

$b^2 - 4ac = 3^2 - 4(1)(5) = 9 - 20 = -11$.

Since the discriminant is negative, the roots are imaginary.

EXAMPLE

Find the quadratic equation whose roots are -2 and 7.

Solution: The factored form is $(x + 2)(x - 7) = 0$. Then, by multiplication and simplification, the answer is $x^2 - 5x - 14 = 0$.

EXAMPLE

Find the quadratic equation whose roots are $\frac{1}{2}$ and 9.

Solution: The factored form is $(x - \frac{1}{2})(x - 9) = 0$. Multiplication and combining similar terms leads to $x^2 - \frac{19}{2}x + \frac{9}{2} = 0$. Multiply by 2 to get the answer $2x^2 - 19x - 9 = 0$.

EXAMPLE

Find the quadratic equation whose only root is $\frac{1}{4}$.

Solution: The factored form is $(x - \frac{1}{4})(x - \frac{1}{4}) = 0$. Multiplication and combining similar terms leads to $x^2 - \frac{1}{2}x + \frac{1}{16} = 0$. Multiply by 16 to get the answer $16x^2 - 8x + 1 = 0$.

EXAMPLE

The sum of the roots of a quadratic equation is 6 and the product of these roots is -16. Write the equation in simplified form.

Solution: Let $a = 1$ in the equation $ax^2 + bx + c = 0$. The equation becomes $x^2 + bx + c = 0$. The sum of the roots equals $-\frac{b}{a} = -b$. Since the sum is 6, this implies that $-b = 6$. So, $b = -6$. The product of the roots $= \frac{c}{a} = c$. Since the product is -16, this means that $c = -16$. The answer $x^2 - 6x - 16 = 0$.

EXAMPLE

The sum of the roots of a quadratic equation is $-\frac{9}{2}$ and the product of these roots is 2. Write the equation in simplified form.

Solution: Let $a = 1$ in the equation $ax^2 + bx + c = 0$. The equation becomes $x^2 + bx + c = 0$. Then $-\frac{b}{1} = -b = -\frac{9}{2}$, so $b = \frac{9}{2}$. Also, $\frac{c}{1} = c = 2$. The equation now reads as $x^2 + \frac{9}{2}x + 2 = 0$. Multiply by 2 to get the answer $2x^2 + 9x + 4 = 0$.

EXAMPLE

If the roots of the equation $x^2 + 5x + c = 0$ are complex numbers, what are the values of c?

Solution: The roots are complex numbers if $b^2 - 4ac < 0$. By substitution, $5^2 - (4)(1)(c) < 0$. Simplifying, this inequality becomes $25 - 4c < 0$. Then $-4c < -25$, so $c > \frac{25}{4}$.

Radical Equation

An equation that has one or more unknowns under a radical is called a radical equation.

To solve a radical equation, isolate the radical term on one side of the equation and move all the other terms to the other side. Then both members of the equation are raised to a power equal to the index of the isolated radical.

After solving the resulting equation, the roots obtained must be checked, since this method often introduces extraneous roots.

These introduced roots must be excluded if they are not solutions.

Given $\sqrt{x^2 + 2} + 6x = x - 4$

$$\sqrt{x^2 + 2} = x - 4 - 6x = -5x - 4$$

$$\left(\sqrt{x^2 + 2}\right)^2 = (-(5x + 4))^2$$

$$x^2 + 2 = (5x + 4)^2$$

$x^2 + 2 = 25x^2 + 40x + 16$

$24x^2 + 40x + 14 = 0$

Applying the quadratic formula, we obtain:

$$x = \frac{-40 \pm \sqrt{1600 - 4(24)(14)}}{2(24)} = \frac{-40 \pm 16}{48}$$

$$x_1 = \frac{-7}{6}, \ x_2 = \frac{-1}{2}$$

Checking roots:

$$\sqrt{\left(\frac{-7}{6}\right)^2 + 2} + 6\left(\frac{-7}{6}\right) \stackrel{?}{=} \left(\frac{-7}{6}\right) - 4$$

$$\frac{11}{6} - 7 \stackrel{?}{=} \frac{-31}{6}$$

$$\frac{-31}{6} = \frac{-31}{6}$$

$$\sqrt{\left(\frac{-1}{2}\right)^2 + 2} + 6\left(\frac{-1}{2}\right) \stackrel{?}{=} \left(\frac{-1}{2}\right) - 4$$

$$\frac{3}{2} - 3 \stackrel{?}{=} \frac{-9}{2}$$

$$\frac{-3}{2} \neq \frac{-9}{2}$$

Hence, $-\frac{1}{2}$ is not a root of the equation, but $\frac{-7}{6}$ is a root.

PROBLEM

Solve for x: $4x^2 - 7 = 0$.

SOLUTION

This quadratic equation can be solved for x using the quadratic formula, which applies to equations in the form $ax^2 + bx + c = 0$ (in our equation $b = 0$). There is, however, an easier method that we can use:

Adding 7 to both sides, $4x^2 = 7$

Dividing both sides by 4, $x^2 = \frac{7}{4}$

Taking the square root of both sides, $x = \pm\sqrt{\frac{7}{4}} = \pm\frac{\sqrt{7}}{2}$.

The double sign $\pm$ (read "plus or minus") indicates that the two roots of the equation are $+\frac{\sqrt{7}}{2}$ and $-\frac{\sqrt{7}}{2}$.

PROBLEM

Solve the equation $2x^2 - 5x + 3 = 0$.

SOLUTION

$2x^2 - 5x + 3 = 0$

The equation is a quadratic equation of the form $ax^2 + bx + c = 0$ in which $a = 2$, $b = -5$, and $c = 3$. Therefore, the quadratic formula $x = \frac{-b \pm \sqrt{b^2 - 4ac}}{2a}$ may be used to find the solutions of the given equation. Substituting the values for a, b, and c in the quadratic formula:

$$x = \frac{-(-5) \pm \sqrt{(-5)^2 - 4(2)(3)}}{2(2)}$$

$$x = \frac{5 \pm \sqrt{1}}{4}$$

$$x = \frac{5 + 1}{4} = \frac{3}{2} \text{ and } x = \frac{5 - 1}{4} = 1$$

Check: Substituting $x = \frac{3}{2}$ in the given equation,

$$2\left(\frac{3}{2}\right)^2 - 5\left(\frac{3}{2}\right) + 3 = 0$$

$$0 = 0$$

Substituting $x = 1$ in the given equation,

$$2(1)^2 - 5(1) + 3 = 0$$

$$0 = 0$$

So the roots of $2x^2 - 5x + 3 = 0$ are $x = \dfrac{3}{2}$ and $x = 1$.

Quadratic Functions

The function $f(x) = ax^2 + bx + c, a \pm 0$, where a, b, and c are real numbers, is called a quadratic function (or a function of second degree) in one unknown.

The graph of $y = ax^2 + bx + c$ is a curve known as a parabola.

The vertex of the parabola is the point $v\left(\dfrac{-b}{2a}, \dfrac{4ac - b^2}{4a}\right)$. The parabola's axis is the line $x = \dfrac{-b}{2a}$.

The graph of the parabola opens upward if $a > 0$ and downward if $a < 0$. If $a = 0$ the quadratic is reduced to a linear function whose graph is a straight line.

Figures below show parabolas with $a > 0$, and $a < 0$, respectively.

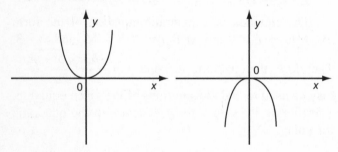

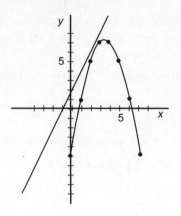

PROBLEM

Solve the system

$$y = -x^2 + 7x - 5 \qquad (1)$$

$$y - 2x = 2 \qquad (2)$$

SOLUTION

Solving Equation (2) for y yields an expression for y in terms of x. Substituting this expression in Equation (1),

$$2x + 2 = -x^2 + 7x - 5 \qquad (3)$$

We have a single equation, in terms of a single variable, to be solved. Writing Equation (3) in standard quadratic form,

$$x^2 - 5x + 7 = 0 \qquad (4)$$

Since the equation is not factorable, the roots are not found in this manner. Evaluating the discriminant will indicate whether Equation (4) has real roots. The discriminant, $b^2 - 4ac$, of Equation (4) equals $(-5)^2 - 4(1)(7) = 25 - 28 = -3$. Since the discriminant is negative, equation (4) has no real roots, and therefore the system has no real solution. In terms of the graph, the figure shows that the parabola and the straight line have no point in common.

PROBLEM

Solve the system

$$y = 3x^2 - 2x + 5 \qquad (1)$$

$$y = 4x + 2 \qquad (2)$$

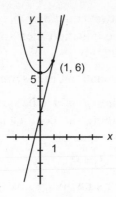

SOLUTION

To obtain a single equation with one unknown variable, x, substitute the value of y from Equation (2) in Equation (1),

$$4x + 2 = 3x^2 - 2x + 5. \tag{3}$$

Writing Equation (3) in standard quadratic form,

$$3x^2 - 6x + 3 = 0. \tag{4}$$

We may simplify equation (4) by dividing both members by 3, which is a factor common to each term:

$$x^2 - 2x + 1 = 0. \tag{5}$$

To find the roots, factor and set each factor $= 0$. This may be done since a product $= 0$ implies one or all of the factors must $= 0$.

$$(x - 1)(x - 1) = 0$$
$$x - 1 = 0 \quad x - 1 = 0$$
$$x = 1 \quad\quad x = 1$$

Equation (5) has two equal roots, each equal to 1. For $x = 1$, from Equation (2), we have $y = 4(1) + 2 = 6$. Therefore, the system has but one common solution:

$$x = 1, \quad y = 6.$$

The figure indicates that our solution is probably correct. We may also check to see if our values satisfy Equation (1) as well:

Substituting in: $y = 3x^2 - 2x + 5$

$$6 \overset{?}{=} 3(1)^2 - 2(1) + 5$$
$$6 \overset{?}{=} 3 - 2 + 5$$
$$6 = 6$$

Quadratic Equations in Two Unknowns and Systems of Equations

A quadratic equation in two unknowns has the general form:

$$ax^2 + bxy + cy^2 + dx + ey + f = 0$$

where a, b, and c are not all zero and a, b, c, d, e, and f are constants.

Graphing: If $b^2 - 4ac < 0$, $b \neq 0$ and $a \neq c$, the graph of $ax^2 + bxy + cy^2 + dx + ey + f = 0$ is a closed curve called an ellipse. If $b = 0$ and $a = c$, the graph $ax^2 + bxy + cy^2 + dx + ey + f = 0$ is a point or a circle, or else it does not exist.

If $b^2 - 4ac > 0$, the graph of $ax^2 + bxy + cy^2 + dx + ey + f = 0$ is a curve called a hyperbola.

If $b^2 - 4ac = 0$, the graph of $ax^2 + bxy + cy^2 + dx + ey + f = 0$ is a parabola or a pair of parallel lines which may be coincident, or else it does not exist.

Solving Systems of Equations Involving Quadratics

Some methods for solving systems of equations involving quadratics are given below:

A) One linear and one quadratic equation

Solve the linear equation for one of the two unknowns, then substitute this value into the quadratic equation.

B) Two quadratic equations

Eliminate one of the unknowns using the method given for solving systems of linear equations.

Example:

$$\begin{cases} x^2 + y^2 = 9 & (1) \\ x^2 + 2y^2 = 18 & (2) \end{cases}$$

Subtracting Equation (1) from (2), we obtain:

$$y^2 = 9, y = \pm 3$$

By substituting the values of y into (1) or (2), we obtain:

$x_1 = 0$ and $x_2 = 0$

So the solutions are:

$x = 0, y = 3$ and $x = 0, y = -3$

C) Two quadratic equations, one homogeneous

An equation is said to be homogeneous if it is of the form

$ax^2 + bxy + cy^2 + dx + ey = 0.$

Consider the system

$$\begin{cases} x^2 + 3xy + 2y^2 = 0 & (1) \\ x^2 - 3xy + 2y^2 = 12 & (2) \end{cases}$$

Equation (1) can be factored into the product of two linear equations:

$x^2 + 3xy + 2y^2 = (x + 2y)(x + y) = 0$

From this we determine that:

$x + 2y = 0 \Rightarrow x = -2y$
$x + y = 0 \Rightarrow x = -y$

Substituting $x = -2y$ into Equation (2), we find:

$(-2y)^2 - 3(-2y)y + 2y^2 = 12$
$\qquad 4y^2 + 6y^2 + 2y^2 = 12$
$\qquad\qquad 12y^2 = 12$
$\qquad\qquad y^2 = 1$
$\qquad\qquad y = \pm 1, \text{ so } x = \pm 2$

Substituting $x = -y$ into Equation (2) yields:

$(-y)^2 - 3(-y)y + 2y^2 = 12$
$\quad y^2 + 3y^2 + 2y^2 = 12$
$\qquad\qquad 6y^2 = 12$
$\qquad\qquad y^2 = 2$
$\qquad\qquad y = \pm\sqrt{2}, \text{ so } x = \pm\sqrt{2}$

So the solutions of Equations (1) and (2) are:

$x = 2, y = -1, x = -2, y = 1, x = \sqrt{2}, y = -\sqrt{2},$
and $x = -\sqrt{2}, y = \sqrt{2}$

D) Two quadratic equations of the form

$ax^2 + bxy + cy^2 = d$

Combine the two equations to obtain a homogeneous quadratic equation then solve the equations by the third method.

E) Two quadratic equations, each symmetrical in x and y

Note: An equation is said to be symmetrical in x and y if by exchanging the coefficients of x and y we obtain the same equation.

Example: $x^2 + y^2 = 9$.

To solve systems involving this type of equations, substitute $u + v$ for x and $u - v$ for y and solve the resulting equations for u and v.

Example: Given the system below:

$$\begin{cases} x^2 + y^2 = 25 & (1) \\ x^2 + xy + y^2 = 37 & (2) \end{cases}$$

Substitute:

$x = u + v$

$y = u - v$

If we substitute the new values for x and y into Equation (2) we obtain:

$(u + v)^2 + (u + v)(u - v) + (u - v)^2 = 37$
$u^2 + 2uv + v^2 + u^2 - v^2 + u^2 - 2uv + v^2 = 37$
$\qquad\qquad 3u^2 + v^2 = 37.$

If we substitute for x and y into Equation (1), we obtain:

$\qquad (u + v)^2 + (u - v)^2 = 25$
$u^2 + 2uv + v^2 + u^2 - 2uv + v^2 = 25$
$\qquad\qquad 2u^2 + 2v^2 = 25.$

The "new" system is:

$\qquad 3u^2 + v^2 = 37$
$\qquad 2u^2 + 2v^2 = 25$

By substituting $a = u^2$ and $b = v^2$, these equations become:

$$\begin{cases} 3a + b = 37 \\ 2a + 2b = 25 \end{cases}$$

and

$$a = \frac{49}{4}, \quad b = \frac{1}{4}$$

So

$$u^2 = \frac{49}{4} \quad \text{and} \quad v^2 = \frac{1}{4}$$

$$u = \pm \frac{7}{2}$$

$$v = \pm \frac{1}{2}$$

$$x = \frac{7}{2} + \frac{1}{2} = 4 \quad \text{or} \quad \frac{-7}{2} - \frac{1}{2} = -4$$

$$y = \frac{7}{2} - \frac{1}{2} = 3 \quad \text{or} \quad \frac{-7}{2} + \frac{1}{2} = -3$$

Since x and y are symmetrical, the possible solutions are $(4, 3)$, $(-4, -3)$, $(3, 4)$, $(-3, -4)$.

Note that if the equation is symmetrical it is possible to interchange the solutions too. If $x = 3$, then $y = 4$ or vice-versa.

PROBLEM

Solve the system:

$$2x^2 - 3xy - 4y^2 + x + y - 1 = 0$$
$$2x - y = 3$$

SOLUTION

A system of equations consisting of one linear and one quadratic is solved by expressing one of the unknowns in the linear equation in terms of the other, and substituting the result in the quadratic equation. From the second equation, $y = 2x - 3$. Replacing y by this linear function of x in the first equation, we find

$$2x^2 - 3x(2x - 3) - 4(2x - 3)^2 + x + 2x - 3 - 1 = 0$$
$$2x^2 - 3x(2x - 3) - 4(4x^2 - 12x + 9) + x + 2x - 3 - 1 = 0$$

Distribute,

$$2x^2 - 6x^2 + 9x - 16x^2 + 48x - 36 + x + 2x - 3 - 1 = 0$$

Combine terms, $\qquad -20x^2 + 60x - 40 = 0$

Divide both side by -20, $\quad \dfrac{20x^2}{-20} + \dfrac{60x}{-20} - \dfrac{40}{-20} = \dfrac{0}{-20}$

$$x^2 - 3x + 2 = 0$$

Factoring, $\qquad\qquad (x - 2)(x - 1) = 0$

Setting each factor equal to zero, we obtain:

$$x - 2 = 0 \qquad\qquad x - 1 = 0$$
$$x = 2 \qquad\qquad\quad x = 1$$

To find the corresponding y-values, substitute the x-values in $y = 2x - 3$:

when $x = 1$, $\qquad\qquad$ when $x = 2$,

$$y = 2(1) - 3 \qquad\qquad y = 2(2) - 3$$
$$y = 2 - 3 \qquad\qquad\quad y = 4 - 3$$
$$y = -1 \qquad\qquad\qquad y = 1$$

Therefore, the two solutions of the system are

$$(1, -1), \qquad\qquad\qquad (2, 1),$$

and the solution set is $\{(1, -1), (2, 1)\}$.

PROBLEM

Solve the system:

$$2x^2 - 3xy + 4y^2 = 3 \qquad (1)$$
$$x^2 + xy - 8y^2 = -6 \qquad (2)$$

SOLUTION

Multiply both sides of the first equation by 2.

$$2\left(2x^2 - 3xy + 4y^2\right) = 2(3)$$
$$4x^2 - 6xy + 8y^2 = 6 \qquad (3)$$

Add Equation (3) to Equation (2):

$$\begin{array}{r} x^2 + xy - 8y^2 = -6 \\ 4x^2 - 6xy + 8y^2 = 6 \\ \hline 5x^2 - 5xy = 0 \end{array} \qquad (4)$$

Factoring out the common factor, $5x$, from the left side of Equation (4):

$$5x(x - y) = 0$$

Whenever a product $ab = 0$, where a and b are any two numbers, either $a = 0$ or $b = 0$ or both. Hence, either

$$5x = 0 \qquad \text{or} \qquad x - y = 0$$
$$x = \frac{0}{5} \qquad\qquad\qquad x = y$$
$$x = 0$$

Substituting $x = 0$ in Equation (1):

$$2(0)^2 - 3(0)y + 4y^2 = 3$$
$$0 - 0 + 4y^2 = 3$$
$$4y^2 = 3$$
$$y^2 = \frac{3}{4}$$

$$y = \pm\sqrt{\frac{3}{4}}$$
$$= \pm\frac{\sqrt{3}}{\sqrt{4}}$$
$$= \pm\frac{\sqrt{3}}{2}$$

Hence, two solutions are: $\left(0, \dfrac{\sqrt{3}}{2}\right), \left(0, -\dfrac{\sqrt{3}}{2}\right)$

Substituting x for y ($x = y$) in equation (1):

$$2x^2 - 3x(x) + 4(x)^2 = 3$$
$$2x^2 - 3x^2 + 4x^2 = 3$$
$$-x^2 + 4x^2 = 3$$
$$3x^2 = 3$$
$$x2 = \frac{3}{3}$$
$$x2 = 1$$
$$x = \pm\sqrt{1} = \pm 1$$

Therefore, when $x = 1$, $y = x = 1$. Also, when $x = -1$, $y = x = -1$. Hence, two other solutions are: $(1, 1)$ and $(-1, -1)$. Thus the four solutions of the system are

$$\left(0, \frac{\sqrt{3}}{2}\right), \left(0, -\frac{\sqrt{3}}{2}\right), (1,1), \text{ and } (-1,-1)$$

Drill: Quadratic Equations

Solve for all values of x.

1. $x^2 - 2x - 8 = 0$

    (A) 4 and –2   (D) –2 and 8

    (B) 4 and 8   (E) –2

    (C) 4

2. $x^2 + 2x - 3 = 0$

    (A) –3 and 2   (D) –3 and 1

    (B) 2 and 1   (E) –3

    (C) 3 and 1

3. $x^2 - 7x = -10$

    (A) –3 and 5   (D) –2 and –5

    (B) 2 and 5   (E) 5

    (C) 2

4. $x^2 - 8x + 16 = 0$

    (A) 8 and 2   (D) –2 and 4

    (B) 1 and 16   (E) 4 and –4

    (C) 4

5. $3x^2 + 3x = 6$

   (A)   3 and –6   (D)   1 and –3

   (B)   2 and 3   (E)   1 and –2

   (C)   –3 and 2

6. $x^2 + 7x = 0$

   (A)   7   (D)   0 and 7

   (B)   0 and –7   (E)   0

   (C)   –7

7. $x^2 – 25 = 0$

   (A)   5   (D)   –5 and 10

   (B)   5 and –5   (E)   –5

   (C)   15 and 10

8. $2x^2 + 4x = 16$

   (A)   2 and –2   (D)   2 and –4

   (B)   8 and –2   (E)   2 and 4

   (C)   4 and 8

9. $2x^2 – 11x – 6 = 0$

   (A)   1 and –3   (D)   –4

   (B)   0 and 4   (E) $-\dfrac{1}{2}$ and 6

   (C)   1

10. $x^2 – 2x – 3 = 0$

   (A)   0   (D)   2

   (B)   –1 and 3   (E)   1 and –2

   (C)   5 and –3

ANSWER KEY

1. (A)
2. (D)
3. (B)
4. (C)
5. (E)

6. (B)
7. (B)
8. (D)
9. (E)
10. (B)

Absolute Value Equations

The absolute value of a, $|a|$, is defined as

$|a| = a$ when $a > 0$,

$|a| = -a$ when $a < 0$,

$|a| = 0$ when $a = 0$.

When the definition of absolute value is applied to an equation, the quantity within the absolute value symbol is considered to have two values. This value can be either positive or negative before the absolute value is taken. As a result, each absolute value equation actually contains two separate equations.

When evaluating equations containing absolute values, proceed as follows:

EXAMPLE

$|5 - 3x| = 7$ is valid if either

$$5 - 3x = 7 \qquad \text{or} \qquad 5 - 3x = -7$$
$$-3x = 2 \qquad\qquad\qquad -3x = -12$$
$$x = -\frac{2}{3} \qquad\qquad\qquad x = 4$$

The solution set is therefore $x = \left(-\frac{2}{3}, 4\right)$.

Remember, the absolute value of a number cannot be negative. So, for the equation $|5x + 4| = -3$, there would be no solution.

Drill: Absolute Value Equations

DIRECTIONS: Find the appropriate solutions.

1. $|4x - 2| = 6$

   (A) -2 and -1 (C) 2

   (B) -1 and 2 (D) No solution

2. $\left|3 - \frac{1}{2}y\right| = -7$

   (A) -8 and 20 (C) 2 and -5

   (B) 8 and -20 (D) No solution

3. $2|x + 7| = 12$

   (A) -13 and -1 (C) -1 and 13

   (B) -6 and 6 (D) No solution

4. $|5x| - 7 = 3$

   (A) 2 and 4 (C) -2 and 2

   (B) $\frac{4}{5}$ and 3 (D) No solution

5. $\left|\frac{3}{4}m\right| = 9$

   (A) 24 and -16 (C) -12 and 12

   (B) $\frac{4}{27}$ and $-\frac{4}{3}$ (D) No solution

Inequalities

An inequality is a statement where the value of one quantity or expression is greater than ($>$), less than ($<$), greater than or equal to ($\geq$), less than or equal to ($\leq$), or not equal to ($\neq$) that of another.

EXAMPLE

$5 > 4$

The expression above means that the value of 5 is greater than the value of 4.

A **conditional inequality** is an inequality whose validity depends on the values of the variables in the expression. That is, certain values of the variables will make the expression true, and others will make it false.

$3 - y > 3 + y$

is a conditional inequality for the set of real numbers, since it is true for any replacement less than zero and false for all others.

$x + 5 > x + 2$

is an **absolute inequality** for the set of real numbers, meaning that for any real value x, the expression on the left is greater than the expression on the right.

$5y < 2y + y$

is inconsistent for the set of non-negative real numbers. For any y greater than 0 the sentence is always false.

An expression is inconsistent if it is always false when its variables assume allowable values.

The solution of a given inequality in one variable x consists of all values of x for which the inequality is true.

The graph of an inequality in one variable is represented by either a ray or a line segment on the real number line.

The endpoint is not a solution if the variable is strictly less than or greater than a particular value.

EXAMPLE

$x > 2$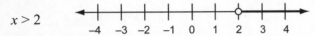

2 is not a solution and should be represented as shown.

The endpoint is a solution if the variable is either (1) less than or equal to or (2) greater than or equal to a particular value.

EXAMPLE

$5 > x \geq 2$

In this case 2 is a solution and should be represented as shown.

Properties of Inequalities

If x and y are real numbers, then one and only one of the following statements is true.

$x > y$, $x = y$, or $x < y$.

This is the order property of real numbers.

If a, b, and c are real numbers, the following statements are true:

A) If $a < b$ and $b < c$ then $a < c$.

B) If $a > b$ and $b > c$ then $a > c$.

This is the transitive property of inequalities.

If a, b, and c are real numbers and $a > b$, then $a + c > b + c$ and $a - c > b - c$. This is the **addition property of inequality.**

Two inequalities are said to have the same **sense** if their signs of inequality point in the same direction.

The sense of an inequality remains the same if both sides are multiplied or divided by the same positive real number.

EXAMPLE

$4 > 3$

If we multiply both sides by 5, we will obtain

$4 \times 5 > 3 \times 5$

$20 > 15$

The sense of the inequality does not change.

The sense of an inequality becomes opposite if each side is multiplied or divided by the same negative real number.

EXAMPLE

$4 > 3$

If we multiply both sides by -5, we would obtain

$4 \times -5 < 3 \times -5$

$-20 < -15$

The sense of the inequality becomes opposite.

If $a > b$ and a, b, and n are positive real numbers, then

$a^n > b^n$ and $a^{-n} < b^{-n}$

If $x > y$ and $q > p$, then $x + q > y + p$.

If $x > y > 0$ and $q > p > 0$, then $xq > yp$.

Inequalities that have the same solution set are called **equivalent inequalities.**

PROBLEM

Solve the inequality $2x + 5 > 9$.

SOLUTION

Add -5 to both sides: $2x + 5 + (-5) > 9 + (-5)$

Additive inverse property: $2x + 0 > 9 + (-5)$

Additive identity property: $2x > 9 + (-5)$

Combine terms: $2x > 4$

Multiply both sides by $\frac{1}{2}$: $\frac{1}{2}(2x) > \frac{1}{2} \times 4$

$x > 2$

The solution set is

$$X = \{x \mid 2x + 5 > 9\}$$
$$= \{x \mid x > 2\}$$

(that is all x, such that x is greater than 2).

Drill: Inequalities

DIRECTIONS: Find the solution set for each inequality.

1. $3m + 2 < 7$

    (A) $m \geq \dfrac{5}{3}$ (C) $m < 2$

    (B) $m > 2$ (D) $m < \dfrac{5}{3}$

2. $\dfrac{1}{2}x - 3 \leq 1$

    (A) $-4 \leq x \leq 8$ (C) $x \leq 8$

    (B) $x \geq -8$ (D) $2 \leq x \leq 8$

3. $-3p + 1 \geq 16$

    (A) $p \geq -5$ (C) $p \leq \dfrac{-17}{3}$

    (B) $p \geq \dfrac{-17}{3}$ (D) $p \leq -5$

4. $-6 < \dfrac{2}{3}r + 6 \leq 2$

    (A) $-6 < r \leq -3$ (C) $r \geq -6$

    (B) $-18 < r \leq -6$ (D) $-2 < r \leq -\dfrac{4}{3}$

5. $0 < 2 - y < 6$

    (A) $-4 < y < 2$ (C) $-4 < y < -2$

    (B) $-4 < y < 0$ (D) $-2 < y < 4$

Graphing Linear Inequalities

These inequalities involve x and y in the traditional coordinate plane. They are often used to model real-life problems such as those related to product consumerism, nutrition, and investments.

We begin with two definitions. The **right half-plane** is represented by the region that lies to the right of the *y*-axis. Similarly, the **left half-plane** is represented by the region that lies to the left of the *y*-axis. Note that the *y*-axis does not lie in either half-plane. Figure 2.1 illustrates these two half-planes.

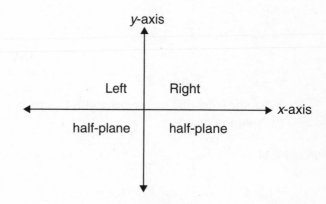

Figure 2.1

An example of a graph that lies entirely in the right-half plane would be $x > 3$. In the *xy*-coordinate plane, the set of points that satisfy this inequality would be any ordered pair in which the *x* value is greater than 3. Note that there is no restriction on the *y* value.

Figure 2.2 shows the graph of $x > 3$.

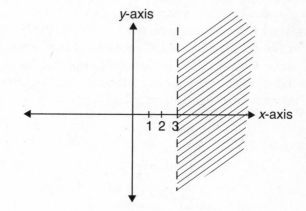

Figure 2.2

Note that the graph of $x > 3$ is represented by a dotted line. This means that any point on this dotted line is <u>not</u> part of the solution to $x > 3$.

As a second example, the graph of $x \leq -2$ lies entirely in the left half-plane. Since the inequality includes the equal sign, a solid line is used in graphing. This is shown in Figure 2.3.

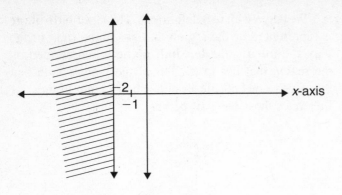

Figure 2.3

Note that the solid line represents points that do belong to the solution of $x \le -2$.

PROBLEM

Graph the solution for the inequality $3x + y \le 7$.

SOLUTION

First, solve this inequality for y, yielding $y \le -3x + 7$. The second step is to graph the equation $y = -3x + 7$. A quick way to graph this line would be to select two values of x, then find the corresponding y values. By selecting $x = 0$ and 1, we determine the two points to be (0, 7) and (1, 4). Finally, since we want all y values less than or equal to $-3x + 7$, we shade the section of the plane that lies below this solid line. (The line is solid because the inequality includes the equal sign.) Figure 2.4 shows the solution.

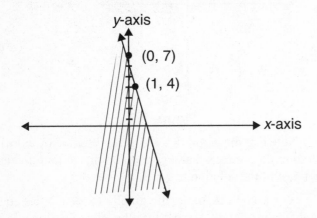

Figure 2.4

PROBLEM

Graph the system of inequalities
$$\begin{cases} 2x + y \le 4 \\ x - 3y < 2 \end{cases}$$

SOLUTION

Solving the first inequality for y leads to $y \le -2x + 4$. To graph the corresponding equation $y = -2x + 4$, let's use the x values of 1 and 2. The two selected points are (1, 2) and (2, 0). If we call the graph of $y = -2x + 4$ line l_1, we will shade the region below the solid line for l_1. Figure 2.5 shows the solution thus far.

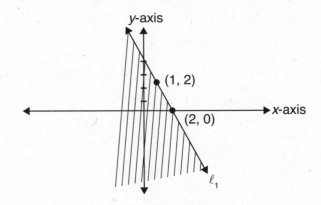

Figure 2.5

Now, in solving the second inequality for y, we first subtract x to get $-3y < -x + 2$. Next, divide by -3 and remember to reverse the inequality sign. This yields $y > \dfrac{1}{3}x - \dfrac{2}{3}$, so the associated equation is $y = \dfrac{1}{3}x - \dfrac{2}{3}$. We'll use x values of 5 and -1. The points to be graphed are (5, 1) and ($-1, -1$). Since the inequality is a "greater than" symbol, we will shade the region above the dotted line, which we will call l_2. The graph is shown in Figure 2.6.

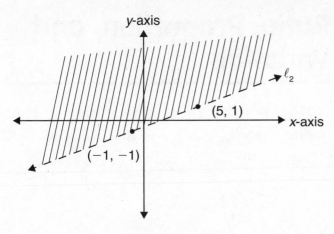

Figure 2.6

The last step is to place these two lines on the same coordinate axes and graph the intersection of the two regions obtained in Figures 3.26 and 3.27. Thus, the solution appears as shown in Figure 2.7.

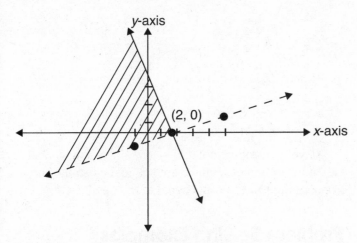

Figure 2.7

Notice that the point (2, 0) represents the intersection of the lines $y = -2x + 4$ and $y = \frac{1}{3}x - \frac{2}{3}$.

Drill: Graphing Linear Inequalities

DIRECTIONS: Find the appropriate solutions.

1. In the graph below, line l_1 represents the equation $y = x - 1$ and line l_2 represents the equation $y = -2x + 8$.

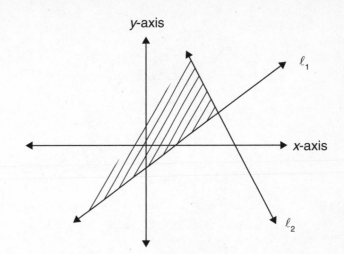

Which of the following systems of inequalities does the shaded region represent?

(A) $\begin{aligned} y \geq x - 1 \\ y \geq -2x + 8 \end{aligned}$ (C) $\begin{aligned} y \leq x - 1 \\ y \leq -2x + 8 \end{aligned}$

(B) $\begin{aligned} y \leq x - 1 \\ y \geq -2x + 8 \end{aligned}$ (D) $\begin{aligned} y \geq x - 1 \\ y \leq -2x + 8 \end{aligned}$

2. Which of the following shaded regions graphically represents the inequalities $0 \leq y \leq 2$ and $-4 \leq x \leq 4$?

A.

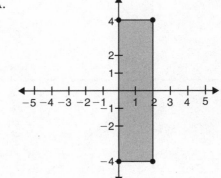

B.

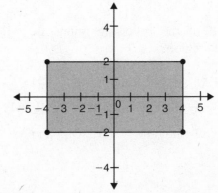

C.

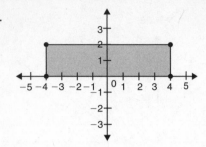

D.

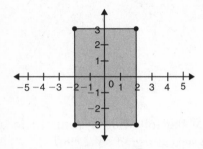

3. Consider the following graph of the intersection of two lines.

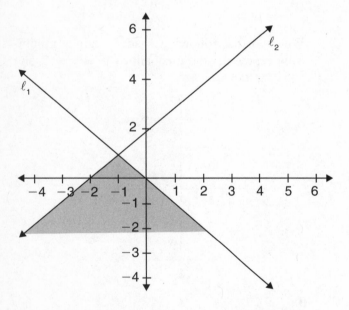

Which of the following points lie within the shaded region?

I. $(-1,3)$ II. $(0.5,0)$ III. $(-2,-1.5)$ IV. $(1,-2)$

(A) Only II and III   (C) Only III and IV

(B) Only I and IV   (D) Only I and II

Ratio, Proportion, and Variation

The ratio of two numbers x and y written $x{:}y$ is the fraction $\dfrac{x}{y}$ where $y \neq 0$. A proportion is an equality of two ratios. The laws of proportion are listed below:

If $\dfrac{a}{b} = \dfrac{c}{d}$, then:

A) $ad = bc$

B) $\dfrac{b}{a} = \dfrac{d}{c}$

C) $\dfrac{a}{c} = \dfrac{b}{d}$

D) $\dfrac{a+b}{b} = \dfrac{c+d}{d}$

E) $\dfrac{a-b}{b} = \dfrac{c-d}{d}$

Given a proportion $a{:}b = c{:}d$, then a and d are called the extremes, b and c are called the means, and d is called the fourth proportional to a, b, and c.

Problem Solving Examples:

PROBLEM

Solve the proportion $\dfrac{x+1}{4} = \dfrac{15}{12}$.

SOLUTION

Cross multiply to determine x; that is, multiply the numerator of the first fraction by the denominator of the second, and equate this to the product of the numerator of the second and the denominator of the first.

$(x + 1)12 = 4 \times 15$

$12x + 12 = 60$

$x = 4$

PROBLEM

If $\dfrac{a}{b} = \dfrac{c}{d}$, $a + b = 60$, $c = 3$, and $d = 2$, find b.

SOLUTION

We are given $\dfrac{a}{b} = \dfrac{c}{d}$. Cross multiplying, we obtain $ad = bc$.

Adding bd to both sides, we have $ad + bd = bc + bd$, which is equivalent to $d(a + b) = b(c + d)$ or

$$\frac{a+b}{b} = \frac{c+d}{d}$$

Replacing $(a + b)$ by 60, c by 3, and d by 2, we obtain

$$\frac{60}{b} = \frac{3+2}{2}$$

$$\frac{60}{b} = \frac{5}{2}$$

Cross multiplying, $5b = 120$

$$b = 24.$$

Variation

A) If x is directly proportional to y, written $x \alpha y$, then $x = ky$ or $\dfrac{x}{y} = k$, where k is called the constant of proportionality or the constant of variation.

B) If x varies inversely as y, then $x = \dfrac{k}{y}$.

C) If x varies jointly as y and z, then $x = kyz$.

Example: If y varies jointly as x and z, and $3x{:}1 = y{:}z$, find the constant of variation.

Solution: A variable s is said to vary jointly as t and v if s varies directly as the product tv, that is, if $s = ktv$ where k is called the constant of variation.

Here the variable y varies jointly as x and z with k as the constant of variation.

$$y = kxz$$

$$3x{:}1 = y{:}z$$

Expressing these ratios as fractions,

$$\frac{3x}{1} = \frac{y}{z}$$

Solving for y by cross-multiplying,

$$y = 3xz$$

Equating both relations for y, we have:

$$kxz = 3xz$$

Solving for the constant of variation, k, we divide both sides by xz,

$$k = 3.$$

PROBLEM

If y varies directly with respect to x and $y = 3$ when $x = -2$, find y when $x = 8$.

SOLUTION

If y varies directly as x, then y is equal to some constant k times x; that is, $y = kx$ where k is a constant. We can now say $y_1 = kx_1$ and $y_2 = kx_2$ or $\dfrac{y_1}{x_1} = k$, $\dfrac{y_2}{x_2} = k$ which implies $\dfrac{y_1}{x_1} = \dfrac{y_2}{x_2}$ which is a proportion. We use the proportion $\dfrac{y_1}{x_1} = \dfrac{y_2}{x_2}$. Thus $\dfrac{3}{-2} = \dfrac{y_2}{8}$. Now solve for y_2:

$$8\left(\frac{3}{-2}\right) = 8\left(\frac{y_2}{8}\right)$$

$$-12 = y_2$$

When $x = 8$, $y = -12$.

PROBLEM

> If y varies inversely as the cube of x, and $y = 7$ when $x = 2$, express y as a function of x.

SOLUTION

The relationship "y varies inversely with respect to x" is expressed as,

$$y = \frac{k}{x}$$

The inverse variation is now with respect to the cube of x, x^3, and we have,

$$y = \frac{k}{x^3}$$

Since $y = 7$ and $x = 2$ must satisfy this relation, we replace x and y by these values,

$$7 = \frac{k}{2^3} = \frac{k}{8}$$

and we find $k = 7 \times 8 = 56$. Substitution of this value of k in the general relation gives,

$$y = \frac{56}{x^3},$$

which expresses y as a function of x. We may now, in addition, find the value of y corresponding to any value of x. If we had the added requirement to find the value of y when $x = 1.2$, $x = 1.2$ would be substituted in the function to give

$$y = \frac{56}{(1.2)^3} = \frac{56}{1.728} = 32.41$$

Other expressions in use are "is proportional to" for "varies directly," and "is inversely proportional to" for "varies inversely."

Drill: Ratios and Proportions

DIRECTIONS: Find the appropriate solutions.

1. Solve for n: $\dfrac{4}{n} = \dfrac{8}{5}$.

    (A) 10   (C) 6

    (B) 8   (D) 2.5

2. Solve for n: $\dfrac{2}{3} = \dfrac{n}{72}$.

    (A) 12   (C) 64

    (B) 48   (D) 56

3. Solve for n: $n : 12 = 3 : 4$.

    (A) 8   (C) 9

    (B) 1   (D) 4

4. Four out of every five students at West High take a mathematics course. If the enrollment at West is 785, how many students take mathematics?

    (A) 628   (C) 705

    (B) 157   (D) 655

5. At a factory, three out of every 1,000 parts produced are defective. In a day, the factory can produce 25,000 parts. How many of these parts would be defective?

    (A) 7   (C) 750

    (B) 75   (D) 7,500

6. A summer league softball team won 28 out of the 32 games they played. What is the ratio of games won to games played?

    (A) $4 : 5$ (C) $7 : 8$

    (B) $3 : 4$ (D) $2 : 3$

Real-World Problems Involving Proportion

PROBLEM

> A chemist is preparing a chemical solution. She needs to add 3 parts sodium and 2 parts zinc to a flask of chlorine. If she has already placed 300 grams of sodium into the flask, how much zinc must she now add?

SOLUTION

Step 1 is to determine the ratio of sodium and zinc. 3 parts sodium, 2 parts zinc = 3:2

Step 2 is to write the problem as a proportion.

$$\frac{3}{2} = \frac{300}{?}$$

Step 3 is to put the proportion in the following format:

$AD = BC \qquad\qquad 3(?) = 2(300)$

Step 4 is to solve the right side of the proportion.

$2(300) = 600$

Step 5 is to rewrite the proportion.

$3(?) = 600$

Step 6 is to find the missing integer that solves the proportion. To do this, divide both sides by the known extreme, 3.

$$\frac{3(?)}{3} = ? \qquad\qquad \frac{600}{3} = 200$$

Step 7 is to rewrite the proportion.

$? = 200$

The solution is 200 grams of zinc.

PROBLEM

An automobile dealer has to sell 3.5 cars for every 1 truck to achieve the optimum profit. This year, it is estimated that 3,500 cars will be sold. How many trucks must he sell to achieve the optimum profit?

SOLUTION

Step 1 is to determine the ratio of cars to trucks.

3.5 cars, 1 truck = 3.5:1

Make both sides of the ratio an integer. To do this, multiply both sides of the ratio by 2.

$2(3.5):2(1) = 7:2$

Step 2 is to write the problem as a proportion.

$$\frac{7}{2} = \frac{3,500}{?}$$

Step 3 is to put the proportion in the following format:

$AD = BC \qquad\qquad 7(?) = 2(3,500)$

Step 4 is to solve the right side of the proportion.

$2(3,500) = 7,000$

Step 5 is to rewrite the proportion.

$7(?) = 7,000$

Step 6 is to find the missing integer that solves the proportion. To do this, divide both sides by the known extreme, 7.

$$\frac{7(?)}{7} = ? \qquad\qquad \frac{7,000}{7} = 1,000$$

Step 7 is to rewrite the proportion.

$? = 1,000$

The solution is 1,000 trucks.

PROBLEM

A baker is making a new recipe for chocolate chip cookies. He decides that for every 6 cups of flour, he needs to add 1 cup of sugar. He puts 30 cups of flour and 2 cups of sugar into the batter. How much more sugar does he need?

SOLUTION

Step 1 is to determine the ratio of flour to sugar.

6 cups flour, 1 cup sugar = 6:1

Step 2 is to write the problem as a proportion.

$$\frac{6}{1} = \frac{30}{?}$$

Step 3 is to put the proportion in the following format:

$AD = BC \qquad\qquad 6(?) = 1(30)$

Step 4 is to solve the right side of the proportion.

1(30) = 30

Step 5 is to rewrite the proportion.

6(?) = 30

Step 6 is to find the missing integer that solves the proportion.

To do this, divide both sides by the known extreme, 6.

$$\frac{6(?)}{6} = ? \qquad\qquad \frac{30}{6} = 5$$

Step 7 is to rewrite the proportion.

? = 5

The solution is that 5 cups of sugar must be added to the batter.

Step 8 is to determine how many more cups of sugar are needed.

5 − 2 = 3

Since only 2 cups have been added so far, the baker must still add 3 cups.

Algebra Review

ANSWER KEY

Drill: Algebraic Terms

1. (B)   2. (C)   3. (C)   4. (A)

Drill: Operations with Polynomials

1. (B)	6. (B)	11. (C)	16. (C)
2. (C)	7. (C)	12. (B)	17. (D)
3. (C)	8. (D)	13. (D)	18. (D)
4. (D)	9. (A)	14. (A)	19. (B)
5. (A)	10. (D)	15. (D)	20. (B)

Drill: Simplifying Algebraic Expressions

1. (C)   3. (B)   5. (D)
2. (D)   4. (A)

Drill: Two Linear Equations

1. (D)   3. (A)   5. (C)
2. (B)   4. (D)

Drill: Formulas

1. (C)   2. (B)   3. (A)

Drill: Absolute Value Equations

1. (B)   3. (A)   5. (C)
2. (D)   4. (C)

Drill: Inequalities

1. (D)   3. (D)   5. (A)
2. (C)   4. (B)

Drill: Graphing Linear Inequalities

1. (D)   2. (C)   3. (C)

Drill: Ratios and Proportions

1. (D)   3. (C)   5. (B)
2. (B)   4. (A)   6. (C)

Detailed Explanations of Answers

Drill: Algebraic Terms

1. (B)

"*x* less than" means that x is being subtracted from a quantity. "Quotient of 5 and *z*" means to divide 5 by *z*.

2. (C)

"The sum of *p* and *q*" means that *p* and *q* are being added. "The product of *w* and *t*" means that *w* and *t* are being multiplied.

3. (C)

$x - 5$ means "five less than *x*." The symbol $>$ means "more than." Note that the symbol $\geq$ means "at least."

4. (A)

$6(c + d)$ means "six multiplied by the sum of *c* and *d*." The symbol $\leq$ means "less than or equal" or equivalently "at most." Note that the symbol $<$ means "less than."

Drill: Operations with Polynomials

1. (B)

$$9a^2b + 3c + 2a^2b + 5c = (9a^2b + 2a^2b) + (3c + 5c)$$
$$= 11a^2b + 8c$$

2. (C)

$$14m^2n^3 + 6m^2n^3 + 3m^2n^3 = 23m^2n^3$$

3. (C)

$$3x + 2y + 16x + 3z + 6y = (3x + 16x) + (2y + 6y) + 3z$$
$$= 19x + 8y + 3z$$

4. (D)

$$(4d^2 + 7e^3 + 12f) + (3d^2 + 6e^3 + 2f) =$$
$$(4d^2 + 3d^2) + (7e^3 + 6e^3) + (12f + 2f)$$
$$= 7d^2 + 13e^3 + 14f$$

5. (A)

$$3ac^2 + 2b^2c + 7ac^2 + 2ac^2 + b^2c =$$
$$(3ac^2 + 7ac^2 + 2ac^2) + (2b^2c + b^2c)$$
$$= 12ac^2 + 3b^2c$$

6. (B)

$$14m^2n - 6m^2n = 8m^2n$$

7. (C)

$$3x^3y^2 - 4xz - 6x^3y^2 = (3x^3y^2 - 6x^3y^2) - 4xz$$
$$= -3x^3y^2 - 4xz$$

8. (D)

$$9g^2 + 6h - 2g^2 - 5h = (9g^2 - 2g^2) + (6h - 5h)$$
$$= 7g^2 + h$$

9. (A)

$$7b^3 - 4c^2 - 6b^3 + 3c^2 = (7b^3 - 6b^3) + (-4c^2 + 3c^2)$$
$$= b^3 - c^2$$

10. (D)

$$11q^2r - 4q^2r - 8q^2r = (11q^2r - 4q^2r) - 8q^2r$$
$$= 7q^2r - 8q^2r$$
$$= -q^2r$$

11. (C)

$$5p^2t \times 3p^2t = (5 \times 3)(p^2 \times p^2)(t \times t)$$
$$= 15p^4t^2$$

12. (B)

$$(2r + s)14r = (2r)(14r) + (s)(14r)$$
$$= 28r^2 + 14sr$$

13. (D)

$$(4m + p)(3m - 2p) = (4m)(3m) + (4m)(-2p)$$
$$+ (p)(3m) + (p)(-2p)$$
$$= 12m^2 [(-8mp) + 3mp] +$$
$$(-2p^2)$$
$$= 12m^2 - 5mp - 2p^2$$

14. (A)

$$(2a + b)(3a^2 + ab + b^2) = (2a)(3a^2) + (2a)(ab) +$$
$$(2a)(b^2) + (b)(3a^2) + (b)(ab) + (b)(b^2)$$
$$= 6a^3 + 2a^2b + 2ab^2 + 3a^2b + ab^2 + b^3$$
$$= 6a^3 + 5a^2b + 3ab^2 + b^3$$

15. (D)

$$(6t^2 + 2t + 1)(3t) = (6t^2)(3t) + (2t)(3t) + (1)(3t)$$
$$= 18t^3 + 6t^2 + 3t$$

16. (C)

$$(x^2 + x - 6) \div (x - 2) = \frac{x^2 + x - 6}{(x - 2)} = \frac{(x + 3)(x - 2)}{(x - 2)}$$
$$= x + 3$$

17. (D)

$$24b^4c^3 \div 6b^2c = \frac{\overset{4}{\cancel{24}} b^{\overset{2}{\cancel{4}}} c^{\overset{2}{\cancel{3}}}}{\cancel{6} \, \cancel{b^2} \, \cancel{c}} = 4b^2c^2$$

18. (D)

$$(3p^2 + pq - 2q^2) \div (p + q) = \frac{3p^2 + pq - 2q^2}{(p + q)}$$
$$= \frac{(3p - 2q)\cancel{(p + q)}}{\cancel{(p + q)}}$$
$$= 3p - 2q$$

19. (B)

$$(y^3 - 2y^2 - y + 2) \div (y - 2) = y - 2 \overline{)\, y^3 - 2y^2 - y + 2}$$

$$\begin{array}{r} y^2 - 1 \\ y - 2 \overline{)\, y^3 - 2y^2 - y + 2} \\ \underline{-(y^3 - 2y^2)} \\ 0 - y + 2 \\ \underline{-(-y + 2)} \\ 0 \end{array}$$

20. (B)

$$(m^2 + m - 14) \div (m + 4) = m + 4 \overline{)\, m^2 + m - 14}$$

$$\begin{array}{r} m - 3 \\ m + 4 \overline{)\, m^2 + m - 14} \\ \underline{-(m^2 + 4m)} \\ -3m - 14 \\ \underline{-(-3m - 12)} \\ -2 \end{array}$$

$$= \frac{-2}{m + 4}$$

$$m - 3 + \frac{-2}{m + 4}$$

Drill: Simplifying Algebraic Expressions

1. (C)

$$16b^2 - 25z^2 = (4b + 5z)(4b - 5z)$$

2. (D)

$$x^2 - 2x - 8 = (x - 4)(x + 2)$$

3. (B)

$$2c^2 + 5cd - 3d^2 = (2c - d)(c + 3d)$$

4. (A)

$$4t^3 - 20t = 4t(t^2 - 5)$$

5. (D)

$$x^2 + xy - 2y^2 = (x - y)(x + 2y)$$

Drill: Two Linear Equations

1. (D)

$$
\begin{aligned}
3x + 4y &= -2 &=& & 3x + 4y &= -2 \\
-3(x - 6y &= -8) &=& & + -3x + 18y &= 24 \\
\hline
& & & & 0 + 22y &= 22 \\
& & & & y &= 1
\end{aligned}
$$

Substitute $y = 1$ in $x - 6y = -8$ to get

$$
\begin{aligned}
x - 6 &= -8 \\
+6 \quad &+6 \\
\hline
x &= 2
\end{aligned}
$$

$$(-2, 1)$$

2. (B)

$$
\begin{aligned}
2x + y &= -10 \\
-2x - 4y &= 4 \\
\hline
0 - 3y &= -6 \\
\frac{-3y}{-3} &= \frac{-6}{-3}
\end{aligned}
$$

$y = 2$ substitute in first equation to get

$$
\begin{aligned}
2x + 2 &= -10 \\
-2 &= -2 \\
\hline
\frac{2x}{2} &= \frac{-12}{2}
\end{aligned}
$$

$$(-6, 2)$$

3. (A)

$$
\begin{aligned}
6x + 5y = -4 &= & 6x + 5y &= -4 \\
(3x - 3y = 9)(-2) &= & \underline{-6x + 6y} &= -18 \\
& & 0 + 11y &= -22 \\
& & \frac{11y}{11} &= \frac{-22}{11} \\
& & y &= -2
\end{aligned}
$$

substitute in the second equation to get

$$
\begin{aligned}
3x - 3(-2) &= 9 \\
3x + 6 &= 9 \\
-6 \quad &-6 \\
\hline
\frac{3x}{3} &= \frac{3}{3} \\
x &= 1
\end{aligned}
$$

$$(1, -2)$$

4. (D)

$$
\begin{aligned}
4x + 3y = 9 &= & 4x + 3y &= 9 \\
(2x - 2y = 8)(-2) &= & \underline{-4x + 4y} &= -16 \\
& & 0 + 7y &= -7 \\
& & y &= -1
\end{aligned}
$$

substitute in the first equation to get

$$4x + 3(-1) = 9$$
$$4x - 3 = 9$$
$$\underline{\quad +3 \quad = +3}$$
$$\frac{4x}{4} = \frac{12}{4}$$
$$x = 3$$

$$(3, -1)$$

5. (C)

$$x + y = 7 \qquad = \qquad x + y = 7$$
$$x = y - 3 \qquad = \qquad \underline{x - y = 3}$$
$$2x = 4$$
$$x = 2$$

substitute in the first equation

$$2 + y = 7$$
$$y = 5$$

$$(2, 5)$$

Drill: Formulas

1. (C)

$$297\pi = \left(\frac{1}{3}\pi\right)(9^2)(h) = 27\pi h. \text{ Thus,}$$

$$h = \frac{297\pi}{27\pi} = 11.$$

2. (B)

$$D = \frac{(30)(27)}{2} = 405.$$

3. (A)

$$24 = \frac{12x^2}{\frac{1}{8}} = 96x^2. \text{ Then, } x^2 = \frac{24}{96} = \frac{1}{4}.$$

Therefore $x = \sqrt{\frac{1}{4}} = \frac{1}{2}.$

Drill: Quadratic Equations

1. (A)

$$(x^2 - 2x - 8) = 0$$
$$(x - 4)(x + 2) = 0$$

The values of x are 4 and -2.

2. (D)

$$x^2 + 2x - 3 = 0$$
$$(x + 3)(x - 1) = 0$$

The values of x are -3 and 1.

3. (B)

$$x^2 - 7x = -10$$
$$x^2 - 7x + 10 = 0$$
$$(x - 5)(x - 2) = 0$$

The values of x are 5 and 2.

4. (C)

$$x^2 - 8x + 16 = 0$$
$$(x - 4)(x - 4) = 0$$
$$(x - 4)^2 = 0$$

The value of x is 4.

5. (E)

$$3x^2 + 3x = 6$$
$$3x^2 + 3x - 6 = 0$$
$$3(x^2 + x - 2) = 0$$
$$3(x + 2)(x - 1) = 0$$

The values of x are -2 and 1.

Drill: Absolute Value Equations

1. **(B)**

$$|4x - 2| = 6 \quad 4x - 2 = 6 \text{ or } 4x - 2 = -6$$
$$4x = 8 \qquad 4x = -4$$
$$x = 2 \text{ or } \qquad x = -1$$

2. **(D)**

$$\left| 3 - \frac{1}{2}y \right| = -7$$

No solution. Absolute value must equal a positive number.

3. **(A)**

$$2|x + 7| = 12$$
$$|x + 7| = 6 \quad x + 7 = 6 \quad \text{or} \quad x + 7 = -6$$
$$x = -1 \quad \text{or} \qquad x = -13$$

4. **(C)**

$$|5x| - 7 = 3$$
$$|5x| = 10 \qquad 5x = 10 \quad \text{or} \quad 5x = -10$$
$$x = 2 \quad \text{or} \quad x = -2$$

5. **(C)**

$$\left| \frac{3}{4}m \right| = 9 \qquad \frac{3}{4}m = 9 \qquad \frac{3}{4}m = -9$$
$$\frac{4}{3}\left(\frac{3}{4}m\right) = 9\left(\frac{4}{3}\right) \quad \frac{4}{3}\left(\frac{3}{4}m\right) = (-9)\left(\frac{4}{3}\right)$$
$$m = 12 \qquad\qquad m = -12$$

Drill: Inequalities

1. **(D)**

$$3m + 2 < 7$$
$$\underline{\quad -2 \;\; -2 \quad}$$
$$\left(\frac{1}{3}\right) 3m \quad < 5 \left(\frac{1}{3}\right)$$
$$m < \frac{5}{3}$$

2. **(C)**

$$\frac{1}{2}x - 3 \le 1$$
$$\underline{\quad +3 +3 \quad}$$
$$\frac{1}{2}x \le 4$$
$$(2)\frac{1}{2}x \le 4(2)$$
$$x \le 8$$

3. **(D)**

$$-3p + 1 \ge 16$$
$$\underline{\quad -1 \quad -1 \quad}$$
$$-3p \ge 15$$
$$\left(-\frac{1}{3}\right) -3p \ge 15 \left(-\frac{1}{3}\right)$$
$$p \le -5$$

4. **(B)**

$$-6 < \frac{2}{3}r + 6 \le 2$$
$$\underline{\; -6 \qquad -6 - 6 \;}$$
$$-12 < \frac{2}{3}r \le \; -4$$
$$\frac{3}{2}\left(-12 < \frac{2}{3}r \le -4\right)$$
$$-18 < r \le -6$$

5. (A)

$$0 < 2 - y < 6$$
$$\underline{-2 - 2 \qquad -2}$$
$$-2 < y \qquad < 4$$
$$-1(-2 < -y < 4)$$
$$-4 < y < 2$$

Drill: Graphing Linear Inequalities

1. (D)

The shaded region lies above line l_1, which implies that $y \geq x - 1$. Also, the shaded region lies below line l_1, which implies that $y \leq -2x + 8$.

2. (C)

The y values must lie between the x-axis and the horizontal line whose equation is $y = 2$. The x values must lie between the vertical lines whose equations are $x = -4$ and $x = 4$.

3. (C)

The shaded region is represented by points that lie below both lines l_1 and l_2. Thus, each of $(-2, -1.5)$ and $(1, -2)$ lie in the shaded region. The point $(1, -3)$ lies above both lines. The point $(0.5, 0)$ lies above line l_1 and below line l_2.

Drill: Ratios and Proportions

1. (D)

$$\frac{4}{n} = \frac{8}{5} \qquad 5(4) = 8n$$
$$\left(\frac{1}{8}\right) 20 = 8n \left(\frac{1}{8}\right)$$
$$\frac{20}{8} = n \Rightarrow 2.5 = n$$

2. (B)

$$\frac{2}{3} = \frac{n}{72} \qquad 2(72) = 3n$$
$$\frac{1}{3}(144) = (3n)\frac{1}{3}$$
$$(2)(24) = n$$
$$48 = n$$

3. (C)

$$n : 12 = 3 : 4 \Rightarrow \qquad \frac{n}{12} = \frac{3}{4}$$
$$4n = (12)(3)$$
$$4n = 36$$
$$n = 9$$

4. (A)

$$4 : 5 = x : 785 \Rightarrow \qquad \frac{4}{5} = \frac{x}{785}$$
$$(785)(4) = 5x$$
$$\left(\frac{1}{5}\right)(785)(4) = (5x)\frac{1}{5}$$
$$(157)(4) = x$$
$$628 = x$$

5. (B)

$$3 : 1000 = y : 25000 \Rightarrow \qquad \frac{3}{1000} = \frac{y}{25,000}$$
$$(3)(25,000) = y(1000)$$
$$\frac{(3)(25,000)}{1000} = y$$
$$75 = y$$

6. (C)

$$28 : 32 \Rightarrow \frac{28}{32} = \frac{7}{8} \Rightarrow 7 : 8$$

Geometry and Measurement

The Customary System of Measurement

Some problems may require you to make conversions for units of measurement (distance, volume, and mass) in both the customary system and the metric system. Following are the most common conversions within each system, including some basic conversions between metric units and customary units.

Distance	1 foot = 12 inches
	1 yard = 3 feet
	1 mile = 5,280 feet
	1 inch = 2.54 centimeters
Capacity (volume)	1 gallon = 4 quarts
	1 quart = 2 pints
	1 pint = 16 fluid ounces
	1 pint = 2 cups
	1 liter = 1.06 quarts
Mass	1 pound = 16 ounces
	1 ton = 2,000 pounds
	1 kilogram = 2.2 pounds

To convert within the standard system, we must multiply or divide. When we convert from a smaller unit to a larger unit (such as inches to feet), we divide. For example, when converting 36 inches to feet, divide 36 by 12 (because there are 12 inches in one foot) for the answer of 3 feet. When converting from a larger unit to a smaller unit (such as gallons to quarts), multiply. For example, when converting 5 gallons to quarts, multiply 5 gallons by 4 quarts (because there are 4 quarts in a gallon), arriving at an answer of 20 quarts.

PROBLEM

> 12 ft. = _____ yd.

SOLUTION

We are converting from a smaller unit to a larger unit, so we use division. Because 3 feet is equivalent to 1 yard, 12 feet = $\frac{12}{3} = 4$ yards.

PROBLEM

> 64 oz. = _____ lbs.

SOLUTION

We are converting from a smaller unit to a larger unit, so we use division. Because 16 ounces is equivalent to 1 pound, 64 ounces $= \dfrac{64}{16} = 4$ pounds.

PROBLEM

7 gal. = _____ qt.

SOLUTION

We are converting from a larger unit to a smaller unit, so we use multiplication. Because 4 quarts is equivalent to 1 gallon, the answer is $7 \times 4 = 28$ quarts.

PROBLEM

Convert 13 feet 7 inches to inches.

SOLUTION

First, convert feet to inches. Because we are converting from a larger unit (feet) to a smaller unit (inches), we use multiplication. Then add the remaining 7 inches. So 13 feet $\times$ 12 inches/foot = 156 inches and 156 inches + 7 inches = 163 inches.

PROBLEM

You have decided to install decorative tiles to line one border of your flower garden. The border measures 15 feet in length. Each tile measures 6 inches in length, and you want to leave 3 inches of space between each tile. How many tiles will you need to construct the border?

SOLUTION

First, convert the 15-foot border to inches: 15 feet $\times$ 12 inches/foot = 180 inches. For each tile, you will need to consider 6 inches plus the 3 inches of space (9 inches total). Then determine how many 9-inch segments are in 180 ($\dfrac{180}{9} = 20$). Thus, you will need 20 tiles to construct the border.

PROBLEM

12 quarts = _____ liters.

SOLUTION

We are converting from a smaller unit to a larger unit, so we use division. Because 1 liter is equivalent to 1.06 quarts, 12 quarts is equivalent to $\dfrac{12}{1.06} \approx 11.32$ liters.

PROBLEM

9.5 kilograms = _____ pounds.

SOLUTION

One kilogram is larger than one pound. Therefore, 9.5 kilograms is equivalent to $(9.5)(2.2) = 20.9$ pounds.

The Metric System of Measurement

The metric system is built on the base of 10, which makes it simpler to understand than the standard system. Knowing the following prefixes will help:

kilo-	=	$\times\ 1{,}000$
hecto-	=	$\times\ 100$
deka-	=	$\times\ 10$
deci-	=	$\times\ 0.10\ \left(\dfrac{1}{10}\right)$
centi-	=	$\times\ 0.01\ \left(\dfrac{1}{100}\right)$
milli-	=	$\times\ 0.001\ \left(\dfrac{1}{1000}\right)$

Metric Units

In the metric system, the basic unit of length is the meter, which is a little longer than a yard in the standard system. Using the prefixes above, a kilometer is 1,000 meters, and a millimeter is $\frac{1}{1,000}$ of a meter.

The basic unit of capacity in the metric system is the liter, which is a little more than a quart in the standard system. A hectoliter is 100 liters, and a centiliter is $\frac{1}{100}$ of a liter.

The basic unit of weight in the metric system is the gram, which is about the weight of a single paper clip. A kilogram is 1,000 grams, and a milligram is $\frac{1}{1,000}$ of a gram.

Converting Within the Metric System

The metric system is built on the base of 10, and to convert within this system, all that is required is to move the decimal point. It may be helpful to use the graphic organizer of a metric chart to help.

PROBLEM

Convert 4 kilometers to meters.

SOLUTION

Just as with our customary system of measurement, we note that we are changing from a larger unit to a smaller unit. Thus, we use multiplication. The answer is $4 \times 1,000 = 4,000$ meters.

PROBLEM

Convert 320 milligrams to dekagrams.

SOLUTION

One milligram is 0.001 of a gram, and a dekagram is equivalent to 10 grams. This implies that one milligram is 0.0001 of a dekagram. Thus, we can use division. The answer is $\frac{320}{10,000} = 0.0320$ dekagrams. (We can also write the answer as 0.032.)

PROBLEM

Convert 123 milliliters to liters.

SOLUTION

We are converting from a smaller unit to a larger unit, which implies the use of division. Thus, the answer is $\frac{123}{1000} = 0.123$.

PROBLEM

Convert 45.6 meters to centimeters.

SOLUTION

We are converting from a larger unit to a smaller unit, which means multiplication. In this case, the answer is $45.6 \times 100 = 4,560$.

Drill: Measurement

1. How many pounds are equivalent to 3.4 kilograms?

    (A) 7.48   (C) 1.54

    (B) 5.6   (D) 1.2

2. A bottle contains 5 liters of water. Half of this bottle is poured into a jar whose capacity is 8 quarts. How many more quarts of liquid could be poured into the jar?

    (A) 2.65   (C) 5.35

    (B) 2.7   (D) 5.5

3. How many fluid ounces could fill a container whose capacity is 1 gallon, 2 quarts, and 1 pint?

   (A) 204   (C) 212

   (B) 208   (D) 216

4. Joan ran 4 miles every day for two weeks. Kelly ran 3080 yards every day for 30 days. Joan ran how many more miles than Kelly?

   (A) 5.5   (C) 3.5

   (B) 4.5   (D) 2.5

5. A recipe calls for 2 grams of water for each cookie that is made. If 28.4 grams is equivalent to 1 ounce, approximately how many ounces of water are needed to make 100 cookies?

   (A) 14   (C) 9

   (B) 12   (D) 7

Points, Lines, and Angles

Geometry is built upon a series of undefined terms. These terms are those that we accept as known in order to define other undefined terms.

A) **Point:** Although we represent points on paper with small dots, a point has no size, thickness, or width.

B) **Line:** A line is a series of adjacent points that extends indefinitely. A line can be either curved or straight; however, unless otherwise stated, the term "line" refers to a straight line.

C) **Plane:** A plane is a collection of points lying on a flat surface that extends indefinitely in all directions.

Definitions

Definition 1

If A and B are two points on a line, then the **line segment** AB is the set of points on that line between A and B and including A and B, which are called the endpoints. The line segment is referred to as $\overline{AB}$.

Definition 2

A **half-line** is the set of all the points on a line on the same side of a dividing point, not including the dividing point, denoted by $\overleftrightarrow{AB}$.

Definition 3

Let A be a dividing point on a line. Then, a **ray** is the set of all the points on a half-line and the dividing point itself. The dividing point is called the endpoint or the vertex of the ray. The ray AB shown below is denoted by $\overrightarrow{AB}$.

Definition 4

Three or more points are said to be collinear if and only if they lie on the same line.

Definition 5

Let X, Y, and Z be three collinear points. If Y is between X and Z, then $\overrightarrow{YX}$ and $\overrightarrow{YZ}$ are called **opposite rays**.

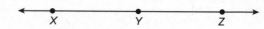

Definition 6

The **absolute value** of x, denoted by $|x|$, is defined as

$$|x| = \begin{cases} x & \text{if } x > 0 \\ 0 & \text{if } x = 0 \\ -x & \text{if } x < 0 \end{cases}$$

Definition 7

The absolute value of the difference of the coordinates of any two points on the real number line is the **distance** between those two points.

Definition 8

The **length** of a line segment is the distance between its endpoints.

Definition 9

Congruent segments are segments that have the same length. The sign for congruent is ≅.

Definition 10

The **midpoint** of a segment is defined as the point of the segment that divides the segment into two congruent segments. (The midpoint is said to bisect the segment.)

PROBLEM

Solve for x when $|x - 7| = 3$.

SOLUTION

This equation, according to the definition of absolute value, expresses the conditions that $x - 7$ must be 3 or -3, since in either case the absolute value is 3. If $x - 7 = 3$, we have $x = 10$; and if $x - 7 = -3$, we have $x = 4$. We see that there are two values of x that solve the equation.

PROBLEM

Find point C between A and B in the figure below such that $\overline{AC} \cong \overline{CB}$.

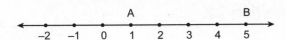

SOLUTION

We must determine point C in such a way that $\overline{AC} \cong \overline{CB}$, or $AC = CB$. We are first given that C is between A and B. Therefore, since the measure of the whole is equal to the sum of the measure of its parts:

(I) $AC + CB = AB$

Using these two facts, we can find the length of AC. From that we can find C.

First, since $AC = CB$, we substitute AC for CB in equation (I)

(II) $AC + AC = AB$

(III) $2(AC) = AB$

Dividing by 2 we have

(IV) $AC = (\frac{1}{2}) AB$

To find AC, we must know AB. We can find AB from the coordinates of A and B. They are 1 and 5, respectively. Accordingly,

(V) $AB = |5 - 1|$

(VI) $AB = 4$

We substitute 4 for AB in equation (IV)

(VII) $AC = (\frac{1}{2}) (4)$

(VIII) $AC = 2$.

Therefore, C is 2 units from A. Since C is between A and B, the coordinate of C must be 3.

Definition 11

The **bisector** of a line segment is a line that divides the line segment into two congruent segments.

Definition 12

An **angle** is a collection of points that is the union of two rays having the same endpoint. An angle such as the one illustrated the accompanying figure can be referred to in any of the following ways:

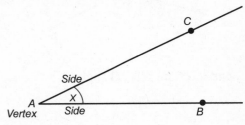

A) by a capital letter that names its vertex, $\angle A$

B) by a lowercase letter or number placed inside the angle, $\angle x$;

C) by three capital letters, where the middle letter is the vertex and the other two letters are not on the same ray, i.e., $\angle CAB$ or $\angle BAC$, both of which represent the angle illustrated in the above figure.

Definition 13

A set of points is **coplanar** if all the points lie in the same plane.

Definition 14

Two angles with a common vertex and a common side, but no common interior points, are called **adjacent angles.**

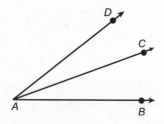

In the above figure, $\angle DAC$ and $\angle BAC$ are adjacent angles; $\angle DAB$ and $\angle BAC$ are not adjacent angles.

Definition 15

Vertical angles are two angles with a common vertex and with sides that are two pairs of opposite rays.

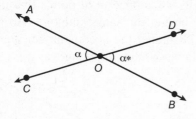

($\angle \alpha$ and $\angle \alpha^*$ are vertical angles.)

Definition 16

An **acute angle** is an angle whose measure is larger that 0° but smaller than 90°.

Definition 17

An angle whose measure is 90° is called a **right angle**.

Definition 18

An **obtuse angle** is an angle whose measure is larger than 90° but less than 180°.

Definition 19

An angle whose measure is 180° is called a **straight angle**. Note: Such an angle is, in fact, a straight line.

Definition 20

An angle whose measure is greater than 180° but less than 360° is called a **reflex angle**.

Definition 21

Complementary angles are two angles, the sum of the measures of which equals 90°.

Definition 22

Supplementary angles are two angles, the sum of the measures of which equals 180°.

Definition 23

Congruent angles are angles of equal measure.

Definition 24

A ray **bisects** (is the bisector of) an angle if the ray divides the angle into two angles that have equal measure.

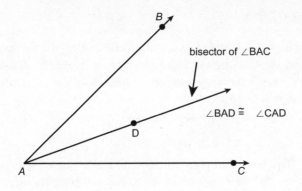

bisector of ∠BAC

∠BAD ≅ ∠CAD

Definition 25

If the two non-common sides of adjacent angles form opposite rays, then the angles are called a **linear pair.** Note that α and β are supplementary.

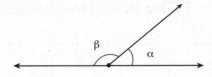

Definition 26

Two lines are said to be **perpendicular** if they intersect and form right angles. The symbol for perpendicular (or, is perpendicular to) is ⊥; $\overleftrightarrow{AB}$ is perpendicular to $\overleftrightarrow{CD}$ is written as $\overleftrightarrow{AB} \perp \overleftrightarrow{CD}$.

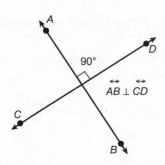

90°

$\overleftrightarrow{AB} \perp \overleftrightarrow{CD}$

Definition 27

A line, a ray, or a line segment that bisects a line segment and is also perpendicular to that segment is called a **perpendicular bisector** of the line segment.

Definition 28

The **distance** from a point to a line is the measure of the perpendicular line segment from the point to that line. Note: This is the shortest possible distance from the point to the line.

Definition 29

Two or more distinct lines are said to be **parallel** (∥) if and only if they are coplanar and they do not intersect.

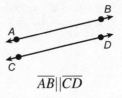

$$\overline{AB} \| \overline{CD}$$

Definition 30

The **projection of a given point** on a given line is the foot of the perpendicular drawn from the given point to the given line.

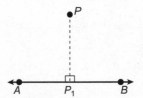

P_1 is the projection of P on $\overleftrightarrow{AB}$

The foot of a perpendicular from a point to a line is the point where the perpendicular meets the line.

Definition 31

The **projection of a segment** on a given line (when the segment is not perpendicular to the line) is a segment with endpoints that are the projections of the endpoints of the given line segment onto the given line.

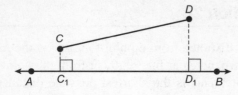

$\overline{C_1 D_1}$ is the projection of $\overline{CD}$ onto $\overleftrightarrow{AB}$

PROBLEM

> The measure of the complement of a given angle is four times the measure of the angle. Find the measure of the given angle.

SOLUTION

By the definition of complementary angles, the sum of the measures of the two complements must equal 90°.

Accordingly,

(1) Let x = the measure of the angle

(2) Then $4x$ = the measure of the complement of this angle.

Therefore, from the discussion above,

$$x + 4x = 90°$$
$$5x = 90°$$
$$x = 18°$$

Therefore, the measure of the given angle is 18°.

PROBLEM

> In the figure, we are given $\overleftrightarrow{AB}$ and triangle *ABC*. We are told that the measure of $\angle 1$ is five times the measure of $\angle 2$. Determine the measures of $\angle 1$ and $\angle 2$.

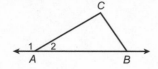

SOLUTION

Since $\angle 1$ and $\angle 2$ are adjacent angles whose non-common sides lie on a straight line, they are, by definition, supplementary. As supplements, their measures must sum to 180°.

If we let x = the measure of $\angle 2$,

then $5x$ = the measure of $\angle 1$.

To determine the respective angle measures, set $x + 5x = 180°$ and solve for x. $6x = 180°$. Therefore, $x = 30°$ and $5x = 150°$.

Therefore, the measure of $\angle 1 = 150°$ and the measure of $\angle 2 = 30°$.

Postulates

Postulate 1 (The Point Uniqueness Postulate)

Let n be any positive number.

Then there exists exactly one point N of $\overrightarrow{AB}$ such that $AN = n$. (AN is the length of n.)

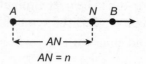

Postulate 2 (The Line Postulate)

Any two distinct points determine one and only one line that contains both points.

Postulate 3 (The Point Betweenness Postulate)

Let A and B be any two points. Then, there exists at least one point (and in fact an infinite number of such points) of $\overleftrightarrow{AB}$ such that P is between A and B, with $AP + PB = AB$.

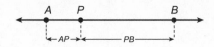

Postulate 4

Two distinct straight lines can intersect at most at only one point.

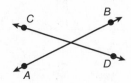

Postulate 5

The shortest line between any two points is a straight line.

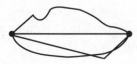

Postulate 6

There is a one-to-one correspondence between the real numbers and the points of a line. That is, to every real number there corresponds exactly one point of the line and to every point of the line there corresponds exactly one real number. (In other words, a line has an infinite number of points between any two distinct points.)

Postulate 7

One and only one perpendicular can be drawn to a given line through any point on that line. Given point O on line $\overleftrightarrow{AB}$, $\overleftrightarrow{OC}$ represents the only perpendicular to $\overleftrightarrow{AB}$ that passes through O.

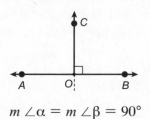

$$m \angle \alpha = m \angle \beta = 90°$$

PROBLEM

In the accompanying figure, point B is between points A and C, and point E is between points D and F. Given that $\overline{AB} \cong \overline{DE}$ and $\overline{BC} \cong \overline{EF}$, prove that $\overline{AC} \cong \overline{DF}$.

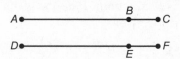

SOLUTION

Two important postulates will be employed in this proof. The Point Betweenness Postulate states that if point Y is between points X and Z, then $XY + YZ = XZ$. Furthermore, the Postulate states that the converse is also true—that is, if $XY + YZ = XZ$, then point Y is between points X and Z.

The Addition Postulate states that equal quantities added to equal quantities yield equal quantities. Thus, if $a = b$ and $c = d$, then $a + c = b + d$.

Given: Point B is between A and C; point E is between points D and F; $\overline{AB} \cong \overline{DE}$; $\overline{BC} \cong \overline{EF}$

Prove: $\overline{AC} \cong \overline{DF}$.

Statement	Reason
1. (For the given, see above)	1. Given.
2. $AB = DE$ $BC = EF$	2. Congruent segments have equal lengths.
3. $AB + BC = DE + EF$	3. Addition Postulate.
4. $AC = DF$	4. Point Between Postulate.
5. $\overline{AC} \cong \overline{DF}$	5. Segments of equal length are congruent.

PROBLEM

Construct a line perpendicular to a given line through a given point on the given line.

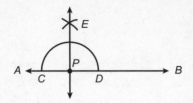

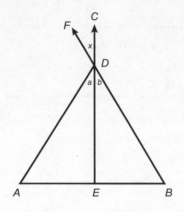

SOLUTION

Let line $\overleftrightarrow{AB}$ and point P be the given line and the given point, respectively.

We notice that $\angle APB$ is a straight angle. A line perpendicular to $\overleftrightarrow{AB}$ from point P will form adjacent congruent angles with $\overleftrightarrow{AB}$, by the definition of a perpendicular. Since $\angle APB$ is a straight angle, the adjacent angles will be right angles. As such, the required perpendicular is the angle bisector of $\angle APB$.

We can complete our construction by bisecting $\angle APB$.

1. Using P as the center and any convenient radius, construct an arc that intersects $\overrightarrow{AB}$ at points C and D.

2. With C and D as centers and with a radius greater in length than the one used in Step 1, construct arcs that intersect. The intersection point of these two arcs is point E.

3. Draw $\overleftrightarrow{EP}$.

$\overleftrightarrow{EP}$ is the required angle bisector and, as such, $\overleftrightarrow{EP} \perp \overleftrightarrow{AB}$.

PROBLEM

> Present a formal proof of the following conditional statement:
>
> If $\overleftrightarrow{CE}$ bisects $\angle a \cong \angle x$, and if $\overleftrightarrow{FDB}$ and $\overleftrightarrow{CDE}$ are straight lines, then $\angle a \cong \angle x$. (Refer to the accompanying figure.)

SOLUTION

In this problem, it will be necessary to recognize vertical angles and be knowledgeable of their key properties. Furthermore, we will need the definition of the bisector of an angle.

Vertical angles are two angles that have a common vertex, and whose sides are two pairs of opposite rays. Vertical angles are always congruent.

Lastly, the bisector of any angle divides the angle into two congruent angles.

Statement	Reason
1. $\overleftrightarrow{CE}$ bisects $\angle ADB$	1. Given.
2. $\angle a \cong \angle b$	2. A bisector of an angle divides the angle into two congruent angles.
3. $\overleftrightarrow{FDB}$ and $\overleftrightarrow{CDE}$ are straight lines	3. Given.
4. $\angle x$ and $\angle b$ are vertical angles	4. Definition of vertical angles.
5. $\angle b \cong \angle x$	5. Vertical angles are congruent.
6. $\angle a \cong \angle x$	6. Transitivity property of congruence of angles.

Note that step 3 is essential because without $\overleftrightarrow{FDB}$ and $\overleftrightarrow{CDE}$ being straight lines, the definition of vertical angles would not be applicable to $\angle x$ and $\angle b$.

Postulate 8

The perpendicular bisector of a line segment is unique.

Postulate 9 (The Plane Postulate)

Any three non-collinear points determine one and only one plane that contains those three points.

Postulate 10 (The Points-in-a-Plane Postulate)

If two distinct points of a line lie in a given plane, then the line lies in that plane.

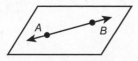

Postulate 11 (Plane Separation Postulate)

Any line in a plane separates the plane into two half planes.

Postulate 12

Given an angle, there exists one and only one real number between 0 and 180 corresponding to it. Note: $m\angle A$ refers to the measurement of angle A.

Postulate 13 (The Angle Sum Postulate)

If A is in the interior of $\angle XYZ$, then

$$m\angle XYZ = m\angle XYA + m\angle AYZ.$$

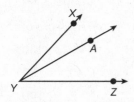

Postulate 14 (The Angle Difference Postulate)

If P is in the exterior of $\angle ABC$ and in the same half-plane (created by edge $\overleftrightarrow{BC}$) as A, then

$$m\angle ABP = m\angle PBC + m\angle ABC.$$

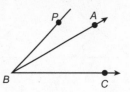

PROBLEM

In the accompanying figure $\overline{SM}$ is the perpendicular bisector of $\overline{QR}$, and $\overline{SN}$ is the perpendicular bisector of $\overline{QP}$. Prove that $SR = SP$.

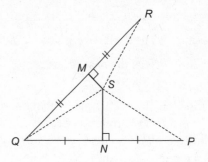

SOLUTION

Every point on the perpendicular bisector of a segment is equidistant from the endpoints of the segment.

Since point S is on the perpendicular bisector of $\overline{QR}$,

(I)　$SR = SQ$

Also, since point S is on the perpendicular bisector of $\overline{QP}$,

(II)　$SQ = SP$

By the transitive property (quantities equal to the same quantity are equal), we have:

(III)　$SR = SP$.

PROBLEM

To construct an angle whose measure is equal to the sum of the measures of two given angles.

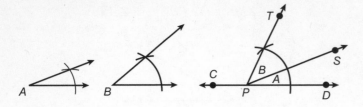

SOLUTION

To construct an angle equal to the sum of the measures of two given angles, we must invoke the theorem that states that the whole is equal to the sum of the parts. The construction, then, will duplicate the given angles in such a way as to form one larger angle equal in measure to the sum of the measures of the two given angles.

The two given angles, $\angle A$ and $\angle B$, are shown in the figure.

1. Construct any line $\overleftrightarrow{CD}$, and mark a point P on it.

2. At P, using $\overrightarrow{PD}$ as the base, construct $\angle DPS \cong \angle A$.

3. Now, using $\overrightarrow{PS}$ as the base, construct $\angle SPT \cong \angle B$ at point P.

4. $\angle DPT$ is the desired angle, equal in measure to $m\angle A + m\angle B$. This follows because the measure of the whole, $\angle DPT$, is equal to the sum of the measure of the parts, $\angle A$ and $\angle B$.

Theorems

Theorem 1

All right angles are equal.

Theorem 2

All straight angles are equal.

Theorem 3

Supplements of the same or equal angles are themselves equal.

Theorem 4

Complements of the same or equal angles are themselves equal.

Theorem 5

Vertical angles are equal.

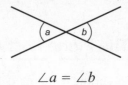

$$\angle a = \angle b$$

Theorem 6

Two supplementary angles are right angles if they have the same measure.

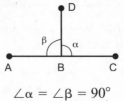

$$\angle \alpha = \angle \beta = 90°$$

Theorem 7

If two lines intersect and form one right angle, then the lines form four right angles.

PROBLEM

Find the measure of the angle whose measure is 40° more than the measure of its supplement.

SOLUTION

By the definition of supplementary angles, the sum of the measures of two supplements must equal 180°. Accordingly,

let x = the measure of the supplement of the angle.

Then $x + 40°$ = the measure of the angle.

Therefore, $x + (x + 40°) = 180°$

$$2x + 40° = 180°$$
$$2x = 140°$$
$$x = 70° \text{ and}$$
$$x + 40° = 110°.$$

Therefore the measure of the angle is 110°.

PROBLEM

What is the measure of a given angle whose measure is half the measure of its complement?

SOLUTION

When two angles are said to be complementary we know that their measures must sum, by definition, to 90°.

If we let x = the measure of the given angle,

then $2x$ = the measure of its complement.

To determine the measure of the given angle, set the sum of the two angle measures equal to 90 and solve for x. Accordingly,

$$x + 2x = 90°$$
$$3x = 90°$$
$$x = 30°$$

Therefore, the measure of the given angle is 30° and its complement is 60°.

PROBLEM

Given that straight lines $\overleftrightarrow{AB}$ and $\overleftrightarrow{CD}$ intersect at point E, that $\angle BEC$ has measure 20° greater than 5 times a fixed quantity, and that $\angle AED$ has measure 60° greater than 3 times this same quantity: Find a) the unknown fixed quantity, b) the measure of $\angle BEC$, and c) the measure of $\angle CEA$. (For the actual angle placement, refer to the accompanying diagram.)

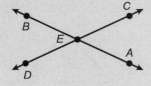

SOLUTION

a) Since $\overleftrightarrow{AB}$ and $\overleftrightarrow{CD}$ are straight lines intersecting at point E, $\angle BEC$ and $\angle AED$ are, by definition, vertical angles. As such, they are congruent and their measures are equal. Therefore, if we let x represent the fixed quantity, $\angle BEC = 5x + 20$ and $\angle AED = 3x + 60$, according to the information given. We can then set up the following equality, and solve for the unknown quantity.

$$5x + 20 = 3x + 60$$
$$5x - 3x = 60 - 20$$
$$2x = 40$$
$$x = 20$$

Therefore, the value of the unknown quantity is 20°.

b) From the information given about $\angle BEC$, we know that $m\angle BEC = (5x + 20)°$. By substitution, we have

$$m\angle BEC = 5(20°) + 20° = 100° + 20° = 120°.$$

Therefore, the measure of $\angle BEC$ is 120°.

c) We know that $\overleftrightarrow{AB}$ is a straight line; therefore, $\angle CEA$ is the supplement of $\angle BEC$. Since the sum of the measure of two supplements is 180°, the following calculation can be made:

$$m\angle CEA + m\angle BEC = 180°$$
$$m\angle CEA = 180° - m\angle BEC.$$

Substituting in our value for $m\angle BEC$, we obtain:

$$m\angle CEA = 180° - 120° = 60°$$

Therefore, the measure of $\angle CEA$ is 60°.

Theorem 8

Any point on the perpendicular bisector of a given line segment is equidistant from the ends of the segment.

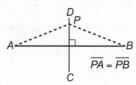

Theorem 9

If a point is equidistant from the ends of a line segment, this point must lie on the perpendicular bisector of the segment.

Theorem 10

If two points are equidistant from the ends of a line segment, these points determine the perpendicular bisector of the segment.

Theorem 11

Every line segment has exactly one midpoint.

Theorem 12

There exists one and only one perpendicular to a line through a point outside the line. Take point C outside line $\overleftrightarrow{AB}$. $\overleftrightarrow{OC}$ represents the only perpendicular to $\overleftrightarrow{AB}$ that passes through C.

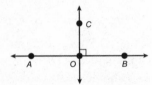

Theorem 13

If the exterior sides of adjacent angles are perpendicular to each other, then the adjacent angles are complementary.

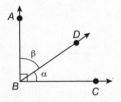

α and β are complementary

Theorem 14

Adjacent angles are supplementary if their exterior sides form a straight line.

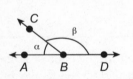

α and β are supplementary

Theorem 15

Two angles that are equal and supplementary to each other are right angles.

Congruent Angles and Congruent Line Segments

Definitions

Definition 1

Two or more geometric figures are congruent when they have the same shape and size. The symbol for congruence is $\cong$; hence, if triangle ABC is congruent to triangle DEF, we write $\triangle ABC \cong \triangle DEF$.

Definition 2

Two line segments are congruent if and only if they have the same measure.

Note: The expression "if and only if" can be used any time both a statement and the converse of that statement are true. Using definition 2, we can rewrite the statement as "two line segments have the same measure if and only if they are congruent." The two statements are identical.

Definition 3

Two angles are congruent if and only if they have the same measure.

PROBLEM

In the figure shown, $\triangle ABC$ is an isosceles triangle, such that $\overline{BA} \cong \overline{BC}$. Line segment $\overline{AD}$ bisects $\angle BAC$ and $\overline{CD}$ bisects $\angle BCA$. Prove that $\triangle ADC$ is an isosceles triangle.

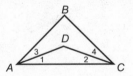

SOLUTION

In order to prove $\triangle ADC$ is isosceles, we must prove that two of its sides, $\overline{AD}$ and $\overline{CD}$, are congruent. To prove $\overline{AD} \cong \overline{CD}$ in $\triangle ADC$, we have to prove that the angles opposite $\overline{AD}$ and $\overline{CD}$, $\angle 1$ and $\angle 2$, are congruent.

Statement	Reason
1. $\overline{BA} \cong \overline{BC}$	1. Given.
2. $\angle BAC = \angle BCA$ or $m\angle BAC = m\angle BCA$	2. If two sides of a triangle are congruent, then the angles opposite them are congruent.
3. $\overline{AD}$ bisects $\angle BAC$ $\overline{CD}$ bisects $\angle BCA$	3. Given.
4. $m\angle 1 = (\frac{1}{2})m\angle BAC$ $m\angle 2 = (\frac{1}{2})m\angle BCA$	4. The bisector of an angle divides the angle into two angles whose measures are equal.
5. $m\angle 1 = m\angle 2$	5. Halves of equal quantities are equal.
6. $\angle 1 \cong \angle 1$	6. If the measure of two angles are equal, then the angles are congruent.
7. $\overline{CD} \cong \overline{AD}$	7. If two angles of a triangle are congruent, then the sides opposite these angles are congruent.
8. $\triangle ADC$ is an isosceles triangle.	8. If a triangle has two congruent sides, then it is an isosceles triangle.

Theorems

Theorem 1

Every line segment is congruent to itself.

Theorem 2

Every angle is congruent to itself.

Let R be a relation on a set A. Then:

R is reflexive if aRa for every a in A.

R is symmetric if aRb implies bRa.

R is anti-symmetric if aRb and bRa imply $a = b$.

R is transitive if aRb and bRc imply aRc.

Note: The term aRa means the relation R performed on a yields a. The term aRb means the relation R performed on a yields b.

Theorem 3

Given a line segment $\overline{AB}$ and a ray $\overrightarrow{XY}$, there exists one and only one point O on $\overrightarrow{XY}$ such that $\overline{AB} \cong \overline{XO}$.

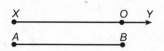

Theorem 4

If $\overline{AB} = \overline{CD}$, Q bisects $\overline{AB}$ and P bisects $\overline{CD}$, then $\overline{AQ} \cong \overline{CP}$ and $\overline{QB} \cong \overline{PD}$.

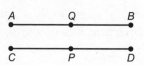

Theorem 5

If $m\angle ABC = m\angle DEF$, and $\overrightarrow{BX}$ and $\overrightarrow{EY}$ bisect $\angle ABC$ and $\angle DEF$, respectively, then $m\angle ABX = m\angle XBC = m\angle DEY = m\angle YEF$.

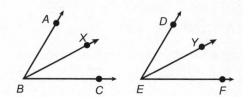

Theorem 6

Let P be in the interior of $\angle ABC$ and Q be in the interior of $\angle DEF$. If $m\angle ABP = m\angle DEQ$ and $m\angle PBC = m\angle QEF$, then $m\angle ABC = m\angle DEF$.

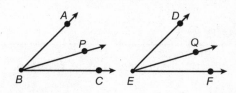

Theorem 7

Let *P* be in the interior of ∠*XYZ* and *Q* be in the interior of ∠*ABC*. If *m*∠*XYZ* = *m*∠*ABC* and *m*∠*XYP* = *m*∠*ABQ* then *m*∠*PYZ* = *m*∠*QBC*.

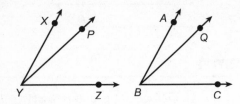

Postulates

By definition, a relation *R* is called an equivalence relation if relation *R* is reflexive, symmetric, and transitive.

Postulate 1

Congruence of segments is an equivalence relation.

(1) Congruence of segments is reflexive.
If $\overline{AB} \cong \overline{AB}$, $\overline{AB}$ is congruent to itself.

(2) Congruence of segments is symmetric.
If $\overline{AB} \cong \overline{CD}$, then $\overline{CD} \cong \overline{AB}$.

(3) Congruence of segments is transitive.
If $\overline{AB} \cong \overline{CD}$ and $\overline{CD} \cong \overline{EF}$, then $\overline{AB} \cong \overline{EF}$.

Postulate 2

Congruence of angles is an equivalence relation, that is, it is reflexive, symmetric, and transitive.

Postulate 3

Any geometric figure is congruent to itself.

Postulate 4

A geometric congruence may be reversed.

Postulate 5

Two geometric figures congruent to the same geometric figure are congruent to each other.

PROBLEM

Given triangle *RST* in the figure shown with $\overline{RT} \cong \overline{ST}$. Points *A* and *B* lie at the midpoint of $\overline{RT}$ and $\overline{ST}$, respectively. Prove that $\overline{RA} \cong \overline{SB}$.

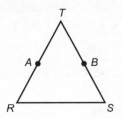

SOLUTION

This solution is best presented as a formal proof.

Statement	Reason
1. $\overline{RT} \cong \overline{ST}$ or $RT = ST$	1. Given.
2. *A* is the midpoint of $\overline{RT}$	2. Given.
3. $RA = (\frac{1}{2})RT$	3. The midpoint of a line segment divides the line segment into two equal halves.
4. *B* is the midpoint of $\overline{ST}$	4. Given.
5. $\overline{SB} = \left(\frac{1}{2}\right)TS$	5. The midpoint of a line segment divides the line segment into two equal halves.
6. $RA = SB$	6. Division Postulate: Halves of equal quantities are equal. Statements 3 and 5.
7. $\overline{RA} \cong \overline{SB}$	7. If two line segments are of equal length, then they are congruent.

Quiz: Congruent Angles

Refer to the diagrams and find the appropriate solutions.

1. Find a.

   (A) 38°

   (B) 68°

   (C) 78°

   (D) 90°

   (E) 112°

2. Find c.

   (A) 32°

   (B) 48°

   (C) 58°

   (D) 82°

   (E) 148°

3. Determine x.

   (A) 21°

   (B) 23°

   (C) 51°

   (D) 102°

   (E) 153°

4. Find z.

   (A) 29°

   (B) 54°

   (C) 61°

   (D) 88°

   (E) 92°

5. In the figure shown, if $\overline{BD}$ is the bisector of angle ABC, and angle ABD is one-fourth the size of angle XYZ, what is the size of angle ABC?

   (A) 21°

   (B) 28°

   (C) 42°

   (D) 63°

   (E) 168°

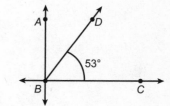

6. $\overrightarrow{BA} \perp \overrightarrow{BC}$ and $m\angle DBC = 53°$.

   Find $m\angle ABD$.

   (A) 27°

   (B) 33°

   (C) 37°

   (D) 53°

   (E) 90°

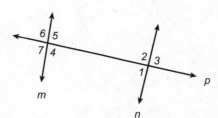

7. If $n \perp p$, which of the following statements is true?

   (A) $\angle 1 \cong \angle 2$

   (B) $\angle 4 \cong \angle 5$

   (C) $m\angle 4 + m\angle 5 > m\angle 1 + m\angle 2$

   (D) $m\angle 3 > m\angle 2$

   (E) $m\angle 4 = 90°$

8. In the figure, if $p \perp t$ and $q \perp t$, which of the following statements is false?

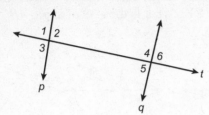

   (A) $\angle 1 \cong \angle 4$

   (B) $\angle 2 \cong \angle 3$

   (C) $m\angle 2 + m\angle 3 = m\angle 4 + m\angle 6$

   (D) $m\angle 5 + m\angle 6 = 180°$

   (E) $m\angle 2 > m\angle 5$

9. If $a \| b$, find z.

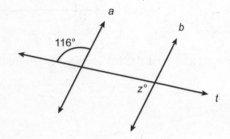

   (A)   26°   (C)   64°   (E)   116°

   (B)   32°   (D)   86°

10. If $m \| n$, which of the following statements is not necessarily true?

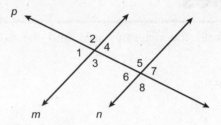

   (A) $\angle 2 \cong \angle 5$

   (B) $\angle 3 \cong \angle 6$

   (C) $m\angle 4 + m\angle 5 = 180°$

   (D) $\angle 1 \cong \angle 6$

   (E) $m\angle 7 + m\angle 3 = 180°$

ANSWER KEY

1. (B)
2. (A)
3. (C)
4. (D)
5. (C)

6. (C)
7. (A)
8. (E)
9. (C)
10. (B)

Regular Polygons (Convex)

A **polygon** is a figure with the same number of sides as angles.

An **equilateral polygon** is a polygon all of whose sides are of equal measure.

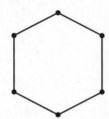

An **equiangular polygon** is a polygon all of whose angles are of equal measure.

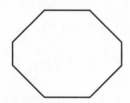

A **regular polygon** is a polygon that is both equilateral and equiangular.

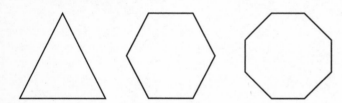

PROBLEM

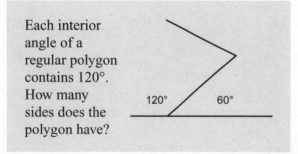

Each interior angle of a regular polygon contains 120°. How many sides does the polygon have?

SOLUTION

At each vertex of a polygon, we can draw an exterior angle that is supplementary to the interior angle, as shown in the diagram.

Since we are told that the interior angle measures 120°, we can deduce that the exterior angle measures 60°.

Each exterior angle of a regular polygon of n sides measure $\dfrac{360^\circ}{n}$ degrees. We know that each exterior angle measures 60°, and, therefore, by setting $\dfrac{360^\circ}{n}$ equal to 60°, we can determine the number of sides in the polygon. The calculation is as follows:

$$\frac{360^\circ}{n} = 60^\circ$$

$$60^\circ n = 360^\circ$$

$$n = 6$$

Therefore, the regular polygon, with interior angles of 120°, has six sides and is called a hexagon.

The **perimeter** of a regular polygon is the product of the length of a side(s) and the number of sides (n) $P = ns$.

The area of a regular polygon can be determined by using the **apothem** and **radius** of the polygon. The apothem (a) of a regular polygon is the segment from the center of the polygon perpendicular to a side of the polygon. The radius (r) of a regular polygon is the segment joining any vertex of a regular polygon with the center of that polygon.

(1) All radii of a regular polygon are congruent.

(2) The radius of a regular hexagon(6 sided) is congruent to a side.

(3) All apothems of a regular polygon are congruent.

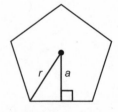

The area of a regular polygon equals one-half the product of the length of the apothem and the perimeter.

$$\text{Area} = \frac{1}{2}a \times p$$

PROBLEM

Find the area of a regular hexagon if one side has length 6.

SOLUTION

Since the length of a side equals 6, the radius also equals 6 and the perimeter equals 36. The base of the right triangle, formed by the radius and apothem, is half the length of a side, or 3. You can find the length of the apothem by using the Pythagorean theorem.

$$a^2 + b^2 = c^2$$
$$a^2 + (3)^2 = (6)^2$$
$$a^2 = 36 - 9$$
$$a^2 = 27$$
$$a = 3\sqrt{3}$$

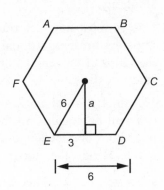

The apothem equals $3\sqrt{3}$. Therefore, the area of the hexagon

$$= \frac{1}{2}a \times p$$
$$= \frac{1}{2}(3\sqrt{3})(36)$$
$$= 54\sqrt{3}$$

Drill: Regular Polygons (Convex)

Angle Measures

DIRECTIONS: Find the appropriate solutions.

1. Find the measure of an interior angle of a regular pentagon.

    (A) 55°   (C) 90°

    (B) 72°   (D) 108°

2. Find the sum of the measures of the exterior angles of a regular triangle.

    (A) 90°   (C) 180°

    (B) 115°   (D) 360°

Area(s) and Perimeter(s)

DIRECTIONS: Find the appropriate solutions.

3. A regular triangle has sides of 24 mm. If the apothem is $4\sqrt{3}$ mm, find the area of the triangle.

    (A) 72 mm²   (C) 144 mm²

    (B) $96\sqrt{3}$ mm²   (D) $144\sqrt{3}$ mm²

4. Find the area of a regular hexagon with sides of 4 cm.

    (A) $12\sqrt{3}$ cm²   (C) $24\sqrt{3}$ cm²

    (B) 24 cm²   (D) 48 cm²

5. Find the area of a regular decagon with sides of length 6 cm and an apothem of length 9.2 cm.

    (A) 55.2 cm²   (C) 138 cm²

    (B) 60 cm²   (D) 276 cm²

Similar Polygons

Definition

Two polygons are similar if there is a one-to-one correspondence between their vertices such that all pairs of corresponding angles are congruent and the ratios of the measures of all pairs of corresponding sides are equal. Note that although they must have the same shape, they may have different sizes.

Theorem 1

The perimeters of two similar polygons have the same ratio as the measure of any pair of corresponding sides of the polygons.

Theorem 2

The ratio of the lengths of two corresponding diagonals of two similar polygons is equal to the ratio of the lengths of any two corresponding sides of the polygons.

Theorem 3

Two polygons composed of the same number of triangles similar each to each, and similarly placed, are similar.

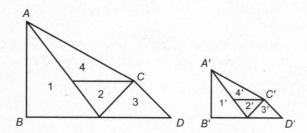

PROBLEM

Prove that any two regular polygons with the same number of sides are similar.

SOLUTION

For any two polygons to be similar, their corresponding angles must be congruent and their corresponding sides proportional. It is necessary to show that these conditions always exist between regular polygons with the same number of sides.

Let us examine the corresponding angles first. For a regular polygon with n sides, each vertex angle is $\frac{(n-2)180}{n}$. Therefore, two regular polygons with the same number of sides will have corresponding vertex angles that are all of the same measure and, hence, are all congruent. This fulfills our first condition for similarity.

We must now determine whether the corresponding sides are proportional. It will suffice to show that the ratios of the lengths of every pair of corresponding sides are the same.

Since the polygons are regular, the sides of each one will be equal. Call the length of the sides of one polygon ℓ_1 and the length of the sides of the other polygon ℓ_2. Hence, the ratio of the lengths of corresponding sides will be $\frac{l_1}{l_2}$. This will be a constant for any pair of corresponding sides and, hence, the corresponding sides are proportional.

Thus, any two regular polygons with the same number of sides are similar.

PROBLEM

The lengths of two corresponding sides of two similar polygons are 4 and 7. If the perimeter of the smaller polygon is 20, find the perimeter of the larger polygon.

SOLUTION

We know, by theorem, that the perimeters of two similar polygons have the same ratio as the measures of any pair of corresponding sides.

If we let s and p represent the side and perimeter of the smaller polygon and s' and p' represent the corresponding side and perimeter of the larger one, we can then write the proportion

$$p : p' = s : s'$$

By substituting the given values, we can solve for p'.

$$20 : p' = 4 : 7$$
$$4\,p' = 140$$
$$p' = 35.$$

Therefore, the perimeter of the larger polygon is 35.

Triangles

A closed three-sided geometric figure is called a **triangle**. The points of the intersection of the sides of a triangle are called the **vertices** of the triangle.

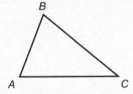

The **perimeter** of a triangle is the sum of the measures of the sides of the triangle.

A triangle with no equal sides is called a **scalene triangle**.

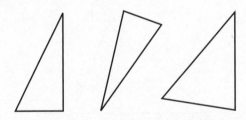

A triangle having at least two equal sides is called an **isosceles triangle**. The third side is called the **base** of the triangle, and the base angles (the angles opposite the equal sides) are equal.

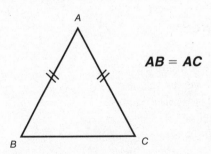

$$AB = AC$$

A side of a triangle is a line segment whose endpoints are the vertices of two angles of the triangle.

An **interior angle** of a triangle is an angle formed by two sides and includes the third side within its collection of points.

An **equilateral triangle** is a triangle having three equal sides. $\overline{AB} \cong \overline{AC} \cong \overline{BC}$. An equilateral, triangle is also **equiangular**, with each angle equaling 60°.

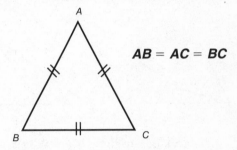

$$AB = AC = BC$$

The sum of the measures of the interior angles of a triangle is 180°.

A triangle with one obtuse angle (greater than 90°) is called an **obtuse triangle**.

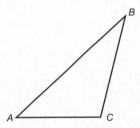

An **acute triangle** is a triangle with three acute angles (less than 90°).

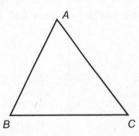

A triangle with a right angle is a **right triangle**. The side opposite the right angle in a right triangle is called the hypotenuse of the right triangle. The other two sides are called arms or legs of the right triangle. By the Pythagorean Theorem, the length of the three sides of a right triangle are related by the formula $c^2 = a^2 + b^2$ where c is the hypotenuse and a and b are the other sides (the legs).

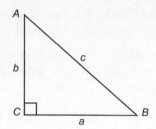

An **altitude** of a triangle is a line segment from a vertex of the triangle perpendicular to the opposite side.

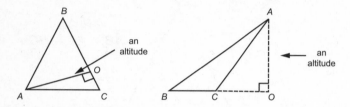

The **area** of a triangle is given by $A = \frac{1}{2}bh$

where h is the altitude and b is the base to which the altitude is drawn.

A line segment connecting a vertex of a triangle and the midpoint of the opposite side is called a **median** of the triangle.

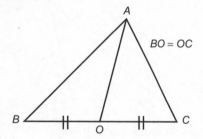

A line that bisects and is perpendicular to a side of a triangle is called a **perpendicular bisector** of that side.

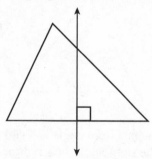

An **angle bisector** of a triangle is a line that bisects an angle and extends to the opposite side of the triangle.

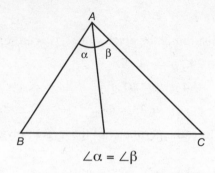

$\angle \alpha = \angle \beta$

The line segment that joins the midpoints of two sides of a triangle is called a **midline** of the triangle.

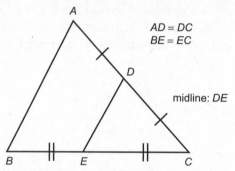

An **exterior angle** of a triangle is an angle formed outside a triangle by one side of the triangle and the extension of an adjacent side.

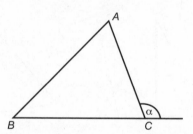

Three or more lines (or rays or segments) are **concurrent** if there exists one point common to all of them, that is, if they all intersect at the same point.

PROBLEM

The measure of the vertex angle of an isosceles triangle exceeds the measurement of each base angle by 30°. Find the value of each angle of the triangle.

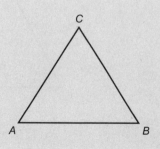

SOLUTION

We know that the sum of the values of the angles of a triangle is 180°. In an isosceles triangle, the angles opposite the congruent sides (the base angles) are, themselves, congruent and of equal value.

Therefore,

(1) Let x = the measure of each base angle.

(2) Then $x + 30$ = the measure of the vertex angle.

We can solve for x algebraically by keeping in mind the sum of all the measures will be 180°.

$$x + x + (x + 30) = 180$$
$$3x + 30 = 180$$
$$3x = 150$$
$$x = 50$$

Therefore, the base angles each measure 50°, and the vertex angle measures 80°.

Drill: Triangles

Angle Measures

DIRECTIONS: Refer to the diagram and find the appropriate solution.

1. In $\triangle PQR$, $\angle Q$ is a right angle. Find $m\angle R$.

   (A) 27°   (C) 54°

   (B) 33°   (D) 67°

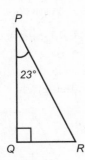

2. $\triangle MNO$ is isosceles. If the vertex angle, $\angle N$, has a measure of 96°, find the measure of $\angle M$.

   (A) 21°

   (B) 42°

   (C) 64°

   (D) 84°

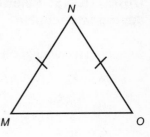

3. Find x.

   (A) 15°

   (B) 25°

   (C) 30°

   (D) 45°

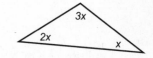

Similar Triangles

DIRECTIONS: Refer to the diagram and find the appropriate solution.

4. The two triangles shown are similar. Find b.

   (A) $2\frac{2}{3}$

   (B) 3

   (C) 4

   (D) 16

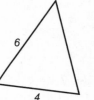

5. The two triangles shown are similar. Find a and b.

   (A) 5 and 10   (C) $4\frac{2}{3}$ and $7\frac{1}{3}$

   (B) 4 and 8   (D) $5\frac{1}{3}$ and 8

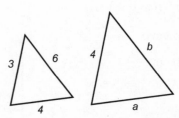

Area

DIRECTIONS: Refer to the diagram and find the appropriate solution.

6.   Find the area of $\triangle MNO$.

    (A)   22

    (B)   49

    (C)   56

    (D)   84

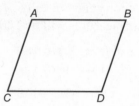

7.   Find the area of $\triangle PQR$.

    (A)   31.5

    (B)   38.5

    (C)   53

    (D)   77

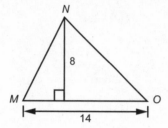

8.   Find the area of $\triangle STU$.

    (A) $4\sqrt{2}$

    (B) $8\sqrt{2}$

    (C) $12\sqrt{2}$

    (D) $16\sqrt{2}$

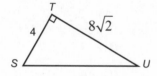

9.   Find the area of $\triangle ABC$.

    (A)   54 cm²

    (B)   81 cm²

    (C)   108 cm²

    (D)   135 cm²

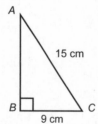

10.   Find the area of $\triangle XYZ$.

    (A)   20 cm²

    (B)   50 cm²

    (C) $50\sqrt{2}$ cm²

    (D)   100 cm²

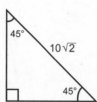

Quadrilaterals

A **quadrilateral** is a polygon with four sides.

Parallelograms

A **parallelogram** is a quadrilateral whose opposite sides are parallel.

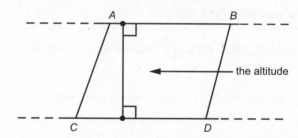

Two angles that have their vertices at the endpoints of the same side of a parallelogram are called consecutive angles.

The perpendicular segment connecting any point of a line containing one side of a parallelogram to the line containing the opposite side of the parallelogram is called the altitude of the parallelogram.

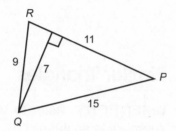

A diagonal of a polygon is a line segment joining any two nonconsecutive vertices.

The area of a parallelogram is given by the formula $A = bh$, where b is the base and h is the height drawn perpendicular to that base. Note that the height equals the altitude of the parallelogram.

$A = bh$

$A = (10)(3)$

$A = 30$

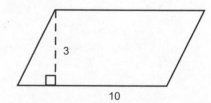

Rectangles

A **rectangle** is a parallelogram with right angles.

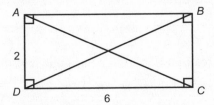

The diagonals of a rectangle are equal.

If the diagonals of a parallelogram are equal, the parallelogram is a rectangle.

If a quadrilateral has four right angles, then it is a rectangle.

The area of a rectangle is given by the formula $A = lw$, where l is the length and w is the width.

$A = lw$

$A = (3)(10)$

$A = 30$

Rhombi

A **rhombus** is a parallelogram that has two adjacent sides that are equal.

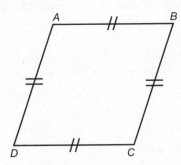

All sides of a rhombus are equal.

The diagonals of a rhombus are perpendicular to each other.

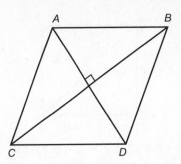

The area of a rhombus can be found by the formula $A = \frac{1}{2}(d_1 \cdot d_2)$ where d_1 and d_2 are the diagonals.

The diagonals of a rhombus bisect the angles of the rhombus.

If the diagonals of a parallelogram are perpendicular, the parallelogram is a rhombus.

If a quadrilateral has four equal sides, then it is a rhombus.

A parallelogram is a rhombus if either diagonal of the parallelogram bisects the angles of the vertices it joins.

Squares

A **square** is a rhombus with a right angle.

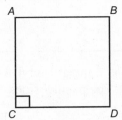

A square is an equilateral quadrilateral.

A square has all the properties of parallelograms and rectangles.

A rhombus is a square if one of its interior angles is a right angle.

In a square, the measure of either diagonal can be calculated by multiplying the length of any side by the square root of 2.

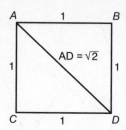

The area of a square is given by the formula $A = s^2$, where s is the side of the square. Since all sides of a square are equal, it does not matter which side is used.

$A = s^2$

$A = 6^2$

$A = 36$

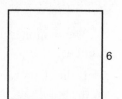

The area of a square can also be found by taking $\frac{1}{2}$ the product of the length of the diagonal squared.

$A = \frac{1}{2}d^2$

$A = \frac{1}{2}(8)^2$

$A = 32$

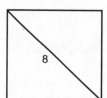

Trapezoids

A **trapezoid** is a quadrilateral with two and only two sides parallel. The parallel sides of a trapezoid are called **bases**.

The **median** of a trapezoid is the line joining the midpoints of the non-parallel sides.

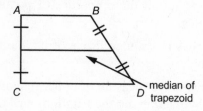

median of trapezoid

The perpendicular segment connecting any point in the line containing one base of the trapezoid to the line containing the other base is the **altitude** of the trapezoid.

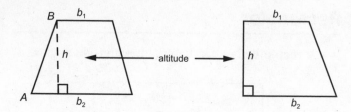

The area of a trapezoid equals one half the altitude times the sum of the bases, or $\frac{1}{2}h(b_1 + b_2)$.

An **isosceles trapezoid** is a trapezoid whose non-parallel sides are equal. A pair of angles including only one of the parallel sides is called a pair of base angles.

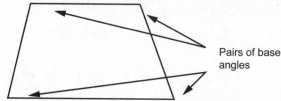

Pairs of base angles

The median of a trapezoid is parallel to the bases and equal to one-half their sum.

The base angles of an isosceles trapezoid are equal.

The diagonals of an isosceles trapezoid are equal.

The opposite angles of an isosceles trapezoid are supplementary.

Drill: Quadrilaterals

DIRECTIONS: Refer to the diagram and find the appropriate solution.

1. Quadrilateral $ABCD$ is a parallelogram. If $m\angle B = (6x + 2)°$ and $m\angle D = 98°$, find x.

   (A) 12

   (B) 16

   (C) $16\frac{2}{3}$

   (D) 18

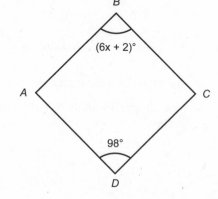

2. Find the area of parallelogram *STUV*.

   (A) 56

   (B) 90

   (C) 108

   (D) 162

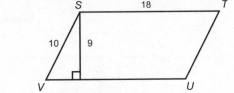

3. In rectangle *ABCD*, $\overline{AD}$ = 6 cm and $\overline{DC}$ = 8 cm. Find the length of the diagonal $\overline{AC}$.

   (A) 10 cm   (C) 20 cm

   (B) 12 cm   (D) 28 cm

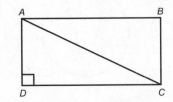

4. Find the area of rectangle *UVXY*.

   (A) 17 cm²

   (B) 34 cm²

   (C) 35 cm²

   (D) 70 cm²

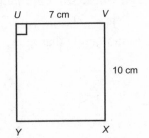

5. Find the length of $\overline{BO}$ in rectangle *BCDE* if the diagonal $\overline{EC}$ is 17 mm.

   (A) 6.55 mm

   (B) 8 mm

   (C) 8.5 mm

   (D) 17 mm

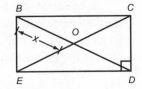

6. In rhombus *GHIJ*, $\overline{GI}$ = 6 cm and $\overline{HJ}$ = 8 cm. Find the length of $\overline{GH}$.

   (A) 3 cm

   (B) 4 cm

   (C) 5 cm

   (D) $4\sqrt{3}$ cm

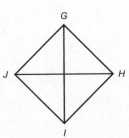

7. Find the area of the trapezoid *RSTU*.

   (A) 80

   (B) 87.5

   (C) 140

   (D) 175

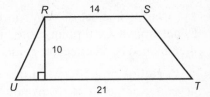

8. *ABCD* is an isosceles trapezoid. Find the perimeter.

   (A) 21 cm   (C) 30 cm

   (B) 27 cm   (D) 50 cm

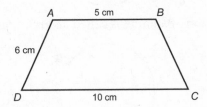

9. Find the area of trapezoid *MNOP*.

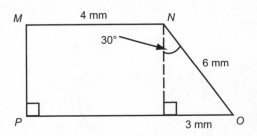

   (A) $(17 + 3\sqrt{3})$ mm²   (C) $\dfrac{33\sqrt{3}}{2}$ mm²

   (B) $\dfrac{33}{2}$ mm²   (D) 33 mm²

10. Trapezoid *XYZW* is isosceles. If $m\angle W$ = 58° and $m\angle Z = (4x - 6)°$, find *x*.

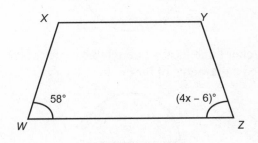

   (A) 8   (C) 13

   (B) 12   (D) 16

Circles

A **circle** is a set of points in the same plane equidistant from a fixed point, called its center. Circles are often named by their center point, circle O.

A **radius** of a circle is a line segment drawn from the center of the circle to any point on the circle.

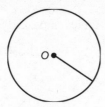

A portion of a circle is called an **arc** of the circle.

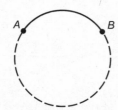

A line that intersects a circle in two points is called a **secant.**

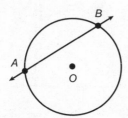

A line segment joining two points on a circle is called a **chord** of the circle.

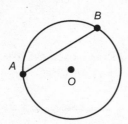

A chord that passes through the center of the circle is called a **diameter** of the circle.

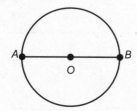

The line passing through the centers of two (or more) circles is called the **line of centers.**

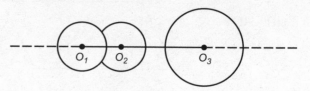

An angle whose vertex is on the circle and whose sides are chords of the circle is called an **inscribed angle** ($\angle$ BAC in the diagrams).

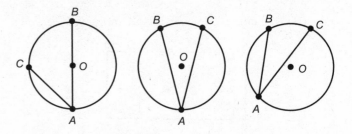

An angle whose vertex is at the center of a circle and whose sides are radii is called a **central angle.**

The measure of a minor arc is the measure of the central angle that intercepts that arc.

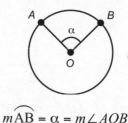

$$m\overgroup{AB} = \alpha = m\angle AOB$$

The distance from a point P to a given circle is the distance from that point to the point where the circle intersects with a line segment with endpoints at the center of the circle and point P.

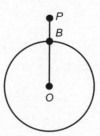

The distance of point P to the diagrammed circle with center O is the line segment $\overline{PB}$ of line segment $\overline{PO}$.

A line that has one and only one point of intersection with a circle is called a tangent to that circle, and their common point is called a **point of tangency.** In the diagram, Q and P are each points of tangency.

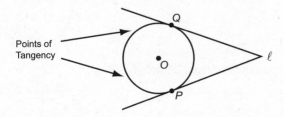

Congruent circles are circles whose radii are congruent.

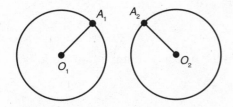

If $O_1A_1 \cong O_2A_2$, then $O_1 \cong O_2$.

The measure of a semicircle is 180°.

A **circumscribed circle** is a circle passing through all the vertices of a polygon. The polygon is said to be **inscribed** in the circle.

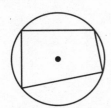

Circles that have the same center and unequal radii are called **concentric circles.**

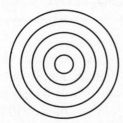

Concentric Circles

The **circumference** of a circle is the length of its outer edge, given by $C = \pi d = 2\pi r$, where r is the radius, d is the diameter, and π(pi) is a mathematical constant approximately equal to 3.14.

The **area** of a circle is given by $A = \pi r^2$. A full circle is 360°. The length of arc intercepted by a central angle has the same ratio to the circle's circumference as the measure of the arc has to be 360°, the full circle. Therefore, arc length is given by $\frac{n}{360} \times 2\pi r$, where $n =$ measure of the central angle. The measure of an arc in degrees, however, is the same as the measure of its central angle.

A sector is the portion of a circle between two radii. Its area is given by $A = \frac{n}{360}(\pi r^2)$ where n is the central angle formed by the radii.

PROBLEM

A and B are points on circle Q such that $\triangle AQB$ is equilateral. If the length of side $\overline{AB} = 12$, find the length of arc AB.

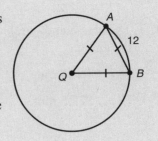

SOLUTION

To find the arc length of arc AB, we must find the measure of the central angle $\angle AQB$ and the measure of the radius $\overline{QA}$. $\angle AQB$ is an interior angle of the equilateral triangle $\triangle AQB$. Therefore,

$$m\angle AQB = 60°.$$

Similarly, in the equilateral $\triangle AQB$,

$$\overline{AQ} = \overline{AB} = \overline{QB} = 12.$$

Given the radius, r, and the central angle, n, the arc length is given by

$$\frac{n}{360} \times 2\pi r.$$

Therefore, by substitution,

Length of arc AB $= \dfrac{60}{360} \times 2\pi \times 12 = \dfrac{1}{6} \times 2\pi \times 12 = 4\pi.$

Drill: Circles

DIRECTIONS: Determine the accurate measure.

1. Find the circumference of circle *A* if its radius is 3 mm.

   (A) 3π mm   (C) 9π mm

   (B) 6π mm   (D) 12π mm

2. Find the area of circle *I*.

   (A) 22 mm²

   (B) 121 mm²

   (C) 121π mm²

   (D) 132 mm²

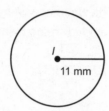

3. The diameter of circle *Z* is 27 mm. Find the area of the circle.

   (A) 91.125 mm²   (C) 191.5π mm²

   (B) 182.25 mm²   (D) 182.25π mm²

4. The area of circle *B* is 225π cm². Find the length of the diameter of the circle.

   (A) 15 cm   (C) 30 cm

   (B) 20 cm   (D) 20π cm

5. The area of circle *X* is 144π mm² while the area of circle *Y* is 81π mm². Write the ratio of the radius of circle *X* to that of circle *Y*.

   (A) 3 : 4   (C) 9 : 12

   (B) 4 : 3   (D) 27 : 12

6. The radius of the smaller of two concentric circles is 5 cm while the radius of the larger circle is 7 cm. Determine the area of the shaded region.

   (A) 7π cm²

   (B) 24π cm²

   (C) 25π cm²

   (D) 36π cm²

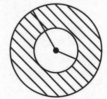

7. Find the measure of arc $\overset{\frown}{MN}$ if $m\angle MON = 62°$.

   (A) 16°

   (B) 32°

   (C) 59°

   (D) 62°

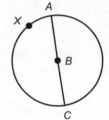

8. Find the measure of arc $\overset{\frown}{AXC}$.

   (A) 150°

   (B) 160°

   (C) 180°

   (D) 270°

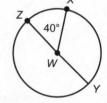

9. Find the measure of arc $\overset{\frown}{XY}$ in circle *W*.

   (A) 40°

   (B) 120°

   (C) 140°

   (D) 180°

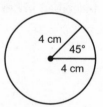

10. Find the area of the sector shown.

    (A) 4 cm²

    (B) 2π cm²

    (C) 16 cm²

    (D) 8π cm²

Perimeters and Areas of Composite Figures

Composite figures are combinations of two or more figures, but each of our examples will contain only two figures. In each case, the two figures will be connected with a common side or one figure will lie entirely within the other figure.

PROBLEM

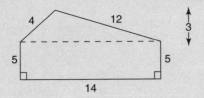

Consider the following composite figure.

What is its perimeter and area?

SOLUTION

The perimeter is $5 + 14 + 5 + 4 + 12 = 40$. The total area (A) is the area of the rectangle added to the area of the triangle. Thus, $A = (14)(5) + \left(\frac{1}{2}\right)(14)(3) = 91$.

PROBLEM

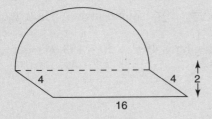

The following composite figure consists of a semicircle on top of a parallelogram.

What is the perimeter and area, to the nearest hundredth?

SOLUTION

The three sides of the parallelogram add up to 24. The length of the semicircle is equivalent to half the circumference of a circle with a radius of 8. This value is 8π, so the perimeter for the entire figure is $24 + 8\pi \approx 49.13$. The area of the parallelogram portion is $(16)(2) = 32$. The area of the semicircle is $\left(\frac{1}{2}\right)(\pi)(8^2) \approx 100.53$. Thus, the area for the entire figure is approximately 132.53.

PROBLEM

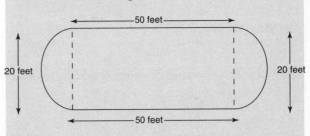

The following figure is a small track consisting of two semicircles that are attached to the widths of a rectangle.

What is the perimeter and area, to the nearest hundredth?

SOLUTION

The perimeter is composed of two lengths of the rectangle and the equivalent of the circumference of a circle. The circumference of a circle with a diameter of 20 feet is 20π feet. Thus, the perimeter for the entire figure is $50 + 50 + 20\pi \approx 162.83$ feet. The area for the entire figure is $(50)(20) + (\pi)(10^2) \approx 1314.16$ square feet.

We now look at areas of shaded regions in which one geometric figure *lies completely inside* another figure.

PROBLEM

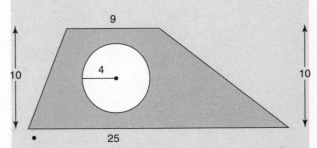

In the following diagram, a circle lies inside a trapezoid.

What is the area of the shaded region, to the nearest hundredth?

SOLUTION

The area of the trapezoid is $\left(\dfrac{1}{2}\right)(10)(25 + 9) = 170$ and the area of the circle is 16π. Thus, the area of the shaded region is $170 - 16\pi \approx 119.73$.

PROBLEM

In the following diagram, a rectangle lies inside a triangle.

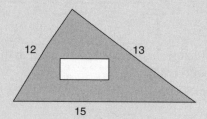

If the length and width of the rectangle are 7 and 3, respectively, what is the area of the shaded region, to the nearest hundredth?

SOLUTION

Heron's formula states that if a, b, and c are the length of the sides of a triangle, and if $s = \dfrac{a+b+c}{2}$, then the area of the triangle is $\sqrt{s(s-a)(s-b)(s-c)}$.

Using Heron's formula, the area of the triangle is $\sqrt{(20)(8)(7)(5)} \approx 74.83$. Since the area of the rectangle is 21, the area of the shaded region is approximately $74.83 - 21 = 53.83$.

PROBLEM

In the following diagram, a rhombus lies inside a circle.

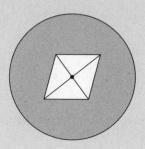

The diameter of the circle is 14 inches and the diagonals of the rhombus are 8 inches and 5 inches.

What is the area of the shaded region, to the nearest hundredth?

SOLUTION

The radius of the circle is 7 inches, so the circle's area is 49π square inches. The area of the rhombus is $\left(\dfrac{1}{2}\right)(8)(5) = 20$ square inches. Thus, the area of the shaded region is $49\pi - 20 \approx 133.94$ square inches.

Drill: Composite Figures

1. In the following diagram, a semicircle lies on top of an equilateral triangle.

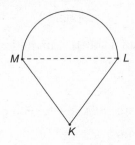

If $KM = 10$, what is the total area?

(A) $12.5\pi + 25\sqrt{3}$　　(C) $12.5\pi + 12.5\sqrt{3}$

(B) $25\pi + 12.5\sqrt{3}$　　(D) $25\pi + 25\sqrt{3}$

2. In the following diagram, a rhombus lies inside a trapezoid.

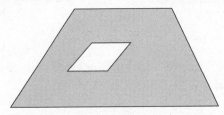

The sum of the bases of the trapezoid is 36 and its height is 9. If the diagonals of the rhombus are 3 and 5, what is the area of the shaded region?

(A) 140.5　　(C) 154.5

(B) 147.5　　(D) 161.5

3. In the following diagram, a triangle lies inside a trapezoid.

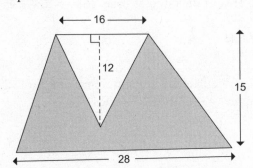

What is the area of the shaded region?

(A) 246　　(C) 222

(B) 234　　(D) 210

4. In the following diagram, an equilateral triangle lies on top of a parallelogram.

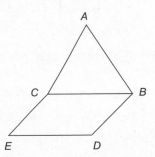

If $AC = 8$ and the total area is 63.7, which of the following is the best approximation for the height to $\overline{DE}$ of the parallelogram?

(A) 3.5　　(C) 5.5

(B) 4.5　　(D) 6.5

Solid Geometry

Cubes, Cylinders

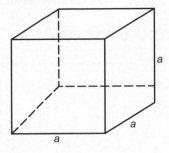

The volume of a cube with edge a is

$$V = a^3.$$

The surface area of a cube with edge a is

$$A = 6a^2.$$

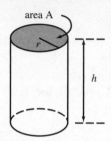

area A

The volume of a right circular cylinder with radius *r* and height *h* is

$$V = \pi r^2 h.$$

The surface area of a right circular cylinder with radius *r* and height *h* is

$$A = 2\pi r^2 + 2\pi rh.$$

Intersecting Planes

If two different planes intersect, they intersect in a straight line.

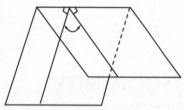

The angle between two planes is the angle between two rays on the two planes, each of which is perpendicular to the line of intersection of the planes.

Volume and Surface Area

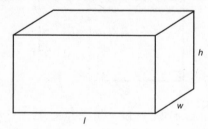

Rectangular solid

The volume of a rectangular solid with length *l*, width *w*, and height *h* is

$$V = lwh.$$

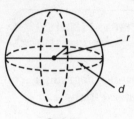

Sphere

The volume of a sphere with radius *r* is

$$V = \frac{4}{3}\pi r^3.$$

The surface area of a sphere with radius *r* is

$$A = 4\pi r^2.$$

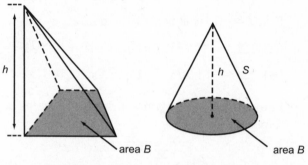

Pyramid   Cone

The volume of a pyramid or cone with base area *B* and height *h* is

$$V = \frac{1}{3}Bh.$$

If the base of the cone is a circle with radius *r*, then

$$A = \pi r^2,$$

so

$$V = \frac{1}{3}\pi r^2 h.$$

The total area of a cone is the sum of the surface area of the conical part (πrs), where *s* is the slant height, plus the area of the circular base, so $A = \pi rs + \pi r^2$.

PROBLEM

Calculate the circumference of a circle that has a radius of 12 inches.

SOLUTION

1. Write the formula for the circumference of a circle.

circumference = $2\pi r$

2. Substitute the known values into the equation. Pi is approximately 3.14. The radius is 12.

circumference = 2(3.14)12

3. Solve the equation.

circumference = 75.4

The correct answer is that the circumference = 75.4 inches.

PROBLEM

Calculate the area of a circle that has a diameter of 10 meters.

SOLUTION

1. Write the formula for the area of a circle.

$A = \pi r^2$.

2. Substitute the known values into the equation. Pi is approximately 3.14. The diameter of the circle is 10 meters, so the radius is 5 meters.

$A = \pi(5)^2$

3. Solve the equation.

$A = 78.5$

The correct answer is that the area of the circle is 78.5 m².

PROBLEM

Calculate the volume of a sphere that has a radius of 2 meters.

SOLUTION

1. Write the formula for the volume of a sphere.

$$V = \frac{4}{3}\pi r^3$$

2. Substitute the known values into the equation. Pi is approximately 3.14 and the radius is 2 meters.

$$V = \frac{4}{3}\pi(2)^3$$

3. Solve the equation.

$V = 33.49$ or ≈ 33.5

The correct answer is that the volume of the sphere is 33.5 m³.

PROBLEM

Calculate the perimeter of the triangle below.

SOLUTION

1. Write the formula for the perimeter of a triangle.

perimeter = length of side 1 + length of side 2 + length of side 3

2. Substitute the known values into the formula.

perimeter = 4 + 3 + 5

3. Solve the equation.

perimeter = 12

The correct answer is that the perimeter of the triangle is 12.

PROBLEM

Calculate the area of the triangle below.

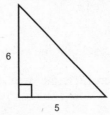

SOLUTION

1. Write the formula for the area of a triangle.

$$A = \frac{1}{2}bh$$

2. Substitute the known values into the formula. The base of the triangle is 5 and the height is 6.

$$A = \frac{1}{2}(5)(6)$$

3. Solve the equation.

$$A = 15$$

The correct answer is that the area of the triangle is 15.

PROBLEM

Calculate the volume of the cube that has a length of 5, a height of 1.5, and a width of 4.

SOLUTION

1. Write the formula for the volume of a cube.

$$V = l \times w \times h$$

2. Substitute the known values into the formula.

$$V = 5 \times 4 \times 1.5$$

3. Solve the equation.

$$V = 30$$

The correct answer is that the volume of the cube = 30.

PROBLEM

Calculate the volume of a pyramid that has a height of 3 feet. The area of the base of the pyramid was calculated to be 15 square feet.

SOLUTION

1. Write the formula for the volume of a pyramid.

$V = \frac{1}{3}Bh$, where B is the area of the base of the pyramid.

2. Substitute the known values into the formula.

$$V = \frac{1}{3}(15)(3)$$

3. Solve the equation.

$$V = 15$$

The correct answer is that the volume of the pyramid is 15 cubic feet.

PROBLEM

Calculate the area of the triangle below.

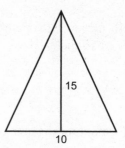

SOLUTION

1. Write the formula for the area of a triangle.

$$A = \frac{1}{2}bh$$

2. Substitute the known values into the formula. The base of the triangle is 10 and the height is 15.

$$A = \frac{1}{2}(10)(15)$$

3. Solve the equation.

$$A = 75$$

The correct answer is that the area of the triangle is 75.

PROBLEM

Calculate the volume of the cone below.

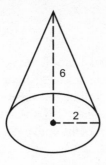

SOLUTION

1. Write the formula for the volume of a cone.

$$V = \frac{1}{3}\pi r^2 h$$

2. Substitute the known values into the equation.

$$V = \frac{1}{3}\pi(2)^2(6)$$

3. Solve the equation.

$$V = 25.12$$

The correct answer is that the volume of the cone is 25.12.

PROBLEM

Calculate the volume of the cylinder below.

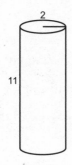

SOLUTION

1. Write the formula for the volume of a cylinder.
$$V = \pi r^2 h$$

2. Substitute the known values into the formula.
$$V = \pi(2)^2(11)$$

3. Solve the equation.

$$V = 138.16$$

The correct answer is that the volume is 138.16.

PROBLEM

Calculate the total area of the cone below. Round to the nearest integer.

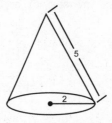

SOLUTION

1. Write the formula for the total area of a cone.
$$A = \pi rs + \pi r^2, \text{ where } s \text{ is the slant height}$$

2. Substitute the known values into the formula.
$$A = \pi(2)(5) + \pi(2)^2$$

3. Solve the equation.
$$A = 10\pi + 4\pi = \pi(10 + 4) = \pi(14)$$
$$A = 44$$

The correct answer is 44.

Similarity for Three-dimensional Figures

For three-dimensional figures, similarity means that pairs of congruent angles and the corresponding linear measurements must be in the same ratio. Many of the linear measurements refer to edges. (*Edges* in three dimensions is equivalent to *sides* in two dimensions.)

Similar Prisms

Let's consider a rectangular prism with length, width and height of 10, 6, and 5, respectively. Its surface area is $(2)(10)(6) + (2)(10)(5) + (2)(6)(5) = 280$, and its volume is $(10)(6)(5) = 300$. Suppose a second rectangular prism has length, width, and height of 30, 18, and 15, respectively. We note that these rectangular prisms are similar. For this second rectangular prism, the surface area is $(2)(30)(18) + (2)(30)(15) + (2)(18)(15) = 2520$. Its volume is $(30)(18)(15) = 8100$.

The ratio of the corresponding edges is $\frac{1}{3}$. We note that the ratio of the surface areas is $\frac{280}{2520} = \frac{1}{9}$ and the ratio of the volumes is $\frac{300}{8100} = \frac{1}{27}$. We note that $\frac{1}{9} = \left(\frac{1}{3}\right)^2$ and $\frac{1}{27} = \left(\frac{1}{3}\right)^3$. It appears that the ratio of the surface areas is the square of the ratio of the linear dimensions. Also, the ratio of the volumes is the cube of the ratio of the linear dimensions.

Similar Cones

Let's consider two similar cones and explore whether we arrive at the same conclusions. The first cone has a radius of 3 and a (perpendicular) height of 4. This means that its lateral height is $\sqrt{3^2 + 4^2} = 5$. The surface area of this cone is $(\pi)(3^2) + (\pi)(3)(5) = 24\pi$, and its volume is $\left(\frac{1}{3}\right)(\pi)(3^2)(4) = 12\pi$.

Suppose a second cone has a radius of 15 and a height of 20. The lateral height is $\sqrt{15^2 + 20^2} = 25$, and the two cones must be similar, since each linear dimension has been multiplied by 5.

For this second cone, the surface area is $(\pi)(15^2) + (\pi)(15)(25) = 600\pi$ and its volume is $\left(\frac{1}{3}\right)(\pi)(15^2)(20) = 1500\pi$. We note that the ratio of the surface areas is $\frac{24\pi}{600\pi} = \frac{1}{25}$ and the ratio of the volumes is $\frac{12\pi}{1500\pi} = \frac{1}{125}$. Noting that $\frac{1}{25} = \left(\frac{1}{5}\right)^2$ and $\frac{1}{125} = \left(\frac{1}{5}\right)^3$, the ratio of the surface areas is the square of the ratio of the linear dimensions. Also, the ratio of the volumes is the cube of the ratio of the linear dimensions.

NOTE:

Without a formal proof, we declare that given two similar three-dimensional figures, the ratio of their surface areas will be the square of the ratio of their linear dimensions. Also, the ratio of their volumes will be the cube of the ratio of their linear dimensions.

PROBLEM

The ratio of the volumes of two similar rectangular prisms is $\frac{8}{27}$. If the surface area of the smaller figure is 48 square inches, what is the surface area of the larger figure?

SOLUTION

The ratio of the linear dimensions is $\sqrt[3]{\frac{8}{27}} = \frac{2}{3}$, so the ratio of their surface areas is $\left(\frac{2}{3}\right)^2 = \frac{4}{9}$. Let x represent the surface area of the larger figure. Then $\frac{4}{9} = \frac{48}{x}$, so $x = 108$ square inches.

Similar Spheres

PROBLEM

The ratio of the radii of two similar spheres is $\frac{6}{1}$. If the volume of the larger sphere is 1620, what is the volume of the smaller sphere?

SOLUTION

The ratio of their volumes is $\left(\frac{6}{1}\right)^3 = \frac{216}{1}$. Using x to represent the volume of the smaller sphere, we can write $\frac{216}{1} = \frac{1620}{x}$. Thus, $x = 7.5$.

Similar Cylinders

PROBLEM

> The height of the larger of two similar cylinders is 20 inches more than the height of the smaller cylinder. If the ratio of their surface areas is $\frac{9}{49}$, what is the height of the larger cylinder?

SOLUTION

The ratio of their heights is $\sqrt{\frac{9}{49}} = \frac{3}{7}$. Let x and $x + 20$ represent the heights of the two cylinders. Then $\frac{3}{7} = \frac{x}{x+20}$, which simplifies to $7x = 3x + 60$. So $x = 15$, which means that the height of the larger cylinder is 35 inches.

Drill: Similarity for Three-Dimensional Figures

1. The ratio of the surface areas of two spheres is $\frac{9}{100}$. The radius of the smaller sphere is 12. What is the surface area of the larger sphere?

    (A) 6400π (C) 3200π

    (B) 4800π (D) 2400π

2. The height of the larger of two similar cylinders is 10 inches less than twice the height of the smaller cylinder. The ratio of their surface areas is $\frac{16}{25}$. If the radius of the smaller cylinder is 6 inches, what is the volume of the smaller cylinder, in cubic inches?

    (A) 512π (C) 360π

    (B) 480π (D) 232π

3. Two cones are similar and the volume of the smaller cone is 54 cubic meters. If the ratio of their surface areas is $\frac{9}{25}$, what is the volume of the larger cone, in cubic meters ?

    (A) 100   (C) 200

    (B) 150   (D) 250

4. Two rectangular prisms are similar. The length for the smaller prism is 4 inches and the ratio of their lengths is $\frac{2}{3}$. If the surface area of the smaller prism is 416 square inches, which of the following could represent the three dimensions, in inches, of the larger prism?

    (A) 8, 20, 24   (C) 8, 15, 18

    (B) 6 , 15, 18   (D) 6, 20, 24

PROBLEM

> Calculate the area of the trapezoid below.

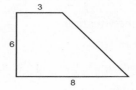

SOLUTION

1. Write the formula for the area of a trapezoid.

$A = \frac{1}{2}h(b_1 + b_2)$, where b_1 and b_2 are the bases

2. Substitute the known values into the formula.

$A = \frac{1}{2}(6)(3 + 8)$

3. Solve the equation.

$A = 33$

The correct answer is that the area of the trapezoid is 33 square feet.

PROBLEM

Given that PR = 5 and QS = 4, calculate the area of the rhombus below.

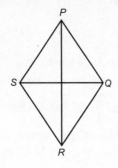

SOLUTION

1. Write the formula for the area of a rhombus.

$A = \frac{1}{2}(d_1 \cdot d_2)$, where d_1 and d_2 are the diagonals of the rhombus.

2. Substitute the known values into the formula.

$$A = \frac{1}{2}(5)(4)$$

3. Solve the equation.

$$A = 10$$

The correct answer is that the area of the rhombus is 10.

PROBLEM

Calculate the area of the parallelogram below.

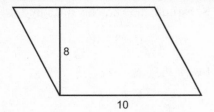

SOLUTION

1. Write the formula for the area of a parallelogram.

$A = bh$, where b is the base and h is the height.

2. Substitute the known values into the formula.

$$A = 10(8)$$

3. Solve the equation.

$$A = 80$$

The correct answer is that the area of the parallelogram is 80.

Problem Solving with Triangles

PROBLEM

Using the Pythagorean theorem, calculate c in the figure below.

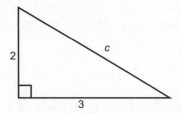

SOLUTION

1. Write the Pythagorean theorem.

$$a^2 + b^2 = c^2$$

2. Substitute the values of a and b into the equation.

$$(3)^2 + (2)^2 = c^2$$

3. Solve the left side of the equation.

$$(3)^2 + (2)^2 = 13$$

4. Rewrite the equation.

$$13 = c^2$$

5. Solve for c.

$$\sqrt{13} = c$$

The correct answer is $c = \sqrt{13}$.

PROBLEM

Using the Pythagorean theorem, calculate a in the figure below.

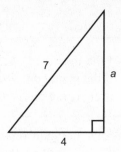

SOLUTION

1. Write the Pythagorean theorem.

$$a^2 + b^2 = c^2$$

2. Substitute the values of b and c into the equation.

$$a^2 + (4)^2 = 7^2$$

3. Simplify the equation.

$$a^2 + 16 = 49$$

4. Subtract 16 from both sides and rewrite the equation.

$$a^2 = 33$$

5. Solve for x.

$$a = \sqrt{33}$$

Applications of the Pythagorean theorem to Special Right Triangles

The figure below shows a 45° - 45° - 90° right triangle. Each of the congruent legs has been labeled as x, and the hypotenuse is labeled c.

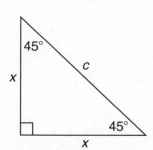

We can prove that the hypotenuse is $\sqrt{2}$ times as long as either leg. By the Pythagorean theorem,

$x^2 + x^2 = c^2$. Then $2x^2 = c^2$, which means that $c = \sqrt{2x^2} = x\sqrt{2}$.

The figure below shows a 30° - 60° - 90° right triangle. The side opposite 30° has been labeled x and the side opposite 90° has been labeled $2x$. The longer side has been labeled b.

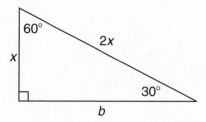

Using the Pythagorean theorem, we can prove that the longer leg is $\sqrt{3}$ times as long as the shorter leg. We have $x^2 + b^2 = (2x)^2$, which simplifies to $x^2 + b^2 = 4x^2$. Then $b^2 = 3x^2$, so $b = \sqrt{3x^2} = x\sqrt{3}$.

Properties of Regular Polygons

A **regular polygon** is one in which all sides are congruent and all angles are congruent. The formula for determining the measure of each angle of a regular polygon of n sides is $\dfrac{(180°)(n - 2)}{n}$. For example, in a regular octagon (8-sided polygon), the measure of each angle is $\dfrac{(180°)(6)}{8} = 135°$.

The **center** of a regular polygon is the point that is equidistant from all vertices.

An **apothem** of a regular polygon is a line segment whose endpoints are the center and the midpoint of one of the sides.

A **radius** of a regular polygon is a line segment whose endpoints are the center and one of the vertices.

Figure 3.1 illustrates a regular pentagon (5-sided polygon) with center P, apothem $\overline{PR}$, and radius $\overline{PQ}$.

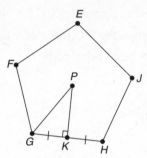

Figure 3.1

NOTE:

There are five apothems and five radii for this pentagon. Also, each apothem is perpendicular to the side to which it is drawn.

Inscribed and Circumscribed Circles

An **inscribed** circle of a polygon is a circle for which each side is a tangent segment.

A **circumscribed** circle of a polygon is a circle that contains each vertex Figures 3.2 and 3.3 illustrate an inscribed circle and a circumscribed circle respectively for the pentagon shown in figure 3.1.

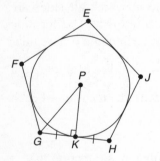

Figure 3.2

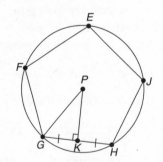

Figure 3.3

NOTE:

The radius of the inscribed circle is the length of an apothem of the pentagon. The radius of the circumscribed circle is the radius of the pentagon.

Given a regular polygon of n sides, in which the length of each side is s and the length of the apothem is a, then the perimeter is ns and the area is $\left(\dfrac{1}{2}\right)(a)(n)(s)$. If the perimeter is known, you can substitute that value for ns in the area formula. In many textbooks, the area formula is shown as $A = \dfrac{1}{2}ap$, where p is the perimeter. Be aware that these formulas apply <u>only</u> to regular polygons.

From our earlier discussion concerning the measure of each angle of a regular polygon, we note that since $EFGHJ$ is a pentagon, $\angle FGK = \dfrac{(180°)(3)}{5} = 108°$. As you would probably guess, $\angle FGK = (2)(\angle PGK)$. Thus $\angle PGK = 54°$. This angle measure will be needed for the next few examples.

PROBLEM

Using Figure 3.1, if the radius is 15 inches, what is the perimeter of the pentagon, to the nearest hundredth of an inch?

SOLUTION

From our knowledge of trigonometry, $\cos 54° = \dfrac{GK}{15}$. Then $GK = (15)(\cos 54°) \approx 8.817$. This means that $GH \approx 17.634$. Thus, the perimeter is approximately $(5)(17.634) \approx 88.17$ inches.

PROBLEM

Using the information of the previous problem, what is the area of $EFGHJ$, to the nearest hundredth?

SOLUTION

We use the relationship $\sin 54° = \dfrac{PK}{15}$. Then $PK = (15)(\sin 54°) \approx 12.135$ Since $\overline{PK}$ represents the apothem, the area of the pentagon is $\left(\dfrac{1}{2}\right)(12.135)$ $(88.17) \approx 534.97$ square inches.

PROBLEM

> Using Figure 3.2, if the area of the circle is 25π, what is the perimeter of the pentagon? (Nearest hundredth)

SOLUTION

The radius of the circle, which is also the value of PK, is 5. Now we note that $\tan 54° = \dfrac{5}{GK}$. So $GK = \dfrac{5}{\tan 54°} \approx 3.633$, which means that $GH \approx 7.266$. Thus, the perimeter is approximately $(5)(7.266) = 36.33$.

PROBLEM

> Using Figure 3.3, if the perimeter of $EFGHJ$ is 80 inches, what is the area of the circumscribed circle, to the nearest hundredth?

SOLUTION

Each side of the pentagon must be 16 inches, which means that GK = 8 inches. Then $\cos 54° = \dfrac{8}{PG}$, so that $PG = \dfrac{8}{\cos 54°} \approx 13.61$. Since $\overline{AB}$ is the radius, the area of the circle is $(\pi)(13.61)^2 \approx 581.92$ square inches.

Regular Hexagon

Figures 3.4 and 3.5 show a regular hexagon with its inscribed circle and circumscribed circle, respectively.

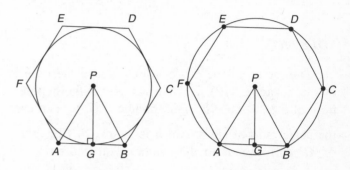

Figure 3.4   **Figure 3.5**

Each angle of a regular hexagon must be $\dfrac{(180°)(4)}{6} = 120°$. This means that for each of Figures 3.4 and 3.5, $\angle PAG = 60°$. As an added bonus, since $\angle PBG = 60°$, ΔPAB must be equilateral. Furthermore, each of ΔPAG and ΔPBG is a 30°-60°-90° right triangle. This implies that the ratio of AG : PG : AP = $1 : \sqrt{3} : 2$. These phenomena make our computations concerning perimeter and area much simpler.

PROBLEM

> Using Figure 3.4, if the radius of the circle is $4\sqrt{3}$, what is the perimeter of the hexagon *ABCDEF*?

SOLUTION

Using the ratio of sides of a 30°-60°-90° right triangle, since $PG = 4\sqrt{3}$, $AG = 4$. Then $AB = 8$, so the perimeter of *ABCDEF* is $(8)(6) = 48$.

PROBLEM

> Using Figure 3.5, if the area of the circle is 144π, what is the length of the apothem of *ABCDEF*, to the nearest hundredth ?

SOLUTION

The radius of the circle, which is also the radius of the hexagon (AP), is 12. Since *AP* is the hypotenuse of the 30°-60°-90° right triangle *PAG*, we can use the basic ratio of sides, which is $1:\sqrt{3}:2$. The value of *AP* corresponds to the number 2 in this ratio, so $PG = 6\sqrt{3} \approx 10.39$.

PROBLEM

> If each side of a regular hexagon is 3 centimeters, what is its area, to the nearest hundredth of a centimeter?

SOLUTION

Even without a diagram, we can consider the apothem as the altitude of an equilateral triangle in which each side is 3 centimeters. From our knowledge of geometry, if *x* represents the side of an equilateral triangle, then $\left(\dfrac{x}{2}\right)(\sqrt{3})$ represents the length of the altitude (height). In this example, the apothem must be $\left(\dfrac{3}{2}\right)(\sqrt{3})$. The perimeter of the hexagon is 18, so its area is $\left(\dfrac{1}{2}\right)\left(\dfrac{3}{2}\right)(\sqrt{3})(18) \approx 23.38$ square centimeters.

NOTE:

There is another method to calculating this answer. The formula $A = \left(\dfrac{x^2}{4}\right)(\sqrt{3})$ can be applied to find the area of any equilateral triangle with a side of *x*. In this problem, this area becomes $\left(\dfrac{9}{4}\right)(\sqrt{3})$. This answer represents the area of $\triangle PAG$. The hexagon contains a total of five other triangles that are congruent to $\triangle PAG$. Each of these triangles would have two consecutive vertices and the point P. Thus, the area of the hexagon is $(6)\left(\dfrac{9}{4}\right)(\sqrt{3}) \approx 23.38$ square centimeters.

Drill: Regular Polygons

1. In a 30°-60°-90° right triangle, the hypotenuse is 12. To the nearest tenth, what is the length of the side opposite the 60° angle?

    (A) 8.5   (C) 10.4

    (B) 9.2   (D) 11.3

2. In a 45°-45°-90° right triangle, the hypotenuse is 20. To the nearest tenth, what is the sum of the lengths of the other two sides?

    (A) 14.1   (C) 24.6

    (B) 18.2   (D) 28.3

3. The following diagram shows a regular hexagon and its inscribed circle.

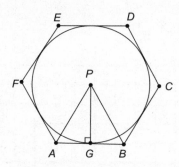

If the radius of the circle is $8\sqrt{3}$, what is the area of hexagon *ABCDEF*?

(A) $96\sqrt{3}$ (C) $288\sqrt{3}$

(B) $192\sqrt{3}$ (D) $384\sqrt{3}$

4. The following diagram shows a regular hexagon and its inscribed circle.

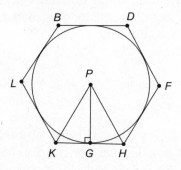

If the perimeter of hexagon *BDFHKL* is 60, what is the area of the circle?

(A) 75π (C) 125π

(B) 100π (D) 180π

5. If the measure of each interior angle of a regular polygon is 162°, how many sides are there?

(A) 16   (C) 20

(B) 18   (D) 22

Coordinate Geometry

Coordinate geometry refers to the study of geometric figures using algebraic principles.

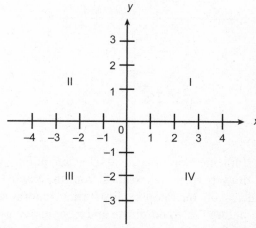

The graph shown is called the Cartesian coordinate plane. The graph consists of a pair of perpendicular lines called **coordinate axes.** The **vertical axis** is the *y*-axis and the **horizontal axis** is the *x*-axis. The point of intersection of these two axes is called the **origin;** it is the zero point of both axes. Furthermore, points to the right of the origin on the *x*-axis and above the origin on the *y*-axis represent positive real numbers. Points to the left of the origin on the *x*-axis or below the origin on the *y*-axis represent negative real numbers.

The four regions cut off by the coordinate axes are, in counterclockwise direction from the top right, called the first, second, third, and fourth quadrant, respectively. The first quadrant contains all points with two positive coordinates.

In the graph shown, two points *A* and *B* are shown. They can be identified by the ordered pair, (*x, y*) of numbers. The *x*-coordinate is the first number and the *y*-coordinate is the second number.

To plot a point on the graph when given the coordinates, draw perpendicular lines from the number-line coordinates to the point where the two lines intersect.

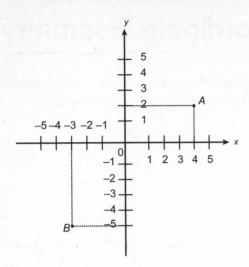

To find the coordinates of a given point on the graph, draw perpendicular lines from the point to the coordinates on the number line. The x-coordinate is written before the y-coordinate and a comma is used to separate the two.

In this case, point A has the coordinates $(4, 2)$ and the coordinates of point B are $(-3, -5)$.

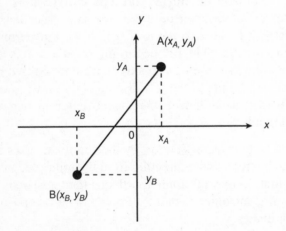

For any two points A and B with coordinates (x_A, y_A) and (x_B, y_B), respectively, the distance between A and B is represented by:

$$d = \sqrt{(x_A - x_B)^2 + (y_A - y_B)^2}$$

This is commonly known as the distance formula.

PROBLEM

Find the distance between the point $A(1, 3)$ and $B(5, 3)$.

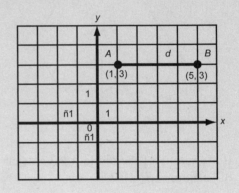

SOLUTION

In this case, where the ordinate of both points is the same, the distance between the two points is given by the absolute value of the difference between the two abscissas. In fact, this case reduces to merely counting boxes, as the figure shows.

Let, x_1 = abscissa of A y_1 = ordinate of A

x_2 = abscissa of B y_2 = ordinate of B

d = the distance

Therefore, $d = |x_1 - x_2|$. By substitution, $d = |1 - 5| = |-4| = 4$. This answer can also be obtained by applying the general formula for distance between any two points.

$$d = \sqrt{(x_1 - x_2)^2 + (y_1 - y_2)^2}$$

By substitution,

$$d = \sqrt{(1 - 5)^2 + (3 - 3)^2}$$

$$= \sqrt{(-4)^2 + (0)^2}$$

$$= \sqrt{16}$$

The distance is 4.

To find the midpoint of a segment between the two given endpoints, use the formula

$$MP = \left(\frac{x_1 + x_2}{2}, \frac{y_1 + y_2}{2}\right)$$

where x_1 and y_1 are the coordinates of one point, and x_2 and y_2 are the coordinates of the other point.

PROBLEM

Find the distance between the points $(-1, 4)$ and $(1, 8)$.

SOLUTION

$$d = \sqrt{(-1-1)^2 + (4-8)^2}$$

$$= \sqrt{(-2)^2 + (-4)^2}$$

$$= \sqrt{20} \text{ or } 2\sqrt{5}$$

PROBLEM

Find the midpoint between the points $(-2, 7)$ and $(10, 3)$.

SOLUTION

$$MP = \left(\frac{-2+10}{2}, \frac{7+3}{2}\right)$$

$$= (4, 5)$$

In many instances, we can estimate the area of a region in the xy-plane by using the areas of well-known geometric figures, such as circles, triangles, squares, rectangles, and so forth.

PROBLEM

Estimate the area of the following region.

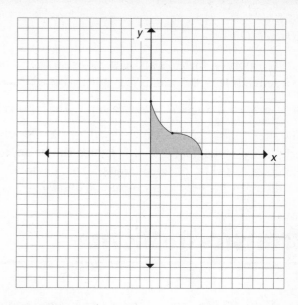

SOLUTION

If we were to draw the line segment that connects the points $(5, 0)$ and $(0, 5)$, part of this region would lie below this segment, but an approximately equal amount of this region would lie above this segment. This means that the area of the region can be approximated by the area of a right triangle with vertices $(0, 0)$, $(5, 0)$, and $(0, 5)$. Therefore, required area would be $(\frac{1}{2})(5)(5) = 12.5$ square units.

PROBLEM

Estimate the area of the following region.

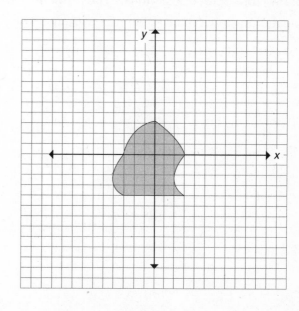

SOLUTION

The portion that lies above the *x*-axis is very close to a semicircle with a radius of 3 units. This area would be $\frac{1}{2}\pi(3^2) = 4.5\pi \approx 14.14$ square units. The portion below the *x*-axis resembles a "twisted" rectangle with a length of 6 and a height of 4. This area can be approximated as $(6)(4) = 24$ square units. Thus, the total area would be $14.14 + 24 = 38.14$ square units.

Transformations

Transformations of geometric figures occur when movement or motion is applied to a figure. The result will be a change in size, orientation, and/or direction. There are three different types of transformations that we will consider: translations, reflections, and rotations.

Translations

A **translation** changes the location but not the size or orientation of a figure. Every point of the original figure is moved the same distance in the same direction along a straight path. Informally, a translation is referred to as a glide. The figures below illustrate translations. The direction of a translation (movement) is shown with an arrow.

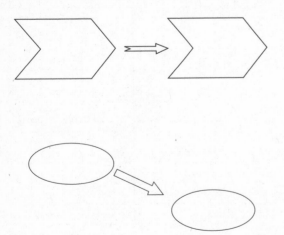

You can also see this in the *xy*- coordinate plane where a translation moves the given figure a specific distance left or right and up or down such that $(x, y) \rightarrow (x + a, y + b)$ indicates a point (x, y) that has been translated horizontally *a* units and vertically *b* units.

PROBLEM

Given $\triangle ABC$ with coordinates *A*: $(-2,5)$, *B*: $(-5,1)$, and *C*: $(-1,1)$, what will be the coordinates of the new triangle after the translation $(x, y) \rightarrow (x + 8, y - 3)$?

SOLUTION

Call the new vertices D, E, and F, that result from the translation from A, B, and C, respectively. The translation means changing the three vertices by adding 8 to the x-coordinate and subtracting 3 from the *y*-coordinate. The coordinates after the translation become D: $(6, 2)$, E: $(3, -2)$, and F: $(7, -2)$. This translation is shown below.

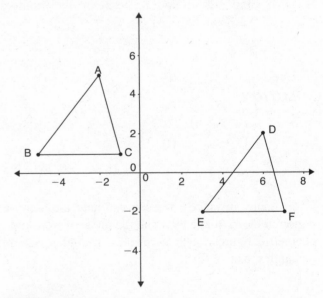

Reflections

A **reflection** (informally referred to as a "flip") of a geometric shape changes location and orientation but not size. A reflection is a mirror image of the shape about a given line called the **axis of reflection**. This can be a horizontal or vertical reflection and within the coordinate plane is typically the *x*-axis or *y*-axis. The figures below illustrate reflections of a line and a trapezoid, respectively. For either figure, the original shape and its reflection are interchangeable. Thus, either figure is a mirror image of the other.

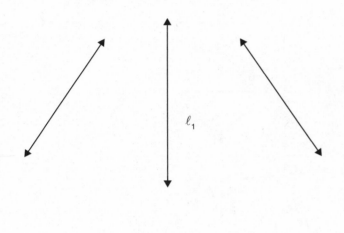

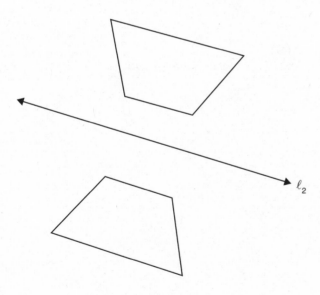

In the *xy*-coordinate system, the points of the reflection can be determined by multiplying either the *y* or *x* coordinate by -1 if the figure is reflected about the *x*-axis or *y*-axis.

PROBLEM

The vertices of a quadrilateral are (1, 6), (3, 4), (6, 5), and (5, 8). If this quadrilateral is reflected about the *x*-axis, what will be the coordinates of the reflected quadrilateral?

SOLUTION

The *x*-coordinates remain the same, but the *y*-coordinates are multiplied by -1. The new vertices are (1, -6), (3, -4), (6, -5), and (5, -8).

PROBLEM

Using the vertices of the original quadrilateral in the previous problem, suppose that the quadrilateral is reflected about the *y*-axis. What will be the coordinates of the midpoint of the reflection of the side that contains (1, 6) and (3, 4)?

SOLUTION

The point (1, 6) becomes (-1, 6), and the point (3, 4) becomes (-3, 4). The midpoint of the segment with endpoints (-1, 6) and (-3, 4) is $\left(\dfrac{-1-3}{2}, \dfrac{6+4}{2} \right) =$ (-2, 5).

Rotations

A **rotation** is a movement of a figure by a number of degrees around a point (called the **center of rotation**) either in a clockwise or counterclockwise direction. A rotation changes location and orientation but not size. When rotations are done in the coordinate plane the origin is usually the center of rotation. Let's look at a few examples in the coordinate plane.

The figure below shows a counterclockwise rotation of 90° about the origin. (The original figure is located in quadrant I.)

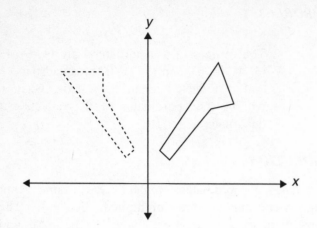

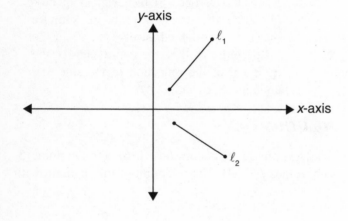

The figure below shows a 90-degree clockwise rotation of line segment l_1 about the origin to become l_2.

Drill: Transformations

1.   Which one of the following illustrates a reflection of $\triangle ABC$ to its image $\triangle A'B'C'$ over line l_1?

(A)

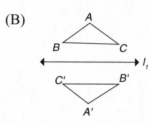

(B)

(C)

(D)

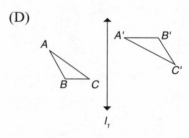

2.   Look at the following diagram.

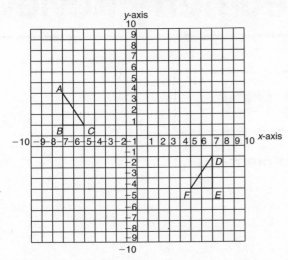

Which transformation will map △*ABC* onto
△*DEF* ?

(A) Reflect △*ABC* over the *y*-axis and slide up
     six spaces.

(B) Reflect △*ABC* over the *x*-axis and slide up
     six spaces.

(C) Reflect △*ABC* over the *y*-axis and slide
     down six spaces.

(D) Reflect △*ABC* over the *x*-axis and slide
     down six spaces

3.   The point *R′*, which is located at (4, 2), is the result
     of a 90°-counterclockwise rotation of the point *R*
     about the origin. What are the coordinates of *R*?

(A) (2, −4)   (C) (2, 4)

(B) (−2, 4)   (D) (−2, −4)

4.   The line segment with endpoints (−1, 2) and (5,
     10) is translated five units to the left and four units
     up. If *M* is the midpoint of the original line seg-
     ment, what are the coordinates of *M′*?

(A) (2, 6)   (C) (−10, −3)

(B) (−6, 2)   (D) (−3, 10)

Geometry Review

ANSWER KEY

Drill: Measurement

1. (A)
2. (C)
3. (B)
4. (C)
5. (D)

Drill: Regular Polygons (Convex)

1. (D)
2. (D)
3. (D)
4. (C)
5. (D)

Drill: Triangles

1. (D)
2. (B)
3. (C)
4. (A)
5. (D)

6. (C)
7. (B)
8. (D)
9. (A)
10. (B)

Drill: Quadrilaterals

1. (B)
2. (D)
3. (A)
4. (D)
5. (C)
6. (C)
7. (D)
8. (B)
9. (C)
10. (D)

Drill: Circles

1. (B)
2. (C)
3. (D)
4. (C)
5. (B)
6. (B)
7. (D)
8. (C)
9. (C)
10. (B)

Drill: Composite Figures

1. (A)
2. (C)
3. (B)
4. (B)

Drill: Similarity for Three-Dimensional Figures

1. (A)
2. (B)
3. (D)
4. (B)

Drill: Regular Polygons

1. (C)
2. (D)
3. (D)
4. (A)
5. (C)

Drill: Transformations

1. (C)
2. (C)
3. (A)
4. (D)

Detailed Explanations of Answers

Drill: Measurement

1. (A)

Since 1 kilogram is equivalent to 2.2 pounds, 3.4 kilograms is equivalent to $(3.4)(2.2) = 7.48$ pounds.

2. (C)

Half the contents of this bottle is 2.5 liters, which is equivalent to $(2.5)(1.06) = 2.65$ quarts. The additional number of quarts that could be poured into the jar is $8 - 2.65 = 5.35$.

3. (B)

1 gallon $= 4$ quarts $= (4)(2) = 8$ pints. Also, 2 quarts $= 4$ pints. So, the given container has a capacity of $8 + 4 + 1 = 13$ pints. Since 1 pint is equivalent to 16 fluid ounces, 13 pints is equivalent to $(13)(16) = 208$ fluid ounces.

4. (C)

There are $\dfrac{5280}{3} = 1760$ yards in one mile. Each day, Kelly ran $\dfrac{3080}{1760} = 1.75$ miles. So, Kelly ran $(1.75)(30) = 52.5$ miles in 30 days. Joan ran a total of $(4)(14) = 56$ miles in two weeks. Thus, Joan ran $56 - 52.5 = 3.5$ more miles than Kelly.

5. (D)

For 100 cookies, $(2)(100) = 200$ grams of water are required. Thus, the number of ounces of water needed is $\dfrac{200}{28.4} \approx 7$.

Drill: Regular Polygons (Convex)

1. (D)

A regular pentagon is both equiangular and equilateral. A pentagon is five sided. Therefore,

$$360° \div 5 = 72° \qquad 180° - 72° = 108°$$

2. (D)

$$(3 \times 180°) - 180° = 360°$$

3. (D)

$$a = 4\sqrt{3} \qquad P = \text{perimeter} = 3(24) = 72$$
$$A = \frac{1}{2}ap = \frac{1}{2}(4\sqrt{3})(72) = 144\sqrt{3}\ \text{mm}^2$$

4. (C)

$s = 4$ therefore, radius $= 4$ too, which makes the apothem

$$\sqrt{(4)^2 - (2)^2} = 2\sqrt{3}$$
$$A = \frac{1}{2}ap = \frac{1}{2}(2\sqrt{3})(6)(4) = 24\sqrt{3}\ \text{cm}^2$$

5. (D)

$$A = \frac{1}{2}ap = \frac{1}{2}a(s)(10) = \frac{1}{2}(9.2)(6)(10) = 276\ \text{cm}^2$$

Drill: Triangles

1. (D)

Since $\angle Q$ is a right angle, $m\angle Q = 90°$. Therefore, $90° - 23° = 67°$

2. (B)

$$\frac{180° - 96°}{2} = \frac{84°}{2} = 42°$$

3. (C)

$$3x + 2x + x = 180°$$
$$6x = 180°$$
$$x = 30°$$

4. (A)

$$6 : 4 = 4 : b \Rightarrow \frac{6}{4} = \frac{4}{b} \Rightarrow 6b = 16$$

$$b = \frac{16}{6} = 2\frac{4}{6} = 2\frac{2}{3}$$

5. (D)

$$3 : 6 = 4 : b \qquad b = 8$$
$$3 : 4 = 4 : a$$
$$\frac{3}{4} = \frac{4}{a}$$
$$3a = 16 \quad a = 16\left(\frac{1}{3}\right) = 5\frac{1}{3}$$

6. (C)

$$A = \frac{1}{2}bh = \frac{1}{2}(14)(8) = 56$$

7. (B)

$$A = \frac{1}{2}bh = \frac{1}{2}(11)(7) = 38\frac{1}{2} \text{ or } 38.5$$

8. (D)

$$A = \frac{1}{2}bh = \frac{1}{2}(4)(8\sqrt{2}) = 16\sqrt{2}$$

9. (A)

Using the Pythagorean theorem,

$$\overline{AB} = \sqrt{(\overline{AC})^2 - (\overline{BC})^2} = \sqrt{(15)^2 - (9)^2} = \sqrt{144} = 12.$$

Then $A = \frac{1}{2}bh = \frac{1}{2}(9)(12) = 54 \text{ cm}^2$

10. (B)

This is an isosceles right triangle, so the legs are equal. Using the Pythagorean theorem,

$$(10\sqrt{2})^2 = a^2 + a^2$$
$$200 = 2a^2$$
$$a^2 = 100$$
$$a = 10$$

so the sides are 10 cm each.

$$A = \frac{1}{2}bh = \frac{1}{2}(10)(10) = 50 \text{ cm}^2$$

Drill: Quadrilaterals

1. (B)

$\angle B$ and $\angle D$ are opposite angles in the parallelogram and are equal. Therefore,

$$6x + 2 = 98$$
$$6x = 96$$
$$x = 16$$

2. (D)

$$A = bh = (18)(9) = 162$$

3. **(A)**

    Using the Pythagorean Theorem,

    $$\overline{AC} = \sqrt{(\overline{AD})^2 + (\overline{DC})^2}$$
    $$= \sqrt{(6)^2 + (8)^2}$$
    $$= \sqrt{36 + 64}$$
    $$= \sqrt{100}$$
    $$= 10 \, \text{cm}$$

4. **(D)**

    $$A = bh = (7)(10) = 70 \, \text{cm}^2$$

5. **(C)**

    $$\overline{EC} = \overline{BD} = 17$$
    $$\overline{BO} = \frac{1}{2}\overline{BD} = \frac{1}{2}(17) = 8.5$$

6. **(C)**

    Using the Pythagorean theorem,

    $$\overline{GH} = \sqrt{\left(\frac{1}{2}GI\right)^2 + \left(\frac{1}{2}HJ\right)^2}$$
    $$= \sqrt{\left[\left(\frac{1}{2}\right)(6)\right]^2 + \left[\left(\frac{1}{2}\right)(8)\right]^2}$$
    $$= \sqrt{(3)^2 + (4)^2}$$
    $$= \sqrt{25} = 5$$

7. **(D)**

    $$A = \frac{1}{2}(b_1 + b_2)h$$

    $$= \frac{1}{2}(14 + 21)(10)$$
    $$= \frac{1}{2}(35)(10)$$
    $$= 175$$

8. **(B)**

    $$\overline{BC} = \overline{AD} = 6$$
    $$P = 6 + 6 + 5 + 10 = 27$$

9. **(C)**

    Use the Pythagorean Theorem to find the height.

    $$6^2 = b^2 + 3^2$$
    $$b^2 = 27$$
    $$b = 3\sqrt{3}.$$

    The area of this trapezoid is the area of the rectangle plus the area of the triangle, or

    $$A = \underset{\text{rectangle}}{bh} + \underset{\text{triangle}}{\frac{1}{2}bh} = (4)\left(3\sqrt{3}\right) + \frac{1}{2}\left(3\sqrt{3}\right)(3)$$

    $$= 12\sqrt{3} + \frac{9}{2}\sqrt{3} = \frac{33}{2}\sqrt{3}$$

10. **(D)**

    The base angles of an isosceles trapezoid are equal.

    Therefore, $\angle W = \angle Z$ so

    $$58 = 4x - 6$$
    $$64 = 4x$$
    $$16 = x$$

Drill: Circles

1. **(B)**

    $$C = 2\pi r = 2(\pi)(3) = 6\pi$$

2. **(C)**

    $$A = \pi r^2 = \pi(11)^2 = 121\pi$$

3. **(D)**

    $$A = \pi r^2 \quad r = \frac{1}{2}d = \frac{1}{2}(27) = 13.5$$
    $$A = \pi(13.5)^2 = 182.25\pi$$

4. (C)

$$A = 225\pi = \pi r^2 \text{ so } r = \sqrt{225} = 15$$
$$d = 2r = 2(15) = 30$$

5. (B)

$$C_X = \pi r^2 = 144\pi \quad r_X = 12$$
$$C_Y = \pi r^2 = 81\pi \quad r_Y = 9$$
$$r_X : r_Y = 12 : 9 = 4 : 3$$

6. (B)

Shaded Area = Larger Area − Smaller Area

$$= \pi r_1^2 - \pi r_2^2$$
$$= \pi(7)^2 - \pi(5)^2$$
$$= 49\pi - 25\pi$$
$$= 24\pi$$

7. (D)

Measure of arc = measure of central angle

8. (C)

The measure of a semicircle is 180°. Therefore, arc $\overset{\frown}{AXC} = 180°$.

9. (C)

Since $\overset{\frown}{XYZ}$ is semicircle, $180° - 40° = 140°$

10. (B)

$$\frac{45}{360}\pi r^2 = \frac{1}{8}\pi(4)^2 = \frac{16}{8}\pi = 2\pi$$

Drill: Composite Figures

1. (A)

The area of triangle KLM is $\frac{10^2}{4}\sqrt{3} = 25\sqrt{3}$. The radius of the semicircle is 5, so its area is $\left(\frac{1}{2}\pi\right)(5^2) = 12.5\pi$.

2. (C)

The area of the trapezoid is $\left(\frac{1}{2}\right)(9)(36) = 162$ and the area of the rhombus is $\left(\frac{1}{2}\right)(5)(3) = 7.5$. Thus, the area of the shaded region is $162 - 7.5 = 154.5$.

3. (B)

The area of the trapezoid is $\left(\frac{1}{2}\right)(15)(28+16) = 330$. The area of the triangle is $\left(\frac{1}{2}\right)(16)(12) = 96$. Thus, the area of the shaded region is $330 - 96 = 234$.

4. (B)

The area of the triangle is $\frac{8^2}{4}\sqrt{3} = 16\sqrt{3} \approx 27.7$. This means that the area of the parallelogram is approximately $63.7 - 27.7 = 36$. The base of the parallelogram ($\overline{DE}$) equals the length of any side of the triangle, which is 8. Let x represent the height of the parallelogram. Then $36 = 8x$, so $x = 4.5$.

Drill: Similarity for Three-Dimensional Figures

1. (A)

The ratio of their radii is $\sqrt{\dfrac{9}{100}} = \dfrac{3}{10}$. Let r represent the radius of the larger sphere. Then $\dfrac{3}{10} = \dfrac{12}{r}$. Cross-multiply to get $3r = 120$, which means $r = 40$. Thus, the surface area of the larger sphere is $(4)(\pi)(40^2) = 6400\pi$.

2 (B)

Let x and $2x - 10$ represent the two heights. Then $\dfrac{x}{2x-10} = \sqrt{\dfrac{16}{25}} = \dfrac{4}{5}$. Cross-multiply to get $5x = 8x - 40$. So $3x = 40$, which leads to $x = \dfrac{40}{3}$. Thus, the volume of the smaller cylinder is $(\pi)(6^2)\left(\dfrac{40}{3}\right) = 480\pi$.

3 (D)

The ratio of their corresponding linear dimensions is $\sqrt{\dfrac{9}{25}} = \dfrac{3}{5}$, so the ratio of their volumes must be $\left(\dfrac{3}{5}\right)^3 = \dfrac{27}{125}$. Let v represent the volume of the larger cone. Then $\dfrac{27}{125} = \dfrac{54}{v}$, which leads to $27v = 6750$. Thus, $v = 250$.

4. (B)

Let x represents the length of the larger prism. Then $\dfrac{4}{x} = \dfrac{2}{3}$, so $x = 6$. This eliminates answer choices (A) and (C). The ratio of their surface areas must be $\left(\dfrac{2}{3}\right)^2 = \dfrac{4}{9}$. Let y represent the surface area of the larger prism. Then $\dfrac{416}{y} = \dfrac{4}{9}$, which means that $y = 936$. Let the width and height of the larger prism be represented by w and h, respectively. We know that $(2)(6)(w) + (2)(6)(h) + (2)(w)(h) = 936$, which simplifies to $6w + 6h + wh = 468$. By substitution of the values in answer choice (B), we can verify that $(6)(15) + (6)(18) + (15)(18) = 468$.

Drill: Regular Polygons

1. (C)

The length of the side opposite 30° is one half the hypotenuse, which is 6. Then the side opposite 60° is equal to the side opposite 30° multiplied by the square root of 3. Thus, the side opposite 60° is $6\sqrt{3} \approx 10.4$.

2. (D)

Each leg of a 45°-45°-90° right triangle is equal to the hypotenuse divided by the square root of 2. Then each leg equals $\dfrac{20}{\sqrt{2}} \approx 14.14$. Thus, the sum of the legs is $28.28 \approx 28.3$.

3. (D)

An apothem, PG, represents the radius of the circle, which is $8\sqrt{3}$. In the 30°-60°-90° right triangle PKG, PK $= \left(8\sqrt{3}\right)\left(\dfrac{2}{\sqrt{3}}\right) = 16$. Then the perimeter of the hexagon is $(16)(6) = 96$. Finally, the area of the hexagon is $\left(\dfrac{1}{2}\right)\left(8\sqrt{3}\right)(96) = 384\sqrt{3}$.

4. (A)

Each side of the regular hexagon must be $\dfrac{60}{6} = 10$. This is also the value of PK and PH. In the 30°-60°-90° right triangle PKG, $PG = 10\left(\dfrac{\sqrt{3}}{2}\right) = 5\sqrt{3}$. Since $\overline{PG}$ is a radius of the circle, the required area is $(\pi)\left(5\sqrt{3}\right)^2 = 75\pi$.

5. (C)

Each exterior angle of this polygon must be 180° 162° = 18°. The sum of the exterior angles must be 360°, so the number of sides is $\dfrac{360°}{18°} = 20$.

Drill: Transformations

1. (C)

Each of the vertices A', B', C' is a mirror image over line l_1 of A, B, and C, respectively.

2. (C)

Reflecting triangle ABC over the y-axis moves it to Quadrant 1. In order to move the triangle to the position of triangle DEF, slide the triangle down six spaces.

3. (A)

Since we already have the coordinates of R', we require a 90°-clockwise rotation to determine the coordinates of R. If a point has the coordinates (x, y), then a 90°-clockwise rotation about the origin results in a point with the coordinates $(y, -x)$. Thus, the coordinates of R are $(2, -4)$.

4. (D)

The coordinates of the midpoint of the original line segment, M, are $\left(\dfrac{-1+5}{2}, \dfrac{2+10}{2}\right) = (2, 6)$. Thus, the coordinates of M' are $(2 - 5, 6 + 4) = (-3, 10)$.

Functions and Their Graphs

4

Elementary Functions

A **function** is any process that assigns a single value of y to each number of x. Because the value of x determines the value of y, y is called the **dependent variable** and x is called the **independent variable**. The set of all the values of x by which the function is defined is called the **domain** of the function. The set of corresponding values of y is called the **range** of the function.

PROBLEM

Is $y^2 = x$ a function?

SOLUTION

Graph the equation. Note that x can have two values of y. Therefore, $y^2 = x$ is not a function.

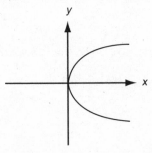

PROBLEM

Find the domain and range for $y = 5 - x^2$.

SOLUTION

First determine if there are any values that would make the function undefined (i.e., dividing by 0). There are none. The domain is the set of real numbers. The range can be found by putting some values in for x.

x	2	1	0	−1	−2
y	1	4	5	4	1

The range is the set of real numbers less than or equal to 5.

PROBLEM

Evaluate $f(1)$ for $y = f(x) = 5x + 2$.

SOLUTION

$$f(x) = 5x + 2$$
$$f(1) = 5(1) + 2$$
$$= 5 + 2$$
$$= 7$$

Functions can be added, subtracted, multiplied, or divided to form new functions.

a. $(f + g)(x) = f(x) + g(x)$

b. $(f - g)(x) = f(x) - g(x)$

c. $(f \times g)(x) = f(x)\, g(x)$

d. $(f / g)(x) = f(x) / g(x)$

PROBLEM

Let $f(x) = 2x^2 - 1$ and $g(x) = 5x + 3$. Determine the following functions:

(1) $f + g$ (2) $f - g$

(3) $f \times g$ (4) f / g

SOLUTION

(1) $(f + g)(x) = f(x) + g(x) = 2x^2 - 1 + 5x + 3$
$$= 2x^2 + 5x + 2$$

(2) $(f - g)(x) = f(x) - g(x) = 2x^2 - 1 - (5x + 3)$
$$= 2x^2 - 1 - 5x - 3$$
$$= 2x^2 - 5x - 4$$

(3) $(f \times g)(x) = f(x)\, g(x) = (2x^2 - 1)(5x + 3)$
$$= 10x^3 + 6x^2 - 5x - 3$$

(4) $(f / g)(x) = f(x) / g(x) = (2x^2 - 1) / (5x + 3)$

Note the domain of (4) is for all real numbers except $-\dfrac{3}{5}$.

The **composite function** $f \circ g$ is defined $(f \circ g)(x) = f(g(x))$.

PROBLEM

Given $f(x) = 3x$ and $g(x) = 4x + 2$. Find $(f \circ g)(x)$ and $(g \circ f)(x)$.

SOLUTION

$$(f \circ g)(x) = f(g(x)) = 3(4x + 2)$$
$$= 12x + 6$$
$$(g \circ f)(x) = g(f(x)) = 4(3x) + 2$$
$$= 12x + 2$$

Note that $(f \circ g)(x) \neq (g \circ f)(x)$.

PROBLEM

Find $(f \circ g)(2)$ if
$$f(x) = x^2 - 3 \text{ and } g(x) = 3x + 1$$

SOLUTION

$$(f \circ g)(2) = f(g(2))$$
$$g(x) = 3x + 1$$

Substitute the value of x.

$$g(2) = 3(2) + 1$$
$$= 7$$
$$f(x) = x^2 - 3$$

Substitute the value of $g(2)$ in $f(x)$.

$$f(7) = (7)^2 - 3$$
$$= 49 - 3$$
$$= 46$$

The **inverse** of a function, f^{-1}, is obtained from f by interchanging the x and y and then solving for y.

Two functions f and g are inverses of one another if $g \circ f = x$ and $f \circ g = x$. To find g when f is given, interchange x and y in the equation $y = f(x)$ and solve for $y = g(x)$. Then replace y with $f^{-1}(x)$.

PROBLEM

Find the inverse of the functions

(1) $f(x) = 3x + 2$

(2) $f(x) = x^2 - 3$

SOLUTION

(1) $f(x) = y = 3x + 2$

To find $f^{-1}(x)$, interchange x and y.

$$x = 3y + 2$$

$$3y = x - 2$$

Solve for y, then replace y with $f^{-1}(x)$.

$$f^{-1}(x) = \frac{x - 2}{3}$$

(2) $f(x) = y = x^2 - 3$.

To find $f^{-1}(x)$, interchange x and y.

$$x = y^2 - 3$$

$$y^2 = x + 3$$

Solve for y, then replace y with $f^{-1}(x)$.

$$f^{-1}(x) = \sqrt{x + 3}$$

Logarithms and Exponential Functions and Equations

An equation

$$y = b^x$$

(with $b > 0$ and $b \neq 1$) is called an **exponential function**. The exponential function with base b can be written as

$$y = f(x) = b^x.$$

The inverse of an exponential function is the **logarithmic function**,

$$f^{-1}(x) = \log_b x.$$

PROBLEM

Write the following equations in logarithmic form:

$3^4 = 81$ and $M^k = 5$.

SOLUTION

The expression $y = b^x$ is equivalent to the logarithmic expression $\log_b y = x$. Therefore, $3^4 = 81$ is equivalent to the logarithmic expression

$$\log_3 81 = 4$$

and $M^k = 5$ is equivalent to the logarithmic expression

$$\log_M 5 = k.$$

PROBLEM

Find the value of $\log_5 25$ and $\log_4 x = 2$.

SOLUTION

$\log_5 25$ is equivalent to $5^x = 25$. Thus $x = 2$, since $5^2 = 25$.

$\log_4 x = 2$ is equivalent to $4^2 = x$. Thus, $x = 16$

Logarithm Properties

If M, N, p, and b are positive numbers and $b = 1$, then

a. $\log_b 1 = 0$

b. $\log_b b = 1$

c. $\log_b b^x = x$

d. $\log_b M N = \log_b M + \log_b N$

e. $\log_b \dfrac{M}{N} = \log_b M - \log_b N$

f. $\log_b M^p = p \log_b M$

PROBLEM

If $\log_{10} 3 = .4771$ and $\log_{10} 4 = .6021$, find $\log_{10} 12$.

SOLUTION

Since $12 = 4(3)$, $\log_{10} 12 = \log_{10} (4)(3)$

Remember

$$\log_b M N = \log_b M + \log_b N.$$

Therefore,

$$\log_{10} 12 = \log_{10} 4 + \log_{10} 3$$

$$= .6021 + .4771$$

$$= 1.0792$$

Properties of Functions

A) A function f is one to one if for every range value there corresponds exactly one domain value of x.

B) A function is even if $f(-x) = f(x)$ or

$$f(x) + f(-x) = 2f(x).$$

C) A function is said to be odd if $f(-x) = -f(x)$ or $f(x) + f(-x) = 0$.

D) Periodicity

A function f with domain X is periodic if there exists a positive real number p such that $f(x + p) = f(x)$ for all $x \in X$.

The smallest number p with this property is called the period of f.

Over any interval of length p, the behavior of a periodic function can be completely described.

E) Inverse of function

Assuming that f is a one-to-one function with domain X and range Y, then a function g having domain Y and range X is called the inverse function of f if:

$$f(g(y)) = y \text{ for every } y \in Y \text{ and}$$

$$g(f(x)) = x \text{ for every } x \in X.$$

The inverse of the function f is denoted f^{-1}.

To find the inverse function f^{-1}, you must solve the equation $y = f(x)$ for x in terms of y.

Be careful: This solution must be a function.

F) The identity function $f(x) = x$ maps every x to itself.

G) The constant function $f(x) = c$ for all $x \in R$.

The "zeros" of an arbitrary function $f(x)$ are particular values of x for which $f(x) = 0$.

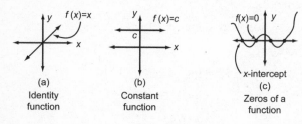

(a) Identity function   (b) Constant function   (c) Zeros of a function

PROBLEM

> Find the domain D and range R of the function
>
> $$\left(x, \frac{x}{|x|}\right).$$

SOLUTION

Note that the y-value of any coordinate pair (x,y) is $\frac{x}{|x|}$. We can replace x in the formula $\frac{x}{|x|}$ with any number except 0, since the denominator, $|x|$, cannot equal 0. This is because division by 0 is undefined. Therefore, the domain D is the set of all real numbers except 0. If x is negative, i.e., $x < 0$, then $|x| = -x$ by definition. Hence, if x is negative, then $\frac{x}{|x|} = \frac{x}{-x} = -1$. If x is positive, i.e. $x > 0$, then $|x| = x$ by definition. Hence, if x is positive, then $\frac{x}{|x|} = \frac{x}{x} = 1$. (The case where $x = 0$ has already been found to be undefined). Thus, there are only two numbers -1 and 1 in the range R of the function; that is, $R = \{-1, 1\}$.

PROBLEM

> If $f(x) = 3x + 4$ and $D = \{x \mid -1 \le x \le 3\}$, find the range of $f(x)$.

SOLUTION

We first prove that the value of $3x + 4$ increases when x increases. If $X > x$, then we may multiply both sides of the inequality by a positive number to obtain an equivalent inequality. Thus, $3X > 3x$. We may also add a number to both sides of the inequality to obtain an equivalent inequality. Thus,

$$3X + 4 > 3x + 4.$$

Hence, if x belongs to D, the function value $f(x) = 3x + 4$ is least when $x = -1$ and greatest when $x = 3$. Consequently, since $f(-1) = -3 + 4 = 1$ and $f(3) = 9 + 4 = 13$, the range is all y from 1 to 13; that is,

$$R = \{y \mid 1 \le y \le 13\}.$$

Graphing a Function

The Cartesian Coordinate System

Consider two lines x and y drawn on a plane region called R.

Let the intersection of x and y be the origin and let us impose a coordinate system on each of the lines.

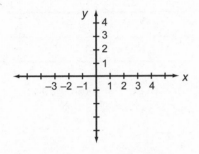

If (x, y) is a point or ordered pair on the coordinate plane R then x is the first coordinate and y is the second coordinate.

To locate an ordered pair on the coordinate plane simply measure the distance of x units along the x-axis, then measure vertically (parallel to the y-axis) y units.

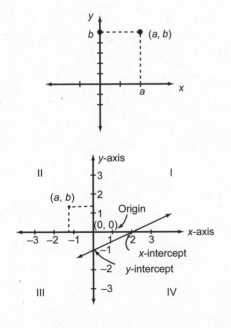

I, II, III, IV are called quadrants in the coordinate plane.

(a, b) is an ordered pair with x-coordinate a and y-coordinate b.

Drawing the Graph

There are several ways to plot the graph of a function. The process of computing and plotting points on the graph is always an aid in this endeavor. The more points we locate on the graph, the more accurate our drawing will be.

It is also helpful if we consider the symmetry of the function. That is,

a) A graph is symmetric with respect to the x-axis if whenever a point (x, y) is on the graph, then $(x, -y)$ is also on the graph.

b) Symmetry with respect to the y-axis occurs when both points $(-x, y)$ and (x, y) appear on the graph for every x and y in the graph.

c) When the simultaneous substitution of $-x$ for x and $-y$ for y does not change the solution of the equation, the graph is said to be symmetric about the origin.

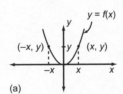

Symmetric about the y-axis

(a)

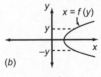

Symmetric about the x-axis
Note: This is not a function of x.

(b)

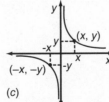

Symmetric about the origin

(c)

Another aid in drawing a graph is locating any vertical asymptotes.

A vertical asymptote is a vertical line $x = a$, such that the functional value $|f(x)|$ grows indefinitely large as x approaches the fixed value a.

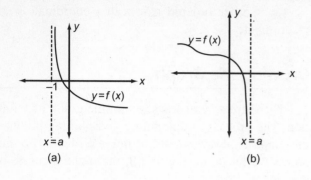

(a)   (b)

$x = a$ is a vertical asymptote for these functions

The following steps encapsulate the procedure for drawing a graph:

a) Determine the domain and range of the function.

b) Find the intercepts of the graph and plot them.

c) Determine the symmetries of the graph.

d) Locate the vertical asymptotes and plot a few points on the graph near each asymptote.

e) Plot additional points as needed.

PROBLEM

> Construct the graph of the function defined by $y = 3x - 9$.

SOLUTION

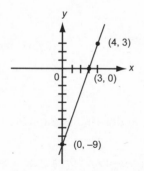

An equation of the form $y = mx + b$ is a linear equation; that is, the equation of a line.

A line can be determined by two points. Let us choose intercepts. The *x*-intercept lies on the *x*-axis and the *y*-intercept on the *y*-axis.

We find the intercepts by assigning 0 to *x* and solving for *y* and by assigning 0 to *y* and solving for *x*. It is helpful to have a third point. We find the third point by assigning 4 to *x* and solving for *y*. Thus we get the following table of corresponding numbers:

x	$y = 3x - 9$	y
0	$y = 3(0) - 9 = 0 - 9 =$	-9
4	$y = 3(4) - 9 = 12 - 9 =$	3

Solving for *x* to get the *x*-intercept:

$$y = 3x - 9$$
$$y + 9 = 3x$$

$$x = \frac{y + 9}{3}$$

When $y = 0$, $x = \dfrac{9}{3} = 3$. The three points are $(0, -9)$, $(4, 3)$, and $(3, 0)$. Draw a line through them (see sketch).

PROBLEM

> Are the following points on the graph of the equation $3x - 2y = 0$?
>
> a) point $(2, 3)$?
>
> b) point $(3, 2)$?
>
> c) point $(4, 6)$?

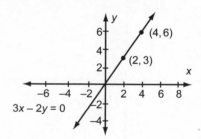

SOLUTION

The point (a, b) lies on the graph of the equation $3x - 2y = 0$ if replacement of *x* and *y* by *a* and *b*, respectively, in the given equation results in an equation which is true.

a) Replacing (x, y) by $(2, 3)$:

$$3x - 2y = 0$$

$$3(2) - 2(3) = 0$$

$$6 - 6 = 0$$

$$0 = 0, \text{ which is true.}$$

Therefore $(2, 3)$ is a point on the graph.

b) Replacing (x, y) by $(3, 2)$:

$$3x - 2y = 0$$

$$3(4) - 2(6) = 0$$

$$9 - 4 = 0$$

$$5 = 0, \text{ which is not true.}$$

Therefore $(3, 2)$ is not a point on the graph.

c) Replacing (x, y) by $(4, 6)$:

$$3x - 2y = 0$$

$$3(4) - 2(6) = 0$$

$$12 - 12 = 0$$

$$0 = 0, \text{ which is true.}$$

Therefore $(4, 6)$ is a point on the graph.

This problem may also be solved geometrically as follows: draw the graph of the line $3x - 2y = 0$ on the coordinate axes. This can be done by solving for y and plotting the points shown in the following table:

x	$y = \dfrac{3}{2}x$
0	0
1	$\dfrac{3}{2} = 1\dfrac{1}{2}$
2	3
−2	−3

Observe that we obtain the same result as in our algebraic solution. The points $(2, 3)$ and $(4, 6)$ lie on the line $3x - 2y = 0$, whereas $(3, 2)$ does not.

Polynomial Functions and Their Graphs

A polynomial in x is an expression of the form

$$a_n x^n + a_{n-1} x^{n-1} + \ldots + a_1 x + a_0,$$

where a_1, a_2, $\ldots$ and a_n are real numbers and where all the exponents are positive integers. When $a_n \neq 0$, this polynomial is said to be of degree n. It is common to let $P(x)$ represent

$$a_n x^n + a_{n-1} x^{n-1} + \ldots + a_1 x + a_0.$$

Then $y = P(x)$ is a polynomial function. A function with the property that

$$P(-x) = P(x)$$

is an even function, while a function with the property

$$P(-x) = -P(x)$$

is an odd function. Even functions are symmetric with respect to the y-axis, while odd functions are symmetric with respect to the origin.

It would be possible to obtain the graph of a polynomial function $y = P(x)$ by simply setting up a table and plotting a large number of points; this is how a computer or a graphing calculator operates. However, it is often desirable to have some basic information about the graph prior to plotting points. The graph of the polynomial function, $y = a_0$ is a line which is parallel to the x-axis and $|a_0|$ units above or below the x-axis, depending on whether a_0 is positive or negative. A function of this type is called a constant function. The graph of the polynomial function

$$y = a_1 x + a_0$$

is a line with slope a_1 and with a_0 as the y-intercept. The graph of the polynomial function

$$y = a_2 x^2 + a_1 x + a_0$$

is a parabola.

It is much more difficult to graph a polynomial function with degree greater than two. However, here are three items which should be investigated.

(1) Find lines (x-axis and y-axis) of symmetry and find out whether the origin is a point of symmetry.

(2) Find out about intercepts. The y-intercept is easy to find but the x-intercepts are usually much more difficult to identify. If possible, factor $P(x)$.

(3) Find out what happens to $P(x)$ when $|x|$ is large. This procedure is illustrated in the following example.

EXAMPLE

Graph

$$y = x^4 - 5x^2 + 4$$

(1) The graph has symmetry with respect to the y-axis.

(2) The y-intercept is at 4. Since

$$x^4 - 5x^2 + 4 = (x^2 - 4)(x^2 - 1)$$
$$= (x - 2)(x + 2)(x - 1)(x + 1),$$

the x-intercepts are at 1, 2, –1, and –2.

(3) As $|x|$ gets large, $P(x)$ gets large.

Here is a sketch of the graph.

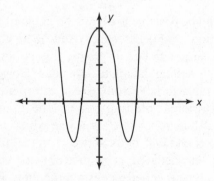

Rational Functions and Their Graphs

When $P(x)$ and $Q(x)$ are polynomials,

$$y = \frac{P(x)}{Q(x)}$$

is called a rational function. The domain of this function is the set of all real numbers x with the property that $Q(x) \neq 0$.

Graphing rational functions is rather difficult. As is the case for polynomial functions, it is desirable to have a general procedure for graphing rational functions. Here is the suggested method for

$$y = \frac{P(x)}{Q(x)}$$

where $P(x) = a_n x^n + a_{n-1} x^{n-1} + \ldots + a_1 x + a_0$ and
$$Q(x) = b_m x^m + b_{m-1} x^{m-1} + \ldots + b_1 x + b_0.$$

(1) Find lines (x-axis and y-axis) of symmetry and determine whether the origin is a point of symmetry.

(2) Find out about intercepts. The y-intercept is at $\dfrac{a_0}{b_0}$ and the x-intercepts will be at values of x where $P(x) = 0$.

(3) Find vertical asymptotes. A line $x = c$ is a vertical asymptote whenever $Q(c) = 0$ and $P(c) \neq 0$.

(4) Find horizontal asymptotes

   (a) If $m = n$, then $y = \dfrac{a_n}{b_m}$ is the horizontal asymptote.

   (b) If $m > n$, then $y = 0$ is the horizontal asymptote.

   (c) If $m < n$, then there is no horizontal asymptote.

This procedure is illustrated in the following example

EXAMPLE

Graph

$$y = \frac{x}{(x - 1)(x + 3)}$$

(1) The axes are not lines of symmetry, nor is the origin a point of symmetry.

(2) The x-intercept and the y-intercept are both at the origin.

(3) The lines $x = 1$ and $x = -3$ are both vertical asymptotes.

(4) The line $y = 0$ is the horizontal asymptote.

Here is a sketch of the graph.

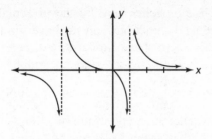

Special Functions and Their Graphs

It is possible to define a function by using different rules for different portions of the domain. The graphs of such functions are determined by graphing the different portions separately. Here is an example.

EXAMPLE

Graph

$$f(x) = \begin{cases} x \text{ if } x \le 1 \\ 2x \text{ if } x > 1 \end{cases}$$

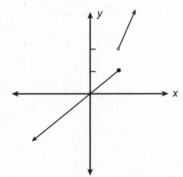

Notice that point (1,1) is part of the graph, but (1, 2) is not.

Functions which involve absolute value can often be completed by translating them to a two-rule form. Consider this example.

EXAMPLE

Graph

$$f(x) = |x| - 1$$

$$|x| = \begin{cases} x \text{ if } x \ge 0 \\ -x \text{ if } x < 0 \end{cases}$$

$f(x)$ can be translated to the following form.

$$f(x) = \begin{cases} x - 1 \text{ if } x \ge 0 \\ -x - 1 \text{ if } x < 0 \end{cases}$$

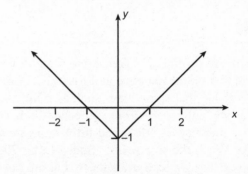

The greatest integer function, denoted by $f(x) = \big[|x| \big]$, is defined by $f(x) = j$, where j is the integer with the property that $j \le x < j + 1$. The graph of this function follows.

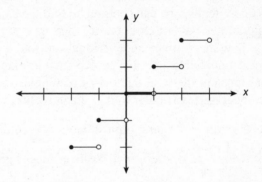

Foundations of Calculus

While middle school mathematics does not usually address formal calculus that includes work with derivatives, integrals, and limits, there are several concepts that are addressed in middle school that provide the foundation for some of these concepts. Among these are ideas concerning limits, rate of change, area, and volume.

Activities that make use of paper folding and other hands-on approaches aid in formulating ideas about limits. For example, one could explore the box problem where you are given a square grid of paper and asked to design an open box by cutting out the corner square grids. First take one square from each corner and then fold up to make a box, then take two, then take three, etc. By determining the volume of each box, looking at a table of values and perhaps graphing the collected data, one can begin to get a sense of maximums, minimums, and limits from this informal approach.

Limits

There are several terms related to calculus concepts that may be helpful to define and illustrate. A **limit** refers to a value that something (such as a function) approaches and either reaches or comes infinitely close to reaching. In everyday life speed-limit signs are a good example. When the sign reads, "Speed-Limit 70 mph," one knows that you can drive up to, but are not to exceed, 70 mph. You are not supposed to exceed the limit!

Consider folding a piece of paper in half, recording the number of sections made, folding in half again and recording sections made, and continue folding in half. Theoretically, one can continue to fold the paper in half indefinitely, although in reality there is a physical limit to how many times an individual can fold a sheet of paper! Interesting patterns evolve such as $f(x) = 2^n$ would represent the total number of rectangles formed on the sheet on a particular fold, n. Each section would be the fraction $\dfrac{1}{2^n}$. Using limit notation we could say that $\lim\limits_{x \to \infty} \dfrac{1}{2^n} = 0$ where n is a positive integer greater than 0. This would be an example of the limit of a func-

tion, which approaches zero but never actually equals zero. In general, functions can (a) have limits, (b) not have a limit, or (c) have limits only at certain points. Even when middle school students graph a function such as $f(x) = \dfrac{1}{x}$, they can visualize a limit since the graph shows that the graph of the function gets infinitely close to both axes but never reaches either. The graph of $f(x) = \dfrac{1}{x}$ is shown below in Figure 4.1.

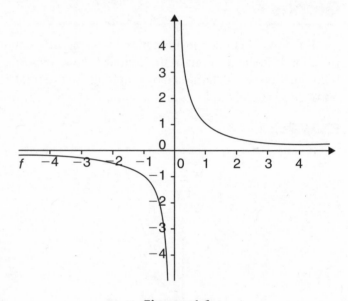

Figure 4.1

Chapter

5

Data, Probability, and Statistical Concepts

Data Description: Graphs

Repeated measurements yield data, which must be organized according to some principle. The data should be arranged in such a way that each observation can fall into one, and only one, category. A simple graphical method of presenting data is the pie chart, which is a circle divided into parts that represent categories.

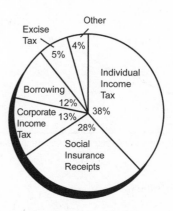

EXAMPLE

2006 Budget

38% came from individual income taxes

28% from social insurance receipts

13% from corporate income taxes

12% from borrowing

5% from excise taxes

4% other

This data can also be presented in the form of a bar chart or bar graph.

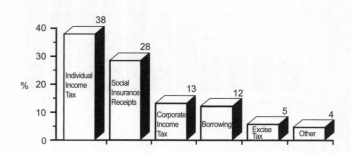

EXAMPLE

The population of the United States for the years 1860 through 1960 is shown in the table below,

Year	Population in millions
1860	31.4
1870	39.8
1880	50.2
1890	62.9
1900	76.0
1910	92.0
1920	105.7
1930	122.8
1940	131.7
1950	151.1
1960	179.3

in this graph,

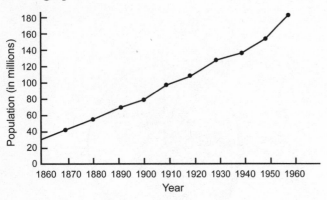

and in this bar chart.

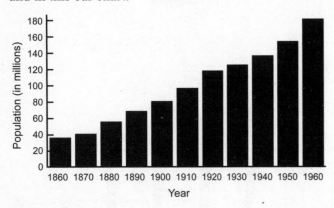

EXAMPLE

A quadratic function is given by

$$y = x^2 + x - 2$$

We compute the values of y corresponding to various values of x.

x	-3	-2	-1	0	1	2	3
y	4	0	-2	-2	0	4	10

From this table, the points of the graph are obtained:

$(-3, 4)$ $(-2, 0)$ $(-1, -2)$ $(0, -2)$ $(1, 0)$ $(2, 4)$ $(3, 10)$

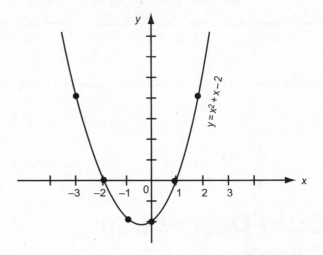

The curve shown is called a parabola. The general equation for a parabola is

$$y = ax^2 + bx + c, \, a \neq 0$$

where a, b, and c are constants.

PROBLEM

Twenty students are enrolled in the foreign language department, and their major fields are as follows: Spanish, Spanish, French, Italian, French, Spanish, German, German, Russian, Russian, French, German, German, German, Spanish, Russian, German, Italian, German, and Spanish.

(a) Make a frequency distribution table.

(b) Make a frequency bar graph.

SOLUTION

(a) The frequency distribution table is constructed by writing down the major field and next to it the number of students.

Major Field	Number of Students
German	7
Russian	3
Spanish	5
French	3
Italian	2
Total	20

(b) A bar graph follows:

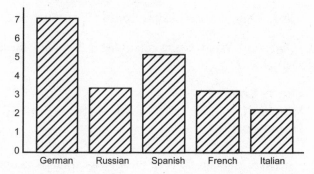

In the bar graph, the fields are listed and spaced evenly along the horizontal axis. Each specified field is represented by a rectangle, and all have the same width. The height of each, identified by a number on the vertical axis, corresponds to the frequency of that field.

A **box-and-whiskers** plot is a graph that displays five statistics. A minimum score, a maximum score, and three percentiles. A percentile value for a score tells you the percentage of scores lower than it. The beginning of the box is the score at the 25th percentile. The end of the box represents the 75th percentile. The score inside of the box is the median, or the score at the 50th percentile. Attached to the box you will find two whiskers. The score at the end of the left whisker is the minimum score. The score at the end of the right whisker is the maximum score.

EXAMPLE

In the box-and-whiskers plot below, the minimum score is 70, the score at the 25th percentile is 78, the median score is 82, the score at the 75th percentile is 90, and the maximum score is 94.

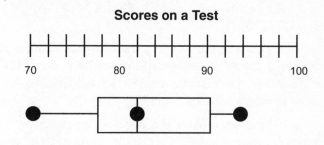

Scores on a Test

PROBLEM

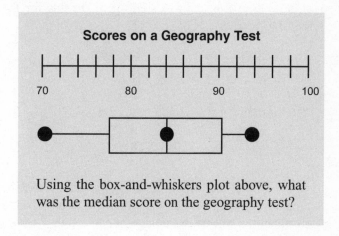

Using the box-and-whiskers plot above, what was the median score on the geography test?

SOLUTION

The median score is 84. On a box-and-whiskers plot, the median score is the score on the inside of the box.

EXAMPLE

A **stem-and-leaf plot** is a way of displaying scores in groups. A stem-and-leaf plot gives you a picture of the scores, as well as the actual numbers themselves in a compact form. In this type of plot, a score is broken into a stem and a leaf. The leaf consists of the smallest digit and the stem consists of the remaining larger digits.

Task: Create a stem and leaf plot using the following scores.

Scores: 64, 48, 61, 81, 63, 59, 70, 54, 76, 61, 55, 31

Solution: The first step is to take these scores and create a set of "ranked ordered scores," ordering the scores from smallest to largest. Notice that the minimum score is 31, while the maximum score is 81.

Ranked Ordered Scores: 31, 48, 54, 55, 59, 61, 61, 63, 64, 70, 76, 81

The second step is to list the range of scores for the stems in a column. The stem of our smallest score (31) is 3, and that of our largest score (81) is 8. List all of the whole numbers between 3 and 8.

The third step is to put the leaves on the stems. Take each score, one at a time and put the last digit in a column next to its stem. For example, the last digit of 31 is 1, so put a 1 next to its stem of 3. The last digit of 48 is 8, so put an 8 next to its stem of 4. Do this for the remaining scores.

Stems	Leaves
8	1
7	0 6
6	1 1 3 4
5	4 5 9
4	8
3	1

A stem-and-leaf plot gives you a picture of how the scores are grouped so that you can begin to understand their meaning. In this example, you can see that 4 people got a score in the 60s. You can also see that the high score was 81, and the low score was 31.

PROBLEM

Stems	Leaves
6	5
5	3 6
4	0 1 7
3	2 9
2	4

The stem-and-leaf plot above was created using what set of scores?

SOLUTION

In this stem-and-leaf plot, the stems are the first digit, and the leaves are the remaining digits. Starting

from the bottom, the first score is 24, the second score is 32, then comes 39, 40, 41, 47, 53, 56, and 65.

EXAMPLE

A **scatter-plot** is a graph that shows the relationship between two variables. A scatter-plot is a set of (x, y) coordinates. Each coordinate is a point on the graph. x represents a value of one variable, while y represents the value of another variable. Remember, a variable is just a measurement that can take on more than one value. A scatter-plot is useful because in one picture you can see if there is a relationship between two variables. It has been said mat, "A picture is worth a thousand words." Likewise, "A graph is worth a thousand numbers."

Given: Variable x represents Grade level. Variable y represents Hours of Homework each week.

Task: Using the data below, construct a scatter-plot.

Question: What is the relationship between these two variables?

| x | **Grade Level** | 1 | 2 | 3 | 4 | 5 | 6 | 7 | 8 | 9 | 10 | 11 | 12 |
| y | **Hours of Homework** | 2 | 3 | 3 | 6 | 4 | 10 | 7 | 10 | 12 | 9 | 14 | 15 |

Answer: You can think of these two variables as one set of (x, y) coordinates on a graph. Remember, a coordinate is just a point. Graph the following points: (1, 2), (2, 3), (3, 3), (4, 6), (5, 4), (6, 10), (7, 7), (8, 10), (9, 12), (10, 9), (11, 14), and (12, 15). This graph shows that as grade level increases, the number of homework hours per week tends to increase.

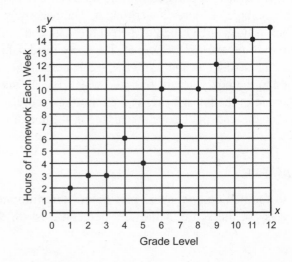

Scatterplot

A statistic called **correlation** tells you if two measurements go together along a straight line. A scatterplot is one way of looking at correlation. There are three different types of correlation.

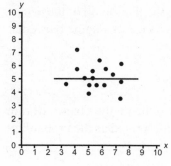

POSITIVE CORRELATION

As one measurement increases, the other measurement also increases.

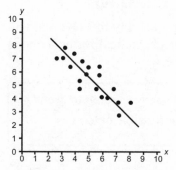

ZERO CORRELATION

The two measurements are not related to each other along a straight line.

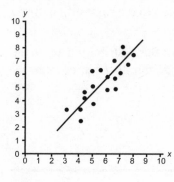

NEGATIVE CORRELATION

As one measurement increases, the other measurement decreases.

Types of Frequency Curves

In applications we find that most of the frequency curves fall within one of the categories listed.

1. One of the most popular is the bell-shaped or symmetrical frequency curve.

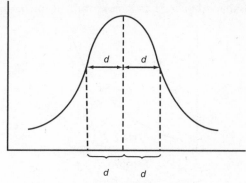

Bell-shaped or Symmetrical

Note that observations equally distant from the maximum have the same frequency. The normal curve has a symmetrical frequency curve.

2. The U-shaped curve has maxima at both ends.

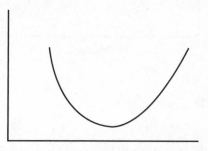

U-shaped

3. A curve can also be skewed to one side. A skew to the left is when the slope to the right of the maximum is steeper than the slope to the left. The opposite holds for the frequency curve skewed to the right.

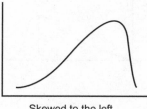
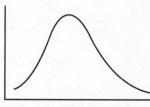

Skewed to the left (negative skew)   Skewed to the right (positive skew)

4. A J-shaped curve has a maximum at one end.

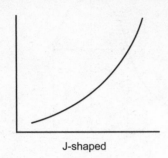

J-shaped

5. A multimodal (bimodal) frequency curve has two or more maxima.

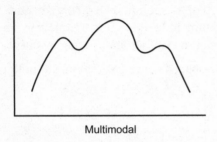

Multimodal

PROBLEM

What are two ways to describe the form of a frequency distribution? How would the following distributions be described?

(a)   (b)

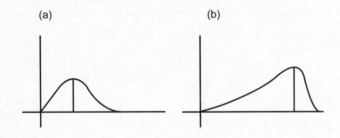

SOLUTION

The form of a frequency distribution can be described by its departure from symmetry or skewness and its degree of peakedness or kurtosis.

If the few extreme values are higher than most of the others, we say that the distribution is "positively skewed" or "skewed" to the right.

If the few extreme values are lower than most of the others, we say that the distribution is "negatively skewed" or "skewed" to the left.

(a) This distribution has extreme values in the upper half of the curve and is skewed to the right or positively skewed.

(b) The extreme values of this distribution are in the lower half of the curve. Thus, the distribution is negatively skewed or skewed to the left.

Probability

Probability is defined as the likelihood of the occurrence of an event or as the chance that some particular event will occur.

EXAMPLE

A weather report might indicate the chance of rain to be 70%, which could be interpreted as the probability of rain = .70.

a) Objective Probability (Calculated)

In most instances, the probability that an event will occur is determined by a mathematical formula and is based on empirical evidence.

$$P(X) = \frac{\text{No. of outcomes corresponding to event } X}{\text{Total no. of possible outcomes}}$$

EXAMPLE

The probability of drawing a queen from a deck of cards is defined as:

$$P(\text{Queen}) = \frac{\text{No. of queens in the deck}}{\text{Total no. of cards in the deck}}$$

$$= \frac{4}{52} = \frac{1}{13} \text{ or } .077$$

b) Subjective Probability

When the probability of an event occurring is based on the personal (or professional) judgment of an individual or group of individuals, the probability is referred to as "subjective."

EXAMPLE

The probability that sales will increase by $500,000 next year if we increase our advertising expenditure by $10,000 is .25.

Properties of Probabilities

The following three properties are characteristics of all probabilities:

1. $0 \leq P(X) \leq 1$; every probability is contained within the range 0 to 1, inclusive, where 0 represents absolute certainty that the event will not occur and 1 represents absolute certainty that the event will occur.

EXAMPLE

P (Head on Coin) $= \dfrac{1}{2}$

P (6 on Die) $= \dfrac{1}{6}$

P (Ace of Spades) $= \dfrac{1}{52}$

2. $\displaystyle\sum_{i=1}^{n} P_i(X) =$ the probabilities of all possible simple events that can occur within a given experiment will sum to 1.

EXAMPLE

coin: $P(\text{Head}) + P(\text{Tail}) = \dfrac{1}{2} + \dfrac{1}{2} = 1$

die: $P(1) + P(2) + P(3) + P(4) + P(5) + P(6) =$
$\dfrac{1}{6} + \dfrac{1}{6} + \dfrac{1}{6} + \dfrac{1}{6} + \dfrac{1}{6} + \dfrac{1}{6} = 1$

cards: $P(\text{Club}) + P(\text{Heart}) + P(\text{Spade}) + P(\text{Diamond})$
$= \dfrac{1}{4} + \dfrac{1}{4} + \dfrac{1}{4} + \dfrac{1}{4} = 1$

3. $P(X) + P(\text{Not } X) = 1$; the probability that event X occurs plus the probability that event X does not occur sums to 1.

EXAMPLE

coin: P (Head) $+ P$ (Not a Head) $= \dfrac{1}{2} + \dfrac{1}{2} = 1$

die: P (6) $+ P$ (Not a 6) $= \dfrac{1}{6} + \dfrac{5}{6} = 1$

cards: P (Spade) $+ P$ (Not a Spade) $= \dfrac{1}{4} + \dfrac{3}{4} = 1$
or $\dfrac{13}{52} + \dfrac{39}{52} = 1$

Methods of Computing Probabilities

a) **Addition**

1. Mutually Exclusive Events—those which cannot occur simultaneously. In order to determine the probability that either event X occurs or event Y occurs, the individual probabilities of event X and event Y are added.

$P(X \text{ or } Y) = P(X) + P(Y)$

EXAMPLE

The probability that either a club or a spade is drawn from a deck of cards in a single draw is defined as:

P (Club or Spade) $= P$ (Club) $+ P$ (Spade)

$= \dfrac{13}{52} + \dfrac{39}{52}$

$= \dfrac{26}{52}$

$= \dfrac{1}{2}$ or .5

Note: That this concept applies to three or more events as well.

2. Non-Mutually Exclusive Events—those which can occur simultaneously. In order to determine the probability that either event X occurs or event Y occurs, the individual probabilities of event X and event Y are added and the probability that the two occur simultaneously is subtracted from the total.

$$P(X \text{ or } Y) = P(X) + P(Y) - P(X \text{ and } Y)$$

EXAMPLE

The probability that either a Queen or a Spade is drawn from a deck of cards in a single draw is defined as:

P (Queen or Spade) $= P$ (Queen) $+ P$ (Spade) $-$
$\qquad\qquad\qquad\qquad P$ (Queen & Spade)

$= \dfrac{4}{52} + \dfrac{13}{52} - \dfrac{1}{52}$

$= \dfrac{16}{52}$

$= \dfrac{4}{13}.$

Notice in this example that we must subtract $\frac{1}{52}$ from the total since the Queen of Spades is counted in the total number of Queens and it is also counted in the total number of Spades. If we do not subtract P (Queen & Spade), we are counting that one card twice.

b) Multiplication

1. Independent Events

Two (or more) events are independent if the occurrence of one event has no effect upon whether or not the other event occurs. In order to determine the probability that event X occurs and event Y occurs, the individual probability of event X and event Y are multiplied together.

$$P(X \text{ and } Y) = P(X) \times P(Y)$$

EXAMPLE

1. The probability of tossing a 6 on a single die followed by the toss of a 3 is:

P (6 and 3) $= P$ (6) $\times P$ (3)

$$= \frac{1}{6} \times \frac{1}{6}$$

$$= \frac{1}{36}.$$

2. The probability of tossing three heads in 3 tosses of a coin:

P (H, H, H) $= P$ (H) $\times P$ (H) $\times P$ (H)

$$= \frac{1}{2} \times \frac{1}{2} \times \frac{1}{2}$$

$$= \frac{1}{8}.$$

3. The probability of drawing a heart from a deck of cards, replacing the first card, and drawing a club on the second draw:

P (H and C) $= P$(H) $\times P$ (C)

$$= \frac{13}{52} \times \frac{13}{52}$$

$$= \frac{1}{4} \times \frac{1}{4}$$

$$= \frac{1}{16}$$

Dependent Events

Two (or more) events are dependent if the occurrence of one event has some effect upon whether or not the other event occurs. In order to determine the probability that event X occurs and event Y occurs, when X and Y are dependent, the formula is:

$$P(X \text{ and } Y) = P(X) \times P(Y \,|\, X)$$

or

$$P(X \text{ and } Y) = P(Y) \times P(X \,|\, Y)$$

where: $P(Y \,|\, X)$ is read as the probability that event Y will occur, given that event X has already occurred.

And: $P(X \,|\, Y)$ is read as the probability that event X will occur given that event Y has already occurred.

EXAMPLE

1. A box contains 6 red balls, 4 green balls, and 5 purple balls. What is the probability that a red ball is drawn on the first draw and a purple ball is drawn on the second draw, if the first ball is not replaced prior to the second ball being drawn

P (Red and Purple) $= P(R) \times P(P \,|\, R)$

$$= \frac{6}{15} \times \frac{5}{14}$$

$$= \frac{30}{210}$$

$$= \frac{1}{7}$$

2. Three cards are drawn from a deck. What is the probability that the first is a Queen, the second is a Queen, and the third is a King? Assume that each card is **not** replaced prior to the next one being drawn.

P ($Q1, Q2, K$) $= P$ ($Q1$) $\times P$ ($Q2 \,|\, Q1$) $\times$ P ($K|Q1$ & $Q2$)

$$= \frac{4}{52} \times \frac{3}{51} \times \frac{4}{50}$$

$$= \frac{4}{132,600}$$

$$\approx .0004$$

3. Two cards are drawn from a deck, one at a time, with no replacement. What is the probability of drawing a picture card, followed by a red king? (In a standard deck of 52 cards, there are 12 picture cards and 2 red kings.)

   Let A = picture card and let R = red king. Then $P(A \text{ and } R) = P(A) \times P(R|A)$

   $$= \frac{12}{52} \times \frac{2}{51} = \frac{3}{13} \times \frac{2}{51} = \frac{6}{663} = \frac{2}{221}$$

4. A jar contains 10 pennies, 20 quarters, and 30 dimes. Two coins will be selected, one at a time, with no replacement. What is the probability of selecting a quarter, followed by a dime?

   Let Q = quarter and let D = dime. Then

   $P(Q \text{ and } D) = P(Q) \times P(D|Q)$

   $$= \frac{20}{60} \times \frac{30}{59} = \frac{1}{3} \times \frac{30}{59} = \frac{30}{177} = \frac{10}{59}$$

Statistics

Definition of Arithmetic Mean

The arithmetic mean, or mean, of a set of measurements is the sum of the measurements divided by the total number of measurements.

The arithmetic mean of a set of numbers $x_1, x_2, \ldots, x_n$ is denoted by $\bar{x}$ (read "x bar").

$$\bar{x} = \frac{\sum_{i=1}^{n} x_1}{n} = \frac{x_1 + x_2 + \ldots + x_n}{n}$$

EXAMPLE

The arithmetic mean of the numbers 3, 7, 1, 24, 11, and 32 is

$$\bar{x} = \frac{3 + 7 + 1 + 24 + 11 + 32}{6} = 13$$

EXAMPLE

Let $f_1, f_2, \ldots, f_n$ be the frequencies of the numbers $x_1, x_2, \ldots, x_n$ (i.e., number x_i occurs f_i times). The arithmetic mean is

$$\bar{x} = \frac{f_1 x_1 + f_2 x_2 + \ldots + f_n x_n}{f_1 + f_2 + \ldots + f_n} = \frac{\sum_{i=1}^{n} f_i x_i}{\sum_{i=1}^{n} f_i}$$

$$= \frac{\sum fx}{\sum f}$$

Note that the total frequency, that is, the total number of cases, is $\sum_{i=1}^{n} f_i$.

EXAMPLE

If the measurements 3, 7, 2, 8, 0, and 4 occur with frequencies 3, 2, 1, 5, 10, and 6, respectively, then the arithmetic mean is

$$\bar{x} = \frac{3 \times 3 + 7 \times 2 + 2 \times 1 + 8 \times 5 + 0 \times 10 + 4 \times 6}{3 + 2 + 1 + 5 + 10 + 6} \approx 3.3$$

Keep in mind that the arithmetic mean is strongly affected by extreme values.

EXAMPLE

Consider four workers whose monthly salaries are $2,500, $3,200, $3,700, and $48,000. The arithmetic mean of their salaries is

$$\frac{\$57,400}{4} = \$14,350$$

The figure $14,350 can hardly represent the typical monthly salary of the four workers.

EXAMPLE

The deviation d_i of x_i from its mean $\bar{x}$ is defined to be

$$d_i = x_i - \bar{x}$$

The sum of the deviations of $x_1, x_2, \ldots, x_n$ from their mean $\bar{x}$ is equal to zero. Indeed,

$$\sum_{i=1}^{n} d_1 = \sum_{i=1}^{n} (x_i - \bar{x}) = 0$$

Thus,

$$\sum_{i=1}^{n}(x_i - \bar{x}) = \sum_{i=1}^{n} x_i - n\bar{x} = \sum x_i - n\frac{\sum x_i}{n}$$

$$= \sum x_i - \sum x_i = 0$$

EXAMPLE

If $z_1 = x_1 + y_1, \ldots, z_n = x_n + y_n$, then $\bar{z} = \bar{x} + \bar{y}$. Indeed,

$$\bar{x} = \frac{\sum x}{n}, \bar{y} = \frac{\sum y}{n}, \text{ and } \bar{z} = \frac{\sum z}{n}$$

We have

$$\bar{z} = \frac{\sum z}{n} = \frac{\sum(x+y)}{n} = \frac{\sum x}{n} + \frac{\sum y}{n} = \bar{x} + \bar{y}.$$

The arithmetic mean plays an important role in statistical inference.

We will be using different symbols for the sample mean and the population mean. The population mean is denoted by μ, and the sample mean is denoted by $\bar{x}$. The sample mean $\bar{x}$ will be used to make inferences about the corresponding population mean μ.

EXAMPLE

Suppose a bank has 500 savings accounts. We pick a sample of 12 accounts. The balance on each account in dollars is

657	284	51
215	73	327
65	412	218
539	225	195

The sample mean $\bar{x}$ is

$$\bar{x} = \frac{\sum_{i=1}^{12} x_i}{12} = \$271.75$$

The average amount of money for the of 12 sampled accounts is $271.75. Using this information, we estimate the total amount of money in the bank to be

$$\$271.25 \times 500 = \$135,875.$$

PROBLEM

The following measurements were taken by an antique dealer as he weighed to the nearest pound his prized collection of anvils. The weights were 84, 92, 37, 50, 50, 84, 40, and 98. What was the mean weight of the anvils?

SOLUTION

The average or mean weight of the anvils is

$$\bar{x} = \frac{\text{sum of observations}}{\text{number of observations}}$$

$$= \frac{84 + 92 + 37 + 50 + 50 + 84 + 40 + 98}{8}$$

$$= \frac{555}{8} = 66.88 \cong 67 \text{ pounds}$$

An alternate way to compute the sample mean is to rearrange the terms in the numerator, grouping the numbers that are the same. Thus,

$$\bar{x} = \frac{(84 + 84) + (50 + 50) + 37 + 40 + 92 + 98}{8}$$

We see that we can express the mean in terms of the frequency of observations. The frequency of an observation is the number of times a number appears in a sample.

$$\bar{x} = \frac{2(84) + 2(50) + 37 + 40 + 92 + 98}{8}$$

The observations 84 and 50 appear in the sample twice, and thus each observation has frequency 2.

PROBLEM

The numbers 4, 2, 7, and 9 occur with frequencies 2, 3, 11, and 4, respectively. Find the arithmetic mean.

SOLUTION

To find the arithmetic mean, $\bar{x}$, multiply each different number by its associated frequency. Add these products, then divide by the total number of numbers.

$$\bar{x} = [(4)(2) + (2)(3) + (7)(11) + (9)(4)] \div 20$$
$$= (8 + 6 + 77 + 36) \div 20$$
$$= 127 \div 20 = 6.35$$

All means can also be computed for the grouped data, that is, when data are presented in a frequency distribution. Then, all values within a given class interval are considered to be equal to the class mark, or midpoint, of the interval.

Measures of Central Tendency

Definition of the Mode

The mode of a set of numbers is that value which occurs most often (with the highest frequency).

Observe that the mode may not exist. Also, if the mode exists, it may not be unique. For example, for the numbers 1, 1, 2, and 2, the mode is not unique.

EXAMPLE

The set of numbers 2, 2, 4, 7, 9, 9, 13, 13, 13, 26, and 29 has mode 13.

The set of numbers that has two or more modes is called **bimodal.**

PROBLEM

Find the mode or modes of the sample 6, 7, 7, 3, 8, 5, 3, and 9.

SOLUTION

In this sample the numbers 7 and 3 both appear twice. There are no other observations that appear as frequently as these two. Therefore, 3 and 7 are the modes of this sample. The sample is called "bimodal."

For grouped data – data presented in the form of a frequency table – we do not know the actual measurements, only how many measurements fall into each interval. In such a case, the mode is the midpoint of the class interval with the highest frequency.

Note that the mode can also measure popularity. In this sense, we can determine the most popular model of car or the most popular actor.

PROBLEM

Find the mode of the sample 14, 19, 16, 21, 18, 19, 24, 15, and 19.

SOLUTION

The mode is another measure of central tendency in a data set. It is the observation or observations that occur with the greatest frequency. The number 19 is observed three times in this sample, and no other observation appears as frequently. The mode of this sample is therefore 19.

PROBLEM

Find the mode of the sample 14, 16, 21, 19, 18, 24, and 17.

SOLUTION

In this sample all the numbers occur with the same frequency. There is no single number that is observed more frequently than any other. Thus, there is no mode. The mode is not a useful concept here.

Definition of Median

The median of a set of numbers is defined as the middle value when the numbers are arranged in order of magnitude.

Usually, the median is used to measure the midpoint of a large set of numbers. For example, we can talk about the median age of people getting married. Here, the median reflects the central value of the data for a large set of measurements. For small sets of numbers, we use the following conventions:

- For an odd number of measurements, the median is the middle value.

- For an even number of measurements, the median is the average of the two middle values.

In both cases, the numbers have to be arranged in order of magnitude.

EXAMPLE

The scores of a test are 78, 79, 83, 83, 87, 92, and 95. Hence, the median is 83.

EXAMPLE

The median of the set of numbers 21, 25, 29, 33, 44, and 47 is $\dfrac{29+33}{2} = 31$.

PROBLEM

Find the median of the sample 34, 29, 26, 37, and 31.

SOLUTION

The median, a measure of central tendency, is the middle number. The number of observations that lie above the median is the same as the number of observations that lie below it.

Arranged in order we have 26, 29, 31, 34, and 37. The number of observations is odd, and thus the median is 31. Note that there are two numbers in the sample above 31 and two below 31.

PROBLEM

Find the median of the sample 34, 29, 26, 37, 31, and 34.

SOLUTION

The sample arranged in order is 26, 29, 31, 34, 34, and 37. The number of observations is even and thus the median, or middle number, is chosen halfway between the third and fourth numbers. In this case, the median is

$$\frac{31+34}{2} = 32.5$$

It is more difficult to compute the median for grouped data. The exact value of the measurements is not known; hence, we know only that the median is located in a particular class interval. The problem is where to place the median within this interval.

For grouped data, the median obtained by interpolation is given by

$$\text{Median} = L + \frac{c}{f_{\text{median}}}\left(\frac{n}{2} - \left(\sum f\right)\text{cum}\right)$$

where

L = the lower class limit of the interval that contains the median

c = the size of the median class interval

f_{median} = frequency of the median class

n = the total frequency

$\left(\sum f\right)_{\text{cum}}$ = the sum of frequencies (cumulative frequency) for all classes before the median class

EXAMPLE

The weight of 50 men is depicted in the table below in the form of frequency distribution.

Weight	Frequency
115 – 121	2
122 – 128	3
129 – 135	13
136 – 142	15
143 – 149	9
150 – 156	5
157 – 163	3
TOTAL	50

Class $136 - 142$ has the highest frequency.

The mode is the midpoint of the class interval with the highest frequency.

$$\text{Mode} = \frac{135.5 + 142.5}{2} = 139$$

The median is located in class $136 - 142$.

We have

$$\text{Median} = L + \frac{c}{f_{\text{median}}}\left[\frac{n}{2} - \left[\sum f\right]_{\text{cum}}\right]$$

where
$$\begin{aligned}
L &= 135.5 \\
c &= 7 \\
f_{\text{median}} &= 15 \\
n &= 50 \\
\left(\sum f\right)_{\text{cum}} &= 2 + 3 + 13 = 18
\end{aligned}$$

Hence,

$$\text{Median} = 135.5 + \frac{7}{15}\left[\frac{50}{2} - 18\right] = 138.77$$

To compute the arithmetic mean for grouped data, we compute midpoint x_i of each of the intervals and use the formula

$$\bar{x} = \frac{\sum\limits_{i=1}^{n} f_i x_i}{\sum\limits_{i=1}^{n} f_i}$$

We have

$$\bar{x} =$$

$$\frac{118 \times 2 + 125 \times 3 + 132 \times 13 + 139 \times 15 + 146 \times 9 + 153 \times 5 + 160 \times 3}{50}$$

$$= 139.42$$

For symmetrical curves, the mean, mode, and median all coincide.

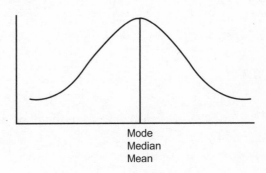

Mode
Median
Mean

For skewed distributions, we have the following.

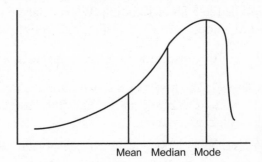

Mean   Median   Mode

The distribution is skewed to the left.

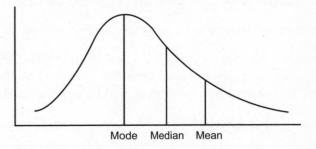

Mode   Median   Mean

The distribution is skewed to the right.

Class Boundaries	Class Weights	Frequencies
58.5 – 61.5	60	4
61.5 – 64.5	63	8
64.5 – 67.5	66	12
67.5 – 70.5	69	13
70.5 – 73.5	72	21
73.5 – 76.5	75	15
76.5 – 79.5	78	12
79.5 – 82.5	81	9
82.5 – 85.5	84	4
85.5 – 88.5	87	2

PROBLEM

Find the median weight from the previous table.

SOLUTION

There are 100 observations in the sample. The median will be the 50th observation. When using an even-numbered sample of grouped data, the convention is to call the $\frac{n}{2}$th observation the median. There are 37 observations in the first four intervals, and the first five intervals contain 58 observations. The 50th observation is in the fifth class interval.

We use the technique of linear interpolation to estimate the position of the 50th observation within the class interval.

The width of the fifth class is three, and there are 21 observations in the class. To interpolate we imagine that each observation takes up $\frac{3}{21}$ units of the interval. There are 37 observations in the first four intervals, and thus the 13th observation in the fifth class will be the median. This 13th observation will be approximately $13\left(\frac{3}{21}\right)$ units from the lower boundary of the fifth class interval. The median is thus the lower boundary of the fifth class plus $13\left(\frac{3}{21}\right)$ or

$$\text{median} = 70.5 + \frac{13}{7} = 72.36$$

PROBLEM

A sample of drivers involved in motor vehicle accidents was categorized by age. The results appear as:

Age	Number of Accidents
16 – 25	28
26 – 35	13
36 – 45	12
46 – 55	8
56 – 65	19
66 – 75	20

What is the value of the median?

SOLUTION

We seek the $\frac{100}{2} = 50$th number, which appears in the third class (36 – 45).

The total number of accidents is 100. The median is the $\frac{100}{2} = 50$th number when the numbers are arranged in ascending order. (In this case, we have intervals of numbers instead of just numbers.) The two intervals 16 – 25 and 26 – 35 consist of 41 count. We need nine numbers from the interval 36 – 45. Use the lower boundary of this interval 36 – 45, which is 35.5, and add $\frac{9}{12}$ of the width of the interval (10).

Then

$$35.5 + \frac{9}{12}(10) = 43$$

Measures of Variability

Range and Percentiles

The degree to which numerical data tend to spread about an average value is called the **variation** or **dispersion** of the data. We shall define various measures of dispersion.

The simplest measure of data variation is the range.

Definition of Range

The **range** of a set of numbers is defined to be the difference between the largest and the smallest number of the set. For grouped data, the range is the difference between the upper limit of the last interval and the lower limit of the first interval.

EXAMPLE

The range of the numbers 3, 6, 21, 24, and 38 is $38 - 3 = 35$.

Definition of Percentiles

The nth percentile of a set of numbers arranged in order of magnitude is that value which has $n\%$ of the numbers below it and $(100 - n)\%$ above it.

EXAMPLE

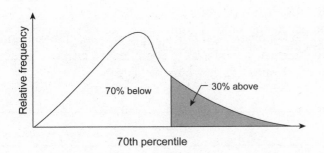

The 70th percentile of a set of numbers

Percentiles are often used to describe the results of achievement tests. For example, someone graduates in the top 10% of the class. Frequently used percentiles are the 25th, 50th and 75th percentiles, which are called the lower quartile, the middle quartile (median), and the upper quartile, respectively.

Definition of Interquartile Range

The interquartile range, abbreviated IQR, of a set of numbers is the difference between the upper and lower quartiles.

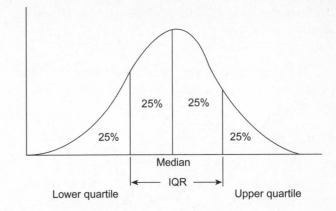

Now, we shall introduce an important concept of deviation.

The deviation of a number x from its mean $\bar{x}$ is defined to be

$$x - \bar{x}$$

Using deviations, we can construct many different measures of variability.

Observe that the mean deviation for any set of measurements is always zero. Indeed, let $x_1, x_2, \ldots, x_n$ be measurements. Their mean is given by

$$\bar{x} = \frac{\sum x_i}{n}$$

The deviations are $x_1 - \bar{x}, x_2 - \bar{x}, \ldots, x_n - \bar{x}$, and their mean is equal to

$$\frac{\sum_{i=1}^{n}(x_i - \bar{x})}{n} = \frac{\sum x_i}{n} - \bar{x} = 0$$

PROBLEM

Find the range of the sample composed of the observations 33, 53, 35, 37, and 49.

SOLUTION

The range is a measure of the dispersion of the sample and is defined to be the difference between the largest and smallest observations.

In our sample, the largest observation is 53 and the smallest is 33. The difference is $53 - 33 = 20$, and the range is 20.

The range is not a very satisfactory measure of dispersion as it involves only two of the observations in the sample.

PROBLEM

In a sample of data, the 75th percentile is the number 23. If the interquartile range is 10, what number represents the 25th percentile?

SOLUTION

The interquartile range = the difference between the 75th percentile and the 25th percentile. If $x = 25$th percentile, we have $23 - x = 10$, so $x = 13$.

Definition of Standard Deviation

The standard deviation of a population $x_1, x_2, \ldots, x_n$ of n numbers is defined by

$$\sigma = \sqrt{\frac{\sum_{i=1}^{n}\left(x_i - \bar{x}\right)^2}{n}}$$

The standard deviation of a sample $x_1, x_2, \ldots, x_n$ of n numbers is defined by

$$s = \sqrt{\frac{\sum_{i=1}^{n}\left(x_i - \bar{x}\right)^2}{n-1}}$$

For data that occurs with multiple frequencies, we can use a modified formula for the standard deviation. Let the frequencies of the numbers $x_1, x_2, \ldots, x_n$ be $f_1, f_2, \ldots, f_n$, respectively. Then

$$\sigma = \sqrt{\frac{\sum_{i=1}^{n} f_i\left(x_i - \bar{x}\right)^2}{\sum_{i=1}^{n} f_i}} \text{ and } s = \sqrt{\frac{\sum_{i=1}^{n} f_i\left(x_i - \bar{x}\right)^2}{\sum_{i=1}^{n} f_i - 1}}$$

Often, in the definition of the standard deviation, the denominator is not n but $n - 1$. For large values of n, the difference between the two definitions is negligible.

Definition of Variance

The sample variance of a set of measurements is defined as the square of the standard deviation. Thus,

$$s^2 = \frac{\sum_{i=1}^{n}(x_i - \bar{x})^2}{n - 1}$$

or

$$s^2 = \frac{\sum_{i=1}^{n} f_i(x_i - \bar{x})^2}{\sum_{i=1}^{n} f_i}$$

Usually, the variance of the sample is denoted by s^2, and the corresponding population variance is denoted by σ^2.

EXAMPLE

A simple manual task was given to six children, and the time each child took to complete the task was measured. Results are shown in the table.

x_i	$x_i - \bar{x}$	$(x_i - \bar{x})^2$
12	2.5	6.25
9	−0.5	0.25
11	1.5	2.25
6	−3.5	12.25
10	0.5	0.25
9	−0.5	0.25
Total 57	0	21.5

For this sample, we shall find the standard deviation and variance.

The average $\bar{x}$ is 9.5.

$$\bar{x} = 9.5$$

The standard deviation is

$$s^2 = \sqrt{\frac{21.5}{5}} = 2.07$$

and the variance is

$$s^2 = 4.3$$

PROBLEM

A couple has six children whose ages are 6, 8, 10, 12, 14, and 16. Find the variance in ages.

SOLUTION

The variance in ages is a measure of the spread or dispersion of ages about the sample mean.

To compute the variance, we first calculate the sample mean.

$$\bar{X} = \frac{\sum X_i}{n} = \frac{\text{sum of observations}}{\text{number of observations}}$$

$$= \frac{6 + 8 + 10 + 12 + 14 + 16}{6} = \frac{66}{6} = 11$$

The variance is defined to be

$$s^2 = \frac{\sum_{i=1}^{n}(X_i - \bar{X})^2}{n - 1}$$

$$= \frac{(6 - 11)^2 + (8 - 11)^2 + (10 - 11)^2 + (12 - 11)^2 + (14 - 11)^2 + (16 - 11)^2}{5}$$

$$= \frac{25 + 9 + 1 + 1 + 9 + 25}{5} = \frac{70}{5} = 14$$

Discrete Mathematics

Chapter 6

Logic

In logic, we concern ourselves only with those sentences that are either true or false, but not both. A statement is a declarative sentence that is either true or false (but not both true and false). For example, the sentences "February has 30 days," "$4 + 2 = 3 \times 2$," and "Ronald Reagan was president of the United States" are statements, but the sentences, "Hand in your paper," "Is it raining," and "Stop the car" are not statements.

The basic type of statement in logic is called a simple statement. A simple statement is a complete sentence that conveys one thought with no connecting words. So, the statements "Five is a counting number," "Today is Monday," and "Sally was late for class" are all simple statements. If we take simple statements and put them together using connecting words, we form sentences that are known as compound or complex statements. The basic connectives are "and" ($\wedge$), "or" ($\vee$), "if...then" ($\rightarrow$), "if and only if" ($\leftrightarrow$), and the negation "not" ($\sim$).

The word "not" does not connect simple statements, but it is still thought of as a connective. It negates a simple statement. A simple statement such as "Today is Monday" is no longer simple if we say "Today is not Monday." The original statement has been negated, so we call the newly formed compound statement a negation.

When we connect two simple statements, p and q, using the word "and" ($\wedge$), we have a compound statement that is called a conjunction ($\wedge$). For example, if p is the statement "Today is Monday," and q is the statement "Tomorrow is Wednesday," then $p \wedge q$ is the sentence "Today is Monday and tomorrow is Wednesday."

The connective "or" is used in forming a compound statement called a disjunction ($\vee$). If p is the statement "I will pass history" and q is the statement "I will be sad," then the statement "I will pass history or I will be sad" is the disjunction $p \vee q$ of the statements p and q.

The connective "if...then" is used in compound statements referred to as conditionals or implications ($\rightarrow$). An example of a conditional is "If you do your homework, then you will pass the exam." The statement between the if and then ("you do your homework") is called the antecedent of the conditional and the part of the sentence that follows "then" ("you will pass the exam") is called the consequence.

The type of statement "Two sides of a triangle are equal if and only if two angles of the triangle are equal" is called a biconditional ($\leftrightarrow$).

A truth table gives us the truth value of a compound statement for each possible combination of the truth or falsity of each simple statement within the compound statement. For example, the following truth table is a truth table for the statement $\sim p \vee q$.

p	q	$\sim p$	$\sim p \vee q$
T	T	F	T
T	F	F	F
F	T	T	T
F	F	T	T

A statement that is always true is called a tautology and a statement that is always false is called a contradiction. Truth tables are also used to determine whether an argument is valid or invalid. An argument is valid if the conclusion follows from the premises. To test whether an argument is valid, we first connect the premises by means of conjunction and then connect the resulting statement to the conclusion to form a conditional. Next, we complete the truth table for this conditional, and if the truth table shows that the conditional is a tautology, then the argument is valid. If the conditional is not a tautology, then the argument is invalid.

The principle of mathematical induction provides a method for proving many theorems. Any such proof by induction involves two parts: we must first show that the formula is true for the natural number 1, and then show that, if the formula is true for any natural number k, then it is also true for the natural number $k + 1$. A proof by induction is complete only if both of these required properties are established.

There are statements that are not true when $n = 1$ but that are true for all natural numbers equal to or greater than some given natural number, say q. In these cases, verify the given statement for $n = q$ in part 1 of the induction proof. After establishing part 2 of the induction proof, the given statement is proved for all natural numbers that are greater than or equal to q.

Sets

If S is a collection of objects, then the objects are called the elements of S. We write $x \in S$ to mean x is an element of S, and we write $x \notin S$ to mean x is not an element of S. So, for instance, if S denotes the set of all positive integers $1, 2, 3, \ldots, n, \ldots$, then $205 \in S$, whereas $-18 \notin S$.

If S and T are two sets such that every element of S is also an element of T, then S is called a subset of T and we write $S \subseteq T$. However, if $S \subseteq T$ and $S \neq T$, then S is called a proper subset of T, and we write $S \subset T$. Thus, if T is the set of all positive integers, and S is the set of all positive even integers, then $S \subset T$. If $S \subseteq T$ and $T \subseteq S$, then S and T are equal sets, that is, $S = T$.

The need also arises for a very peculiar set, namely one having no elements. This is called the empty or null set and is denoted by $\varnothing$; $\varnothing$ has the property that is a subset of every set.

It is helpful to regard all sets under consideration as being subsets of some constant set, called the universal set, U. If S is a subset of U that satisfies a certain property P, we write

$$S = \{x \in U : x \text{ satisfies } P\}$$

There are several important ways in which sets may be combined with one another. If S and T are subsets of some universal set, U, then the operations of union, intersection, and difference are defined as follows:

1) Union: $S \cup T = \{x : x \in S \text{ or } x \in T\}$

2) Intersection: $S \cap T = \{x : x \in S \text{ and } x \in T\}$

3) The difference of S and T: $S - T = \{x : x \in S \text{ but } x \notin T\}$

In the particular case when S is a subset of U, then $U - S$ is called the complement of S in U and is written S'. That is,

$$S' = U - S = \{x : x \in U \text{ and } x \notin S\}$$

We represent these three operations pictorially by what are called Venn Diagrams. If S is Ⓢ and T is Ⓣ, then

$S \cup T =$ is the shaded region.

$S \cap T =$ is the shaded region.

$S - T =$ is the shaded region.

Another construction of new sets from the old is the cartesian product of two sets, S and T, defined by

$$S \times T = \{(s, t): s \in S \text{ and } t \in T\}$$

where we define the ordered pair (s_1, t_1) is equal to the ordered pair (s_2, t_2) if and only if $s_1 = s_2$ and $t_1 = t_2$.

For the sets $S = \{1, 2\}$, and $T = \{5, 10\}$, we have

$$S \times T = \{(1, 5), (1, 10), (2, 5), (2, 10)\}$$

Counting Methods

Sampling and Counting

There are many instances in the application of probability theory where it is desirable and necessary to count the outcomes in the sample space and the outcomes in an event. For example, in the special instance of a uniform probability function, the probability of an event is known when the number of outcomes that comprises the event is known; that is, as soon as the number of outcomes in the subset that defines the event is known.

If a sample space $S = \{e_1, e_2, \ldots, e_n\}$ contains n simple events, $E_i = \{e_i\}$, $i = 1, 2, \ldots, n$, then using a uniform probability model, we assign probability $\dfrac{1}{n}$ for each point in S; that is, $P(E_i) = \dfrac{1}{n}$. To determine the probability of an event A, we need,

1. The number of possible outcomes in S.
2. The number of outcomes in the event A.

   Then,

   $$P(A) = \frac{\text{number of outcomes correspondings to } A}{\text{number of possible outcomes in } S}$$

Frequently, it may be possible to enumerate fully all the sample space points in S and then count how many of these correspond to the event A. For example, if a class consists of just three students, and the instructor always calls on each student once and only once during each class, then if we label the students 1, 2, and 3, we can easily enumerate the points in S as

$$S = \{(1, 2, 3), (1, 3, 2), (2, 1, 3), (2, 3, 1), (3, 1, 2), \\ (3, 2, 1)\}$$

Assume that the instructor chooses a student at random, it would seem reasonable to adopt a uniform probability model and assign probability $\dfrac{1}{6}$ to each point in S. If A is the event that John is selected last, then

John = 3

$$A = \{(1, 2, 3), (2, 1, 3)\}$$
$$P(A) = \frac{2}{6} = \frac{1}{3}$$

It would be most unusual for a class to consist of only three students. The total enumeration of the sample space becomes more complicated even if we increase the class size to 6 students. To deal with these situations in which the sample space contains a large number of points, we need to have an understanding of basic counting or combinatorial procedures.

The Fundamental Principle of Counting

Suppose a man has four ways to travel from New York to Chicago, three ways to travel from Chicago to Denver, and six ways to travel from Denver to San Francisco, how many ways can he go from New York to San Francisco via Chicago and Denver?

If we let A_1 be the event "going from New York to Chicago," A_2 be the event "going from Chicago to Denver," and A_3 be the event "going from Denver to San Francisco," then because there are four ways to accomplish A_1, 3 ways to accomplish A_2, and 6 ways to accomplish A_3, the number of routes the man can follow is

$$(4) \times (3) \times (6) = 72$$

We can now generalize these results and state them formally as the fundamental principle or multiplication rule of counting.

If an operation consists of a sequence of k separate steps of which the first can be performed in n_1 ways, followed by the second in n_2 ways, and so on until the kth can be performed in n_k ways, then the operation consisting of k steps can be performed in

$$n_1 \times n_2 \times n_3 \ldots \ldots n_k$$

ways.

Tree Diagrams

A tree diagram is a device that can be used to list all possible outcomes of a sequence of experiments where each experiment can occur only in a finite number of ways.

The following tree diagram list the different ways three different flavors of ice cream, chocolate (*c*), vanilla (*v*), and strawberry (*s*), can be arranged on a cone, with no flavor used more than once.

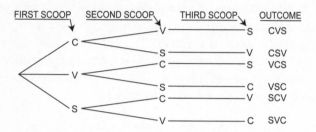

The tree starts with three branches in the first stage, representing the three possibilities for first stage. For each outcome at the first stage, there are two possibilities at the second stage. Then, for each outcome in the second stage, there is only one possibility at the third stage. Consequently, there are 3 × 2 × 1, or 6, different arrangement.

Using a tree diagram, we can develop the sample space for an experiment consisting of tossing a fair coin and then rolling a die as follows:

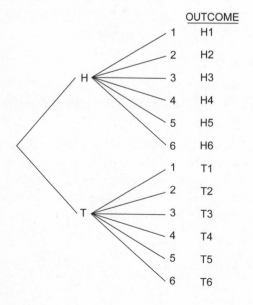

Factorial Notation

Consider how many ways the owner of an ice cream parlor can display ten ice cream flavors in a row along the front of the display case. The first position can be filled in ten ways, the second position in 9 ways, and the third position in 8 ways, and so on. By the fundamental counting principle, there are

$$(10) \times (9) \times (8) \times (7) \times \ldots \times (2) \times (1)$$

or 3,628,800 ways to display the flavor. If there are 16 flavors, there would be $(16) \times (15) \times (14) \times \ldots \times (3) \times (2) \times (1)$ ways to arrange them. In general

If *n* is a natural number, then the product from 1 to *n* inclusive is denoted by the symbol *n*! (read as "*n* factorial" or as "factorial *n*") and is defined as

$$n! = n(n - 1)(n - 2) \ldots (3)(2)(1)$$

where *n* is a positive natural number.

There are two fundamental properties of factorials:

1. By definition, $0! = 1$

2. $n(n - 1)! = n!$

   For example, $(6)(5!) = 6!$

Counting Procedures Involving Order Restrictions (Permutations)

Suppose a class consists of 5 students. The instructor calls on exactly three students out of the 5 students during each class period to answer three different questions. To apply the uniform probability model, we need to know how many points there are in the sample space *S*. Note that each point in *S* is an ordered triplet; that is, the point (3, 5, 1) is different from the point (5, 3, 1). The same three people were called upon to respond, but the order of response is different. Such arrangement is referred to as a permutation.

A permutation of a number of objects is any arrangement of these objects in a definite order.

For example if a class consists of 3 students, then there are 3 × 2 × 1 = 6 ways in which the students might be called upon.

In general, if the class had consisted of n students and all of them had been called upon, then the responses could have taken place in

$$n(n-1)(n-2)\ldots(3)(2)(1)$$

ways. Hence,

The number of permutations of a set of n distinct objects, taken all together, is $n!$

In our example of the class consisting of five students, only three students were to be called on to respond; that is, we are interested in an ordered subset.

An arrangement of r distinct objects taken from a set of n distinct objects, $r \le n$, is called a permutation of n objects taken r at a time. The total number of such orderings is denoted by nPr, and defined as

$$nPr = \frac{n!}{(n-r)!}$$

In our example, $n=5$, $r=3$,

$$_5P_3 = \frac{5!}{(5-3!)} = 5 \times 4 \times 3 = 60$$

If we have n items with r objects alike, then the number of distinct permutations taking all n at a time is

$$\frac{n!}{r!}$$

In general,

In a set of n elements having r_1 elements of one type, r_2 elements of a second type and so on to r_k element of a kth type, then the number of distinct permutations of the n elements, taken all together, is given by

$$\frac{n!}{r_1!r_2!r_3!\ldots r_k!}$$

where $\sum_{i=1}^{k} r_i = n$

For example, the number of ways a group of 10 of which 6 are females and 4 are males can line up for theatre tickets, if we are interested only in distinguishing between sexes, is given by

$$\frac{10!}{6!4!} = 210$$

Counting Procedures Not Involving Order Restrictions (Combinations)

Suppose that a class of 12 students selects a committee of 3 to plan a party. A possible committee is John, Sally, and Joe. In this situation, the order of the three is not important because the committee of John, Sally, and Joe, is the same as the committee of Sally, Joe, and John.

When choosing committee members and in other cases of selection where order is not important, we are interested in combinations, not permutations.

A subset of r objects selected without regard to order from a set of n different objects, $r \le n$, is called a combination of n objects taken r at a time. The total number of combinations of n things taken r at a time is denoted by nCr or $\binom{n}{r}$ and is defined as

$$nCr = \binom{n}{r} = \frac{n!}{r!(n-r)!}$$

In our example, the number of possible committees that could plan the party can be calculated by

$$_{12}C_3 = \binom{12}{3} = \frac{12!}{3!(12-3)!} = 220$$

A well-known triangular array in mathematics is called Pascal's triangle, the first 14 rows of which are shown below. Note that the first row is labeled "Row 0."

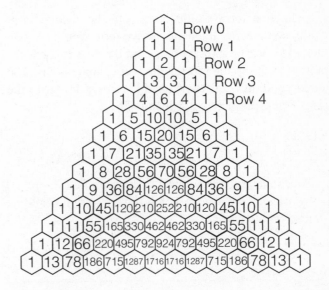

Each row contains numbers, called elements. Row 0 contains the number 1. Each row has one more element than the previous row. The first and last elements of each row contain the number 1. Each of the other elements are calculated by adding the two elements nearest to it in the previous row. As an example, in row 4, the number 6 is calculated by adding the two 3's in row 3. As another example, in row 7, there are two 21's, each of which is calculated by adding 6 and 15 from row 6. There are many applications for the pattern of numbers found in Pascal's triangle.

PROBLEM

What is the sum of the numbers in row 10 of Pascal's triangle?

SOLUTION

You could simply add the numbers 1, 10, 45, 120, ..., but one of the properties of this triangle is that the sum of the numbers in row n is 2^n. Thus, the sum of the numbers in row 10 is $2^{10} = 1024$.

PROBLEM

What is the coefficient of the fourth term of the expansion of $(x + y)^8$?

SOLUTION

The first term would be x^8 and the second term would contain x^7y. Each successive term would contain the next lowest exponent for x and the next highest exponent for y. So the fourth term would contain x^5y^3. The corresponding coefficient for this term is found in the fourth element of row 8, which is 56.

NOTE:

We could write the complete expansion for $(x + y)^8$ by using all the elements of the eighth row. It would read as follows:

$(x + y)^8 = x^8 + 8x^7y + 28x^6y^2 + 56x^5y^3 + 70x^4y^4 + 56x^3y^5 + 28x^2y^6 + 8xy^7 + y^8$.

PROBLEM

Given a group of 12 people, how many different groups of five people can be formed?

SOLUTION

Using Pascal's triangle, identify row 12. Ignore the first number (1) and then count until you reach the fifth number, which will be the correct answer 792.

NOTE:

The technique of selecting a group of five from 12 is called a combination. So, Example 3 could also be solved with the expression

$$_{12}C_5 = \frac{12!}{(5!)(7!)} = 792.$$

PROBLEM

A deck of playing cards is thoroughly shuffled and a card is drawn from the deck. What is the probability that the card drawn is the ace of diamonds?

SOLUTION

The probability of an event occurring is

$$\frac{\text{the number of ways the event can occur}}{\text{the number of possible outcomes}}$$

In our case there is one way the event can occur, for there is only one ace of diamonds and there are 52 possible outcomes (for there are 52 cards in the deck). Hence, the probability that the card drawn is the ace of diamonds is $\frac{1}{52}$.

PROBLEM

A bag contains four black and five blue marbles. A marble is drawn and then replaced, after which a second marble is drawn. What is the probability that the first is black and the second blue?

SOLUTION

Let C = event that the first marble drawn is black.

D = event that the second marble drawn is blue.

The probability that the first is black and the second is blue can be expressed symbolically:

$P(C \text{ and } D) = P(CD).$

We can apply the following theorem. If two events, A and B, are independent, then the probability that A and B will occur is

$P(A \text{ and } B) = P(AB) = P(A) \times P(B).$

Note that two or more events are said to be independent if the occurrence of one event has no effect upon the occurrence or non-occurrence of the other. In this case the occurrence of choosing a black marble has no effect on the selection of a blue marble and vice versa; since, when a marble is drawn it is then replaced before the next marble is drawn. Therefore, C and D are two independent events.

$P(CD) = P(C) \times P(D)$

$P(C) = \dfrac{\text{number of ways to choose a black marble}}{\text{number of ways to choose a marble}}$

$= \dfrac{4}{9}$

$P(D) = \dfrac{\text{number of ways to choose a blue marble}}{\text{number of ways to choose a marble}}$

$= \dfrac{5}{9}$

$P(CD) = P(C) \times P(D) = \dfrac{4}{9} \times \dfrac{5}{9} = \dfrac{20}{81}$

PROBLEM

A traffic count at a highway junction revealed that out of 5,000 cars that passed through the junction in one week, 3,000 turned to the right. Find the probability that a car will turn (A) to the right and (B) to the left. Assume that the cars cannot go straight or turn around.

SOLUTION

(A) If an event can happen in s ways and fail to happen in f ways, and if all these ways ($s + f$) are assumed to be equally likely, then the probability (p) that the event will happen is

$p = \dfrac{s}{s + f} = \dfrac{\text{successful ways}}{\text{total ways}}.$

In this case $s = 3,000$ and $s + f = 5,000$. Hence,

$p = \dfrac{3,000}{5,000} = \dfrac{3}{5}.$

(B) If the probability that an event will happen is $\dfrac{a}{b}$, then the probability that this event will not happen is $1 - \dfrac{a}{b}$. Thus, the probability that a car will not turn right, but left, is $1 - \dfrac{3}{5} = \dfrac{2}{5}$. This same conclusion can also be arrived at using the following reasoning:

Since 3,000 cars turned to the right, $5,000 - 3,000 = 2,000$ cars turned to the left. Hence, the probability that a car will turn to the left is

$\dfrac{2,000}{5,000} = \dfrac{2}{5}.$

Drill: Pascal's Triangle

1. Using Pascal's triangle, solve the following problem: Given a group of nine people, how many different groups of six people can be formed?

   (A) 56   (C) 84

   (B) 70   (D) 126

2. Using Pascal's triangle, solve the following problem: What is the coefficient of the fifth term of the expression $(a + b)^{11}$?

   (A) 462   (C) 252

   (B) 330   (D) 210

3. Using Pascal's triangle, solve the following problem: The sum of the numbers in Row P is 2,097,152. What is the value of P?

   (A) 24   (C) 22

   (B) 23   (D) 21

ANSWER KEY

1. (C)   3. (D)
2. (B)

Detailed Explanations of Answers

Drill: Pascal's Triangle

1. (C)

Row 9 begins with the numbers 1, 9, 36, 84, …. Ignore the first number and then count six more numbers. The number you will reach is 84.

2. (B)

Row 11 begins with the numbers 1, 11, 55, 165, …. The fifth number in this row is 330.

3. (D)

The sum of the numbers in row P is 2^P. Then 2^P = 2,097,152. Using logarithms, $(P)(\log_{10} 2) = \log_{10} 2,097,152$. Thus, $P = \dfrac{\log_{10} 2,097,152}{\log_{10} 2} = 21$.

Discrete Mathematics Sequences and Series

A sequence is a function whose domain is the set of all natural numbers. All the sequences described in this section will have a subset in the set of all real numbers as their range. It is common to let a_n represent the nth term of the sequence. For example, if

$$a_n = 10n$$

then the sequence is 10, 20, 30, 40 . . .

The sum of the first n terms of the sequence,

$$a_1, a_2, a_3, \ldots a_n,$$

is indicated by

$$a_1 + a_2 + a_3 + \ldots + a_n,$$

and the sum of these terms is called a series. The Greek letter Σ is used to represent this sum as indicated below.

$$\sum_{k=1}^{n} a_k = a_1 + a_2 + a_3 + \ldots + a_n$$

For a fixed number a and a fixed number d, the sequence

$$a, a + d, a + 2d, a + 3d, \ldots$$

is called an arithmetic sequence, and the nth term of this sequence is given by

$$a_n = a + (n - 1)d$$

The number a is called the first term and d is called the common difference. The symbol S_n is used to represent the corresponding series and

$$\sum_{k=1}^{n} a + (K - 1)d$$

$$\text{or } S_n = n \left(\frac{a_1 + a_n}{2} \right)$$

A sequence of the form

$$a, ar, ar^2, \ldots$$

is called a geometric sequence, where a is the first term and r is the common ratio. The nth term of such a sequence is

$$a_n = ar^{n-1}$$

The symbol S_n is used to represent the corresponding series and

$$S_n = \frac{a(1 - r^n)}{1 - r}.$$

Expressions of the form

$$a + ar + ar^2 \ldots$$

are called infinite geometric series. When $|r| < 1$, the sum S of the infinite geometric series exists and

$$S = \frac{a}{1 - r}.$$

PROBLEM

In an arithmetic sequence, $a_1 = 29$ and $a_8 = 78$. Find the common difference d and the sixth term a_6.

SOLUTION

The nth term in an arithmetic sequence is given by $a_n = a + (n - 1)d$ where a is the initial term and d is the common difference. Using the given information we can first find d.

$$78 = 29 + (8 - 1)d$$
$$78 = 29 + 7d$$
$$49 = 7d$$
$$7 = d$$

Thus the common difference is 7. We may now use this information to obtain a_6.

$$a_6 = 29 + (6 - 1)(7)$$
$$= 29 + 35$$
$$= 64$$

thus the sixth term is 64.

Linear Equations and Matrices

A linear equation is an equation of the form $a_1 x_1 + a_2 x_2 + \ldots + a_n x_n = b$, where $a_1, \ldots, a_n$ and b are real constants.

EXAMPLES

a) $2x + 6y = 9$
b) $x_1 + 3x_2 + 7x_3 = 5$
c) $x - 2 = 0$

Linear equations in two variables are always straight lines.

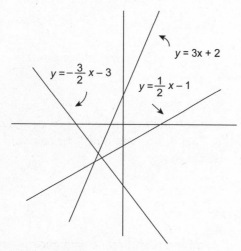

$y = 3x + 2$

$y = -\dfrac{3}{2} x - 3$

$y = \dfrac{1}{2} x - 1$

A system of linear equations is a finite set of linear equations, all of which use the same set of variables.

EXAMPLES

a) $2x_1 + x_2 + 5x_3 = 4$

   $x_2 + 3x_3 = 0$

   $7x_1 + 3x_2 + x_3 = 9$

b) $y - z = 5$

   $z = 1$

The solution of a system of linear equations is that set of real numbers which, when substituted into the set of variables, satisfies each equation in the system. The set of all solutions is called the solution set S of the system.

EXAMPLE

$y + z = 9 \qquad\qquad S = \{5, 4\}$
$z = 4$

A consistent system of linear equations has at least one solution, while an inconsistent system has no solutions.

EXAMPLES

(a) $y + z = 9 \qquad S = \{5, 4\}$ (consistent system)
   $z = 4$

Consistent System

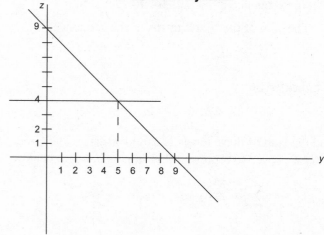

b) $x_1 + x_2 = 7 \qquad S = \varnothing$ (inconsistent system)
   $x_1 = 3$
   $x_1 - x_2 = 7$

Inconsistent System

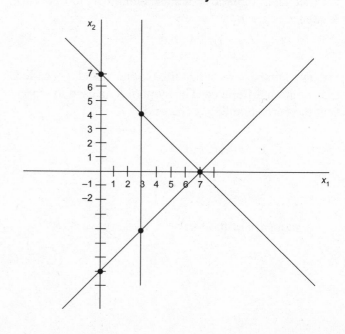

Every system of linear equations has either one solution, no solution, or infinitely many solutions.

A system of linear equations with infinitely many solutions is called a dependent system of linear equations.

The augmented matrix for a system of linear equations is the matrix of the form:

$$\begin{bmatrix} a_{11} & a_{12} & \dots & a_{1n} & b_1 \\ a_{21} & a_{22} & \dots & a_{2n} & b_2 \\ & \vdots & & & \\ a_{m1} & a_{m2} & \dots & a_{mn} & b_m \end{bmatrix}$$

where a_{ij} represents each coefficient in the system and b_i represents each constant in the system.

EXAMPLE

$$\begin{array}{rcl} x_1 + 6x_2 - 2x_3 &=& 4 \\ 3x_1 \quad\quad + x_3 &=& 7 \\ 5x_1 - 3x_2 + x_3 &=& 0 \end{array} \quad \begin{bmatrix} 1 & 6 & -2 & 4 \\ 3 & 0 & 1 & 7 \\ 5 & -3 & 1 & 0 \end{bmatrix}$$

Elementary row operations are operations on the rows of an augmented matrix, which are used to reduce that matrix to a more solvable form. These operations are the following:

a) Multiply a row by a non-zero constant.

b) Interchange two rows.

c) Add a multiple of one row to another row.

PROBLEM

By forming the augmented matrix and row reducing, determine the solutions of the following system:

$$\begin{array}{rcl} 2x - y + 3z &=& 4 \\ 3x \quad\quad + 2z &=& 5 \\ -2x + y + 4z &=& 6 \end{array}$$

SOLUTION

The augmented matrix of the system is:

$$\begin{bmatrix} 2 & -1 & 3 & 4 \\ 3 & 0 & 2 & 5 \\ -2 & 1 & 4 & 6 \end{bmatrix}.$$

Add the first row to the third row:

$$\begin{bmatrix} 2 & -1 & 3 & 4 \\ 3 & 0 & 2 & 5 \\ 0 & 0 & 7 & 10 \end{bmatrix}$$

This is the augmented matrix of:

$$\begin{array}{rcl} 2x - y + 3z &=& 4 \\ 3x \quad\quad + 2z &=& 5 \\ 7z &=& 10 \end{array}$$

The system has been sufficiently simplified now so that the solution can be found.

From the last equation we have $z = \dfrac{10}{7}$. Substituting this value into the second equation and solving for x gives $x = \dfrac{5}{7}$. Substituting $x = \dfrac{5}{7}$ and $z = \dfrac{10}{7}$ into the first equation and solving for y yields $y = \dfrac{12}{7}$. The solution to the system is, therefore,

$$x = \frac{5}{7}, y = \frac{12}{7}, z = \frac{10}{7}.$$

PROBLEM

Solve the following linear system of equations:

$$\begin{array}{rcl} 2x + 3y - 4z &=& 5 \\ -2x \quad\quad + z &=& 7 \\ 3x + 2y + 2z &=& 3 \end{array}$$

SOLUTION

The augmented matrix for the system is:

$$\begin{bmatrix} 2 & 3 & -4 & 5 \\ -2 & 0 & 1 & 7 \\ 3 & 2 & 2 & 3 \end{bmatrix}$$

which can be reduced by using the following sequence of row operations:

Add the first row to the second row.

$$\begin{bmatrix} 2 & 3 & -4 & 5 \\ 0 & 3 & -3 & 12 \\ 3 & 2 & 2 & 3 \end{bmatrix}$$

Divide the first row by 2 and the second row by 3.

$$\begin{bmatrix} 1 & \frac{3}{2} & -2 & \frac{5}{2} \\ 0 & 1 & -1 & 4 \\ 3 & 2 & 2 & 3 \end{bmatrix}$$

Add -3 times the first row to the third row.

$$\begin{bmatrix} 1 & \frac{3}{2} & -2 & \frac{5}{2} \\ 0 & 1 & -1 & 4 \\ 0 & -\frac{5}{2} & 8 & -\frac{9}{2} \end{bmatrix}$$

Add $\dfrac{5}{10}$ times the second row to the third row.

$$\begin{bmatrix} 1 & \frac{3}{2} & -2 & \frac{5}{2} \\ 0 & 1 & -1 & 4 \\ 0 & 0 & \frac{11}{2} & \frac{11}{2} \end{bmatrix}$$

This is the augmented matrix for the system:

$$x + \frac{3}{2}y - 2z = \frac{5}{2}$$
$$y - z = 4$$
$$\frac{11}{2}z = \frac{11}{2}$$

Now the solution to this system can be easily found. From the last equation we have $z = 1$. Substituting $z = 1$ in the second equation gives $y = 5$. Next, substitute $y = 5$ and $z = 1$ into the first equation. This gives $x = -3$. Therefore, the solution to the system is $x = -3$, $y = 5$, $z = 1$.

PROBLEM

Solve the following system:

$$x + y + 2z = 9$$
$$2x + 4y - 3z = 1$$
$$3x + 6y - 5z = 0$$

SOLUTION

The augmented matrix for the system is:

$$\begin{bmatrix} 1 & 1 & 2 & 9 \\ 2 & 4 & -3 & 1 \\ 3 & 6 & -5 & 0 \end{bmatrix}.$$

It can be reduced by elementary row operations.

Add -2 times the first row to the second row and -3 times the first row to the third row.

$$\begin{bmatrix} 1 & 1 & 2 & 9 \\ 0 & 2 & -7 & -17 \\ 0 & 3 & -11 & -27 \end{bmatrix}$$

Multiply the second row by $\dfrac{1}{2}$.

$$\begin{bmatrix} 1 & 1 & 2 & 9 \\ 0 & 1 & -\frac{7}{2} & -\frac{17}{2} \\ 0 & 3 & -11 & -27 \end{bmatrix}$$

Add -3 times the second row to the third row.

$$\begin{bmatrix} 1 & 1 & 2 & 9 \\ 0 & 1 & -\frac{7}{2} & -\frac{17}{2} \\ 0 & 0 & -\frac{1}{2} & -\frac{3}{2} \end{bmatrix}$$

Multiply the third row by -2 to obtain

$$\begin{bmatrix} 1 & 1 & 2 & 9 \\ 0 & 1 & -\frac{7}{2} & -\frac{17}{2} \\ 0 & 0 & 1 & 3 \end{bmatrix}.$$

This is the augmented matrix for the system:

$$x + y + 2z = 9$$
$$y - \frac{7}{2}z = -\frac{17}{2}$$
$$z = 3$$

Solving this system gives $x = 1$, $y = 2$, and $z = 3$.

PROBLEM

For the following system, find the augmented matrix; then, by reducing, determine whether the system has a solution.

$$3x - y + z = 1$$
$$7x + y - z = 6 \qquad (1)$$
$$2x + y - z = 2$$

SOLUTION

The augmented matrix for the system is

$$\begin{bmatrix} 3 & -1 & 1 & | & 1 \\ 7 & 1 & -1 & | & 6 \\ 2 & 1 & -1 & | & 2 \end{bmatrix}.$$

This can be reduced by performing the following row operations. Divide the first row by 3.

$$\begin{bmatrix} 1 & -\frac{1}{3} & \frac{1}{3} & | & \frac{1}{3} \\ 7 & 1 & -1 & | & 6 \\ 2 & 1 & -1 & | & 2 \end{bmatrix}$$

Now add -7 times the first row to the second row and -2 times the first row to the third row.

$$\begin{bmatrix} 1 & -\frac{1}{3} & \frac{1}{3} & | & \frac{1}{3} \\ 0 & \frac{10}{3} & -\frac{10}{3} & | & \frac{11}{3} \\ 0 & \frac{5}{3} & -\frac{5}{3} & | & \frac{4}{3} \end{bmatrix}$$

Divide the second row by $\frac{10}{3}$.

$$\begin{bmatrix} 1 & -\frac{1}{3} & \frac{1}{3} & | & \frac{1}{3} \\ 0 & 1 & -1 & | & \frac{11}{10} \\ 0 & \frac{5}{3} & -\frac{5}{3} & | & \frac{4}{3} \end{bmatrix}$$

Add $-\frac{5}{3}$ times the second row to the third row.

$$\begin{bmatrix} 1 & -\frac{1}{3} & \frac{1}{3} & | & \frac{1}{3} \\ 0 & 1 & -1 & | & \frac{11}{10} \\ 0 & 0 & 0 & | & -\frac{1}{2} \end{bmatrix}$$

Since the third row contains zeros in the first 3 columns, there is no solution.

Networks

A network is a system of interconnected people or things (for example, a system of interconnected computers). It can be system of intersecting lines or channels such as a railroad network or a network of canals. Networks can be graphed using vertices and lines. The vertices represent the person or thing, while the lines represent a connection.

EXAMPLE

An executive at a big company wants to communicate with her manager. The manager wants to be able to communicate with his two employees. The two employees can communicate with each other but *not* with the executive. Draw a graph of a network that satisfies these requirements.

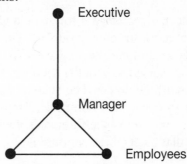

The executive, on top, can communicate with her manager. The manager can communicate with his two employees. The two employees can communicate with each other but not with the executive.

EXAMPLE

Long Line Railroad Company is planning to build a railroad line from Greenville to Stuckyville, then on to Mountain View. Close to Stuckyville, there are three other towns. Long Line Railroad would like Stuckyville to be directly connected to the other three towns. Construct a network that meets these conditions.

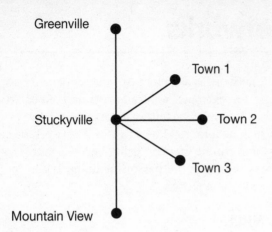

This network meets the conditions described. The railroad line can travel from Greenville to Stuckyville, then on to Mountain View. Also, Stuckyville is connected to the other three towns.

PROBLEM

An architect, a secretary, a foreman, and a carpenter all work at a construction company. Their computers are connected in the following way. The architect's computer is connected to both the secretary's computer and the foreman's computer. The secretary's computer is connected to everyone's computer. The carpenter's computer is connected to the foreman's. Draw a graph of a network that meets these conditions.

SOLUTION

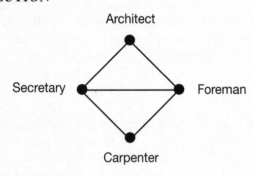

Algorithms

An algorithm is a set of rules that always leads to the correct solution. There are different algorithms for different things.

EXAMPLE

The algorithm for calculating the total cost of an item at a store goes like this:

1. Multiply the price of the item times the sales tax expressed in decimal form to find the amount of the tax.

2. Add the sales tax to the price of the item to find the total cost.

EXAMPLE

The prime factorization of a number is when a number is expressed in terms of prime numbers. A prime number is a number that can only be divided evenly by one and itself. A factor is a number that can be divided evenly into another number. The process of prime factorization is breaking down a number into parts. The algorithm for finding the prime factored form of a number goes like this.

1) Divide the number by 2 as many times as possible.

2) Divide the remaining factor by 3 as many times as possible.

3) Divide the remaining factor by 5 as many times as possible.

4) Divide the remaining factor by 7 as many times as possible.

5) Continue factoring using prime numbers (for example, 11, 13, 17, 19, …) until the number is expressed in terms of all its prime factors.

Using this algorithm, find the prime factored form of the number 2,520.

$$2{,}520 \div 2 = 1{,}260$$

$$1{,}260 \div 2 = 630$$

$$630 \div 2 = 315$$

$$315 \div 3 = 105$$

$$105 \div 3 = 35$$

$$35 \div 5 = 7$$

The prime factored form of 2,520 is $2 \times 2 \times 2 \times 3 \times 3 \times 5 \times 7$.

Flow Charts

A flow chart is a graphical representation of the successive steps in solving a problem. A flow chart uses symbols connected by lines.

EXAMPLE

This flow chart shows the percent income tax paid depending upon how much income a person earned last year. Find the percent income tax for someone who earned $40,000 last year.

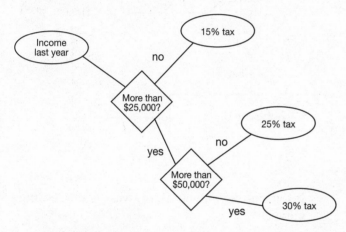

Consulting the flow chart, we see that a person with an income of $40,000 last year would have to pay 25% in income tax.

PROBLEM

This flow chart shows a series of mathematical operations. If the starting number is 100, what is the result?

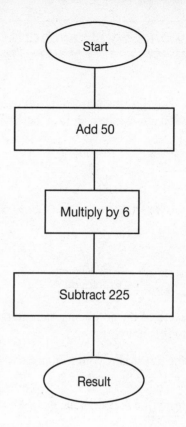

SOLUTION

Start with 100

$$100 + 50 = 150$$

$$150 \times 6 = 900$$

$$900 - 225 = 675$$

The result is 675.

Drill: Networks and Flowcharts

1. Look at the following network involving formal communication among the people at the *XYZ* company.

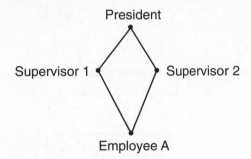

Which one of the following statements would *not* apply to this network?

(A) The President communicates with Supervisor 1 and Supervisor 2.

(B) Employee A communicates with Supervisor 2.

(C) Supervisor 1 communicates with Employee A.

(D) Supervisor 1 communicates with Supervisor 2.

2. Look at the following network involving the paths that Susan can take in traveling from her home to the Post Office.

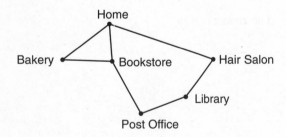

Which one of the following is *not* a path that she can use?

(A) Home – Bookstore – Hair Salon – Library– Post Office

(B) Home – Bakery – Bookstore – Post Office

(C) Home – Hair Salon – Library – Post Office

(D) Home – Bookstore – Post Office

3. Look at the following flowchart that shows a series of mathematical operations for given starting number.

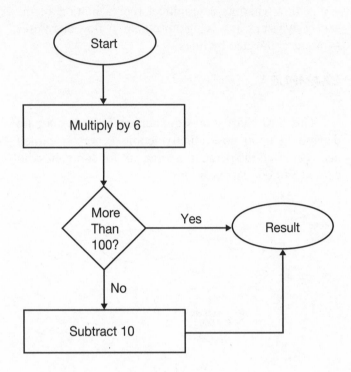

If the starting number is 15, what is the resulting number?

(A) 75   (C) 85

(B) 80   (D) 90

4. Look at the following flowchart that illustrates the monthly property tax that a homeowner must pay, based on the value of his/her home.

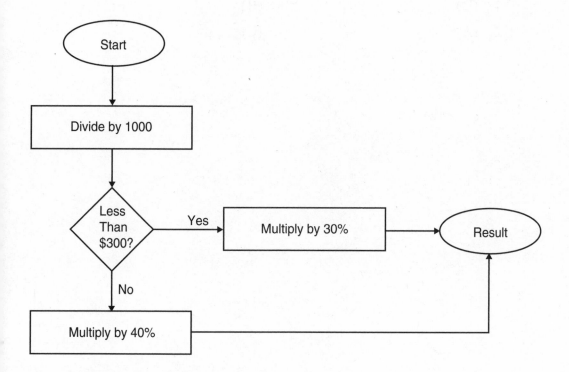

If the value of a home is $280,000, what is the monthly property tax?

(A) $112

(B) $98

(C) $84

(D) $70

ANSWER KEY

1. (D)

2. (A)

3. (B)

4. (C)

Detailed Explanations of Answers

Drill: Networks and Flowcharts

1. (D)

There is no line segment between Supervisors 1 and 2. Therefore these two supervisors do not communicate with each other.

2. (A)

There is no line segment between the Bookstore and the Hair Salon.

3. (B)

The first step is to multiply 15 by 6, which yields 90. Since 90 is not more than 100, the next step is to subtract 10 from 90 to get the result of 80.

4. (C)

The first step is to divide $280,000 by 1000 to get $280. Since this amount is less than $300, the next step is to multiply $280 by 30% to get the result of $84.

Mathematical Reasoning, Proof, Connections

Basic Concepts of Logic

Sentences

Logic is concerned with declarative sentences that are unambiguous and definite, and either true or false (though we may not know which).

Truth Values

There are two truth values: Truth and Falsity.

Every sentence to which standard logic applies has exactly one of the two truth values (that is, is either true or false, but not both). No sentence can be both true and false.

Arguments

An *argument* is a set of sentences, one of which is the *conclusion*. The remaining sentences are the *premises* of the argument, where the *premises* are taken to present evidence or reasons in support of the *conclusion*.

Conclusion-Indicator Words

To identify arguments in a text or conversation, it is important to understand what function each sentence in the discourse is performing. English offers some "indicator words" as clues to help identify what function sentences are serving. These serve only as a guide and do not guarantee that an argument is present. (This is because these words, like most words of English, have several different meanings.)

Conclusion-indicator words include: *therefore, thus, hence, so, consequently, it follows that.*

Premise-Indicator words

Premise-indicator words include: *since, because, for, given that, inasmuch as, for the reason that, on account of.*

Evaluating Arguments

Arguments may be evaluated according to a variety of criteria or standards.

One such standard is the FACT standard: Are all of the premises true? Is the data (evidence) offered in the premises actually, as a matter of fact, true? Are the reasons offered correct? Logic generally offers no help regarding the question of the truth or falsity of premises.

Logic is concerned with the LOGIC question: the evaluation of arguments in terms of the strength of support the premises provide for the conclusion. That is, logic develops standards for determining how strongly the premises, if all true, support the conclusion. This is an evaluation of how relevant the evidence or reasons given in the premises is to the claim made by the conclusion. Deductive logic formulates the most demanding standards by which to evaluate arguments.

Deductive Validity and Invalidity

An argument is (deductively) valid if and only if it is *impossible* that all its premises be true while its conclusion is false. That is, the premises of a valid argument, if they were all true, *guarantee* the truth of the conclusion; to accept all the premises and deny the conclusion would be inconsistent.

An argument is invalid if and only if it is not valid. That is, even if the premises are or were assumed (imagined) to be all true, the conclusion could still be false.

The relationship of evidential strength that premises lend to a conclusion can be seen in the following table:

The premises of a valid argument are said to entail its conclusion.

The table below summarizes these relationships between truth values of premises and conclusion and the validity and invalidity of arguments.

Premises	Conclusion	Validity
all true	true	can't tell
all true	false	invalid
one or more false	true	can't tell
one or more false	false	can't tell

Inductive Strength and Weakness

Invalid arguments may still be good arguments when evaluated by other acceptable standards. Inductive logic develops different standards by which arguments are evaluated.

An argument is *inductively strong* if and only if it is *improbable* that all its premises be true while its conclusion is false. Inductive strength is typically measured as a real number value from zero (false) to one (certain).

An argument is inductively weak if and only if it is not inductively strong.

Examples:

The following argument is invalid, but inductively strong:

Evidential Strength between Premises and Conclusion		
Example of an argument that . . .	**Valid** (The truth of the premises guarantees the truth of the conclusion.)	**Invalid** (The truth of the premises does not guarantee the truth of the conclusion.)
All true premises, true conclusion	If Chicago is in Illinois, then it is in the USA. Chicago is in Illinois. Therefore, Chicago is in the USA.	Clinton was President in 1995. Therefore, Washington was the 1st US President.
All true premises, false conclusion	**By definition of "valid," none exist**	Either Bush or Clinton have been presidents. Bush was a president. Therefore, Clinton has not been President.
One or more false premises, true conclusion	Either Reagan was a President or Bush was a Vice-President. Reagan was not a President. Therefore, Bush was a Vice President.	Bush was not a President. Therefore, Bush was a Vice President.
One or more false premises, false conclusion	Clinton was a President and Dukakis was a President. Therefore, Dukakis was a President.	Bush was not a President. Therefore, Bush was not a Vice President.

Ninety percent of restaurants in Chicago are owned by Greeks.

Lou Mitchell's is a restaurant in Chicago.

Therefore, Lou Mitchell's is owned by Greeks.

This argument is inductively strong, because given the truth of the premises, the chances are that Lou Mitchell's will be among the 90 percent of restaurants that are Greek-owned. The argument is invalid because there is some chance that Lou Mitchell's may be among the 10 percent that are not Greek-owned; so it is not *impossible* that even should the premises be true, the conclusion may still be false.

The following argument is valid:

100 percent (that is, all) of restaurants in Chicago are owned by Greeks.

Lou Mitchell's is a restaurant in Chicago.

Therefore, Lou Mitchell's is owned by Greeks.

Note that while the premises in fact are not true, if they were, the conclusion would have to be true. Also note that any percentage in the first premise less than 100 percent would give an invalid argument; as long as the percentage is greater than 0 percent, the argument has some inductive strength; as the percentage approaches 0 percent, the reason to accept the conclusion, given the evidence supplied by the premises, approaches no reason at all.

Symbolic logic is concerned only with deductive standards for evaluating arguments and with matters related to these standards.

Logical Properties of Sentences

Consistency

A sentence is *consistent* if and only if it is *possible* that it is true.

A sentence is *inconsistent* if and only if it is not consistent; that is, if and only if it is *impossible* that it is true.

Example: At least one odd number is not odd.

Logical Truth

A sentence is *logically true* if and only if it is *impossible* for it to be false; that is, the denial of the sentence is inconsistent.

Example: Either Mars is a planet or Mars is not a planet.

Logical Falsity

A sentence is *logically false* if and only if it is *impossible* for it to be true; that is, the sentence is inconsistent.

Example: Mars is a planet and Mars is not a planet.

Logical Indeterminacy (Contingency)

A sentence is *logically indeterminate* (*contingent*) if and only if it is neither logically true nor logically false.

Example: Einstein was a physicist and Pauling was a chemist.

Logical Equivalence of Sentences

Two sentences are *logically equivalent* if and only if it is *impossible* for one of the sentences to be true while the other sentence is false; that is, if and only if it is impossible for the two sentences to have different truth values.

Example: "Chicago is in Illinois and Pittsburgh is in Pennsylvania" is logically equivalent to "Pittsburgh is in Pennsylvania and Chicago is in Illinois."

Method of Proof

Logic

Definition 1

A statement is a sentence which is either true or false, but not both.

Definition 2

If a and b are statements, then a statement of the form "a and b" is called the conjunction of a and b, denoted by $a \wedge b$.

Definition 3

The disjunction of two statements *a* and *b* is shown by the compound statement "*a* or *b*," denoted by $a \vee b$.

Definition 4

The negation of a statement *q* is the statement "not *q*," denoted by $\sim q$.

Definition 5

The compound statement "if *a*, then *b*," denoted by $a \rightarrow b$, is called a conditional statement or an implication.

"If *a*" is called the hypothesis or premise of the implication, "then *b*" is called the conclusion of the implication.

Further, statement *a* is called the antecedent of the implication, and statement *b* is called the consequent of the implication.

Definition 6

The converse of $a \rightarrow b$ is $b \rightarrow a$.

Definition 7

The contrapositive of $a \rightarrow b$ is $\sim b \rightarrow \sim a$.

Definition 8

The inverse of $a \rightarrow b$ is $\sim a \rightarrow \sim b$.

Definition 9

The statement of the form "*p* if and only if *q*," denoted by $p \leftrightarrow q$, is called a biconditional statement.

Definition 10

An argument is valid if the truth of the premises means that the conclusion must also be true.

Definition 11

Intuition is the process of making generalizations on insight.

PROBLEM

Write the inverse for each of the following statements. Determine whether the inverse is true or false. (a) If a person is stealing, he is breaking the law. (b) If a line is perpendicular to a segment at its midpoint, it is the perpendicular bisector of the segment. (c) Dead men tell no tales.

SOLUTION

The inverse of a given conditional statement is formed by negating both the hypothesis and conclusion of the conditional statement.

(a) The hypothesis of this statement is "a person is stealing;" the conclusion is "he is breaking the law." The negation of the hypothesis is "a person is not stealing." The inverse is "if a person is not stealing, he is not breaking the law."

The inverse is false, since there are more ways to break the law than by stealing. Clearly, a murderer may not be stealing but he is surely breaking the law.

(b) In this statement, the hypothesis contains two conditions: (1) the line is perpendicular to the segment; and (2) the line intersects the segment at the midpoint. The negation of (statement a *and* statement b) is (not statement a *or* not statement b). Thus, the negation of the hypothesis is "The line is not perpendicular to the segment or it doesn't intersect the segment at the midpoint." The negation of the conclusion is "the line is not the perpendicular bisector of a segment."

The inverse is "if a line is not perpendicular to the segment or does not intersect the segment at the midpoint, then the line is not the perpendicular bisector of the segment."

In this case, the inverse is true. If either of the conditions holds (the line is not perpendicular; the line does not intersect at the midpoint), then the line cannot be a perpendicular bisector.

(c) This statement is not written in if-then form, which makes its hypothesis and conclusion more difficult to see. The hypothesis is implied to be "the man is dead"; the conclusion is implied to be "the man tells no tales." The inverse is, therefore, "If a man is not dead, then he will tell tales."

The inverse is false. Many witnesses to crimes are still alive but they have never told their stories to the police, either out of fear or because they didn't want to get involved.

Basic Principles, Laws, and Theorems

1. Any statement is either true or false. (The law of the Excluded Middle)

2. A statement cannot be both true and false. (The Law of Contradiction)

3. The converse of a true statement is not necessarily true.

4. The converse of a definition is always true.

5. For a theorem to be true, it must be true for all cases.

6. A statement is false if one false instance of the statement exists.

7. The inverse of a true statement is not necessarily true.

8. The contrapositive of a true statement is true and the contrapositive of a false statement is false.

9. If the converse of a true statement is true, then the inverse is true. Likewise, if the converse is false, the inverse is false.

10. Statements which are either both true or false are said to be logically equivalent.

11. If a given statement and its converse are both true, then the conditions in the hypothesis of the statement are both necessary and sufficient for the conclusion of the statement.

If a given statement is true but its converse is false, then the conditions are sufficient but not necessary for the conclusion of the statement.

If a given statement and its converse are both false, then the conditions are neither sufficient nor necessary for the statement's conclusion.

Deductive Reasoning

An arrangement of statements that would allow you to deduce the third one from the preceding two is called a syllogism. A syllogism has three parts:

The first part is a general statement concerning a whole group. This is called the major premise.

The second part is a specific statement which indicates that a certain individual is a member of that group. This is called the minor premise.

The last part of a syllogism is a statement to the effect that the general statement which applies to the group also applies to the individual. This third statement of a syllogism is called a deduction.

Example A: Properly Deduced Argument

A) Major Premise: All birds have feathers.

B) Minor Premise: An eagle is a bird.

C) Deduction: An eagle has feathers.

The technique of employing a syllogism to arrive at a conclusion is called deductive reasoning.

If a major premise which is true is followed by an appropriate minor premise which is true, a conclusion can be deduced which must be true, and the reasoning is valid. However, if a major premise which is true is followed by an inappropriate minor premise which is also true, a conclusion cannot be deduced.

Example B: Improperly Deduced Argument

A) Major Premise: All people who vote are at least 18 years old.

B) Improper Minor Premise: Jane is at least 18.

C) Illogical Deduction: Jane votes.

The flaw in example B is that the major premise stated in A makes a condition on people who vote, not on a person's age. If statements B and C are interchanged, the resulting three-part deduction would be logical.

Indirect Proof

Indirect proofs involve considering two possible outcomes—the result we would like to prove and its negative—and then showing, under the given hypothesis, that a contradiction of prior known theorems, postulates, or definitions is reached when the negative is assumed.

Postulate 1

A proposition contradicting a true proposition is false.

Postulate 2

If one of a given set of propositions must be true, and all except one of those propositions have been proved to be false, then this one remaining proposition must be true.

The method of indirect proof may be summarized as follows:

Step 1. List all the possible conclusions.

Step 2. Prove all but one of those possible conclusions to be false (use Postulate 1 given).

Step 3. The only remaining possible conclusion is proved true according to Postulate 2.

• EXAMPLE

When attempting to prove that in a scalene triangle the bisector of an angle cannot be perpendicular to the opposite side, one method of solution could be to consider the two possible conclusions:

1) the bisector can be perpendicular to the opposite side, or

2) the bisector cannot be perpendicular to the opposite side.

Obviously, one and only one of these conclusions can be true; therefore, if we can prove that all of the possibilities, except one, are false, then the remaining possibility must be a valid conclusion. In this example, it can be proven that, for all cases, the statement which asserts that the bisector of an angle of a scalene triangle can be perpendicular to the opposite side is false. Therefore, the contradicting possibility—the bisector cannot be perpendicular to the opposite side—is in fact true.

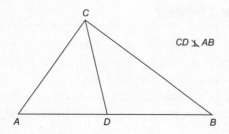

$CD \perp AB$

PROBLEM

Prove, by indirect method, that if two angles are not congruent, then they are not both right angles.

SOLUTION

Indirect proofs involve considering two possible outcomes, the result we would like to prove and its negative, and then showing, under the given hypothesis, that a contradiction of prior known theorems, postulates, or definitions is reached when the negative is assumed.

In this case, the outcomes can be that the two angles are not right angles or that the two angles are right angles. Assume the negative of what we want to prove—that the two angles are right angles.

The given hypothesis in this problem is that the two angles are not congruent. A previous theorem states that all right angles are congruent. Therefore, the conclusion we have assumed true leads to a logical contradiction. As such, the alternative conclusion must be true. Therefore, if two angles are not congruent, then they are not both right angles.

Inductive Reasoning

Inductive reasoning is a method of reasoning by which one draws a conclusion or generalization based on a pattern of specific cases. Observing a well-defined pattern can lead us to predict an answer for the unknown portion of the pattern.

For example, observing the numbers 2, 5, 8, 11, . . ., we find that a pattern is defined based on a difference of 3 between each two consecutive numbers. Extrapolating this pattern, we can conclude that the number immediately following 11 is $11 + 3 = 14$.

In mathematics, we use the following steps as the general method of inductive reasoning.

Let $P(n)$ be a statement or proposition, where n is a positive integer.

Try to verify that $P(1)$ is a true statement. That is, replace n with 1 in the given statement or proposition to see whether the statement is true or false. If the statement is true, assume that it is also true for all the following values of n, up to k. That is, assume that $P(n)$ is true for $n = k$.

Next, using the true statements $P(1)$ and $P(k)$, try to verify that $P(n)$ is true for $n = k + 1$ as well. If you succeed in verifying this step, you can claim that the statement or proposition $P(n)$ is true for all integer values of n.

PROBLEM

> Prove by mathematical induction that
> $1 + 7 + 13 + \ldots + (6n - 5) = n(3n - 2)$.

SOLUTION

Denote $1 + 7 + 13 + \ldots + (6n - 5)$ by $P(n)$.

So, (1) $P(n) = 1 + 7 + 13 + \ldots + (6n - 5)$

Step 1. Check the statement to see whether it is true for $n = 1$. To do so, simply replace n with 1 in the given statement.

(2) $P(1) = [6(1) - 5] = 1[3(1) - 2]$

Computing both sides of (2) indicates the statement is true for $n = 1$.

Step 2. Assume that the statement is true for $n = k$. This means that

(3) $P(k) = 1 + 7 + 13 + \ldots + (6k - 5) = k(3k - 2)$.

Step 3. Now, try to prove that the statement is true for $n = k + 1$ as well. To do so, add $6k + 1$ to the right side equation in (3).

(4) $1 + 7 + 13 + \ldots + (6k - 5) + 6k + 1 = k(3k - 2) + 6k + 1$

We know that

(5) $(6k - 5) + 6k + 1 = 6k - 5 + 6k + 1 - 6 + 6$

$= (6k - 5) + (6k + 6) - 5$

$= (6k - 5) + [6(k + 1) - 5]$

Next, simplify and rearrange the right side of (4) as follows

(6) $k(3k - 2) + 6k + 1 = 3k^2 - 2k + 6k + 1$

$= 3k^2 + 4k + 1$

$= 3k^2 + 3k + k + 1$

$= 3k(k + 1) + (k + 1)$

$= (k + 1)(3k + 1)$

$= (k + 1)[3(k + 1) - 2]$

$= (k + 1)(3k + 3 - 2)$

$= (k + 1)[3(k + 1) - 2]$

Placing the final results obtained through (5) and (6) into (4), we get

(7) $1 + 7 + 13 + \ldots + (6k - 5) + [6(k + 1) - 5]$

$= k(3k - 2) + (k + 1)[3(k + 1) - 2]$.

That is, $P(n)$ is true for $n = k + 1$.

Defined and Undefined Terms: Axioms, Postulates, and Assumptions; Theorems and Corollaries

To build a logical system of mathematics, the first step is to take a known and then move to what is not known. The terms which we will accept as known are called undefined terms. We accept certain basic terms as undefined, since their definition would of necessity include other undefined terms. Examples of some important undefined terms with characteristics that you must know are:

A) Set: The sets we will be concerned with will have clearly defined characteristics.

B) Point: Although we represent points on paper with small dots, a point has no size, thickness, or width. A point is denoted by a capital letter.

C) Line: A line is a series of adjacent points which extends indefinitely. A line can be either curved or straight; however, unless otherwise stated, the term "line" refers to a straight line. A line is denoted by listing two points on the line and drawing a line with arrows on top, i.e., $\overleftrightarrow{AB}$.

D) Plane: A plane is the collection of all points lying on a flat surface which extends indefinitely in all directions. Imagine holding a record cover in a room and imagine that the record cover divides the entire room. Remember that a plane has no thickness.

We use these undefined terms to construct defined terms so we can describe more sophisticated expressions.

Necessary characteristics of a good definition are:

A) It names the term being defined.

B) It uses only known terms or accepted undefined terms.

C) It places the term into the smallest set to which it belongs.

D) It states the characteristics of the defined term which distinguish it from the other members of the set.

E) It contains the least possible amount of information.

F) It is always reversible.

Axioms, postulates, and assumptions are the statements in geometry which are accepted as true without proof, whereas theorems are the statements in geometry which are proven to be true.

A corollary is a theorem that can be deduced easily from another theorem or from a postulate.

In this text, the term postulate is used exclusively, instead of axiom or assumption.

Postulate 1

A quantity is equal to itself (reflexive law).

Postulate 2

If two quantities are equal to the same quantity, they are equal to each other (transitive law).

Postulate 3

If a & b are any quantities, and $a = b$, then $b = a$ (symmetric law).

Postulate 4

The whole is equal to the sum of its parts.

Postulates 5

If equal quantities are added to equal quantities, the sums are equal quantities.

Postulate 6

If equal quantities are subtracted from equal quantities, the differences are equal quantities.

Postulate 7

If equal quantities are multiplied by equal quantities, the products are equal quantities.

Postulate 8

If equal quantities are divided by equal quantities (not 0), the quotients are equal quantities.

Postulates 9

There exists one and only one straight line through any two distinct points.

Postulate 10

Two straight lines can intersect at only one point.

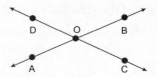

PROBLEM

In the figure shown, the measure of ∢DAC equals the measure of ∢EAC and the measure of ∢1 equals the measure of ∢2. Show that the measure of ∢3 equals the measure of ∢4.

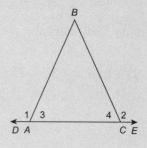

SOLUTION

This proof will require the subtraction postulate, which states that if equal quantities are subtracted from equal quantities, the differences are equal.

Given: $\angle DAC \cong \angle ECA$, $\angle 1 \cong \angle 2$

Prove: $\angle 3 \cong \angle 4$

Statement	Reason
1. $m\angle DAC = m\angle ECA$ $\quad$ $m\angle 1 = m\angle 2$	1. Given.
2. $m\angle DAC - m\angle 1 =$ $\quad m\angle ECA - m\angle 2$	2. Subtraction Postulate.
3. $m\angle 3 = m\angle 4$	3. Substitution Postulate.

Mathematics as Communication

The teacher has knowledge of the nature of mathematics as a form of communication and is able to apply this knowledge to provide meaningful instruction to the student.

- Identify statements that correctly communicate mathematical definitions or concepts.

- Interpret written presentations of mathematics.

- Select or interpret appropriate concrete examples, pictorial illustrations, and symbolic representations in developing mathematical concepts.

It is necessary for students, parents, and teachers to understand that mathematics is a means of communication, complete with its own syntax, grammar, dialects, and slang. A simple and common rule that many math teachers share is the translation of the word 'is' into '=' when teaching students to decode word problems. This is a useful piece of information but it is just a very small example of what it means to communicate using mathematics. Although mathematics is indeed a language in which symbols can be translated into nouns and verbs and equations into sentences, it is also pictures, graphs, proofs, diagrams, and abstractions. Teachers must appreciate and understand the complexity and importance of mathematical language and language about mathematics. Moreover, being able to effectively communicate about and communicate with mathematics allows teachers to reach more students in more meaningful ways.

Defining Objects and Concepts in Mathematics

One of the most attractive and yet daunting characteristics of mathematics is that the rules and objects used in doing math in Moscow are the same as in Singapore or in Kigali or in Miami. The emphases in curricula may differ and the styles of teaching may reflect different cultural norms but a *square* in London must also be a *square* in New Delhi. Therefore, a mathematics teacher should be knowledgeable of the necessary and sufficient conditions required to define mathematical objects and concepts and be careful in the sharing of this knowledge with students.

Of key importance is the difference between descriptions and definitions. A description may in its fullness accidentally include enough information to define a mathematical object but will likely contain information that is not essential and may lack information that is. A good definition in mathematics provides the information that is necessary to distinguish one object or concept from another—no more and no less. In the table below are some likely 'definitions' of a square along with an evaluation of each.

Many advocates of education reform, including the *National Council of Teachers of Mathematics*, suggest that teachers introduce content-related jargon after students have developed a need for the term in order to make communication about the problem that they are solving or the idea that they are exploring more coherent. This is quite different from the tradition of providing students with a list of terms and definitions at the start of each chapter or section. However, regardless of instructional strategy, mathematics teachers need to ensure that the definitions students develop or work with are good ones.

Possible Definition of a Square

Definitions	Comments
A shape with four right angles.	Does not contain sufficient information to determine that the shape is a quadrilateral or the necessary information to distinguish the shape from a rectangle. This is not an adequate definition.
A four-sided quadrilateral with opposite sides parallel, all sides congruent, and four right angles.	Although accurate the definition is unwieldy and contains redundant and, therefore, unnecessary information. This is not a good definition.
A quadrilateral with congruent sides and four right angles.	Contains the necessary and sufficient information to distinguish a shape as square or not a square. This is a good definition.

The Language of Mathematics

Along with a careful approach to defining terms and concepts, teachers of mathematics should be accurate and precise in their understanding and use of language when talking or writing about math. Beyond being able to recite definitions, axioms, and formulas, teachers need to have a working knowledge of mathematical jargon. Teachers need to understand and be able to use terms like *at least one, direct variation, rate of change, if and only if, or mutually exclusive*. It is this ability that will help tie one mathematical concept to another. Also, teachers need to recognize the difference between mathematical terminology, like *rate of change*, and mathematical slang, such as *rise over run*. The use of mathematical slang is not necessarily a bad thing but meaning and understanding are more important than expedient turns of phrase.

Beyond Words

In addition to using concise mathematical language, a skilled mathematics teacher often uses analogies and concrete examples to illustrate ideas or to help students make connections. Physical representations, even if they are approximations to the mathematical ideal, are a powerful tool in engaging minds. A good example is the concept of *slope*. Math teachers commonly use a hill or a flight of stairs as a model and then equate the slope of a line with the *steepness* of the model. Physical experiences of doing mathematics or observing mathematical constructs afford students with an immediacy of experience that often goes beyond words. The same is true for pictorial representations of an idea. For example, Leonardo da Vinci's anatomical sketch *Vitruvian Man* is great for the study of proportions or a guided discovery of the golden mean.

Although an effective mathematics teacher will choose appropriate physical and pictorial examples, the careful teacher should ensure that student understanding is rooted in the mathematics. The teacher needs to be sure that the learner can go beyond the model or representation to use his or her mathematical knowledge of the concept in a meaningful way. Being able to compare slope to steepness is valuable but if the student can not calculate the slope of a line—or the steepness of a flight of stairs—then the mathematics has been lost.

Finally, it is important that teachers foster this attention to the language of mathematics among their students. Carelessness or ambiguity in language is a good indicator of insufficient understanding.

Mathematical Connections

The teacher understands the connections within the structure of mathematics and is able to use those connections to further student understanding as well as provide more avenues of access to mathematics ideas.

- Identify equivalent representations of the same concept or procedure (e.g., graphical, algebraic, verbal, numeric).

- Interpret relationships between mathematical topics (e.g., multiplication as repeated addition, powers as repeated multiplication).

- Interpret descriptions, diagrams, and representations of arithmetic operations.

Mental Connections

The study of mathematics has developed over several millennia into ever more specialized fields. In our public schools, the distinctions are being made even at the middle and elementary school levels but are most pronounced in high schools where students receive mathematics instruction in year-long doses of algebra, geometry, or calculus. This is advantageous with regard to course scheduling and high mobility rates among students but it neglects the interconnectedness of mathematics as a whole and limits student exploration of the field. An effective mathematics teacher should have knowledge of these connections and use them to give students a more comprehensive picture of mathematics.

Using these *mathematical* connections, teachers will be able to give students more chances to make mental connections to multiple ideas resulting in an increase in retention and more depth in understanding. Furthermore, teachers that understand these links in the underlying structure of mathematics are better able to make meaningful long-term instructional and curricular plans by using already mastered concepts to develop new ones.

Equivalent Representations

A good test for depth of understanding of any topic is a person's ability to communicate about the subject in multiple ways. Teachers should use several different but equivalent representations of a concept or procedure to build mathematical understanding and encourage flexible thinking. For example, in creating a lesson on linear relationships, a teacher can have students a) collect and organize data using a chart or table, b) explore the data using graphs or pictograms, c) analyze the graphs for more information, d) develop a symbolic model for the phenomenon and e) write an evaluation of the experiment and a summary of conclusions. Throughout the process, the teacher needs to reinforce the concept of linearity as it manifests in each of the representations.

It is also essential that students learn how each representation highlights different aspects of the same idea. Numeric information draws our attention to patterns within data and the degree of the relationship between variables. Tables and charts allow us to organize data in ways that make looking for patterns easier. Graphs or pictograms afford us with a way to see trends in data as well as provide visual information that can sometimes match the actual physical behavior of objects. Written or verbal communications offer the opportunity for providing explanations or setting conditions. Symbolic representations allow us to make generalizations and explore the phenomenon under different conditions. Students should be able to determine what representation is best to highlight the periodic behavior in a pendulum or the possible permutations of a 5-letter combination.

Finally, the teacher needs to use multiple representations often enough that students become competent in selecting and constructing the most appropriate representation or representations for their needs. Students should come to see the multitude of representations as tools that they can create and then use to explore and solve concrete, real-world problems.

Relationships Between Mathematical Topics

In addition to being able to represent one idea or procedure in multiple ways, teachers must understand that topics within and between fields of mathematical study are connected. The seemingly disjointed courses of algebra and geometry are rife with connections such as the concept of linearity, the usefulness of co-ordinate systems, number sequences and the properties of geometric shapes, etc. Sometimes the connections are so important that one concept is actually defined by the other. A good example is the relationship between addition and multiplication. At the elementary level, the fact that multiplication is simply *multiple* additions helps students construct an understanding of what multiplication is and does. However, at more advanced levels this understanding can help students simplify or manipulate complex expressions.

It is also important for teachers to recognize themes and behaviors that extend throughout mathematics. For example, dilation and translation are concepts that appear in Algebra I, Geometry, and Algebra II again and again. Teachers should plan for and take advantage of the repetition.

The idea of building models from collected data is another important, ongoing theme that becomes increasingly important in the study of mathematics and its applications. Furthermore, mathematics teachers should be aware of the connections between mathematics and other fields of study. The vast majority of our students will not become theoretical mathematicians. They will become users of mathematics in the social, life, and physical sciences as well as in business, marketing, and service industries.

Representations of Arithmetic Operations

Teachers of elementary mathematics have long used base-ten blocks, multiplication rectangles, and pictograms to help students learn the basic add, subtract, multiply, and divide operations. These diagrams and representations of the basic operations can be directly transferred to the teaching of algebra.

Teachers should be able to interpret and use these models to develop procedures such as distributing through a quantity or factoring an equation. Algebra tiles can take the place of base-ten blocks and the multiplication rectangles can be set up in similar fashion to provide a model for the multiplication problem $(x + 3)(x + 1)$ or the factoring problem $3x^2 - 4x - 4$. Understanding these connections to the elementary models can help demystify many of these algebra procedures.

For in-depth explanations of the base-ten blocks and multiplication rectangles see J. A. Van de Walle's *Elementary and Middle School Mathematics: Teaching Developmentally* and for information on the use of algebra tiles see the manuals accompanying the tiles or visit one of the many dedicated sites on the internet.

Praxis II

Middle School
Mathematics Test (0069)

Practice Test 1

This test is also on CD-ROM in our interactive TestWare® for this Praxis II Assessment. We strongly recommend that you first take this exam on computer. You will then have the benefits of enforced time conditions, individual diagnostic analysis, and instant scoring.

Sample Mathematics Definitions and Formulas

NOTATION

(a, b)	$\{x: a < x < b\}$
$[a, b)$	$\{x: a \leq x < b\}$
$(a, b]$	$\{x: a < x \leq b\}$
$[a, b]$	$\{x: a \leq x \leq b\}$
gcd (m, n)	<u>greatest common divisor</u> of two integers m and n
lcm (m, n)	<u>least common multiple</u> of two integers m and n
$[x]$	<u>greatest integer</u> m such that $m \leq x$
$m \equiv k \pmod{n}$	m and k are <u>congruent modulo n</u> (m and k have the same remainder when divided by n, or equivalently, $m - k$ is a multiple of n)
f^{-1}	<u>inverse</u> of an invertible function f (<u>not</u> the same as $\dfrac{1}{f}$)
$\lim\limits_{x \to a^+} f(x)$	<u>right-hand limit</u> of $f(x)$; limit of $f(x)$ as x approaches a from the right
$\lim\limits_{x \to a^-} f(x)$	<u>left-hand limit</u> of $f(x)$; limit of $f(x)$ as x approaches a from the left
$\varnothing$	the empty set
$x \in S$	x is an element of set S
$S \subset T$	set S is a proper subset of set T
$S \subseteq T$	either set S is a proper subset of set T or $S = T$
$S \cup T$	union of sets S and T
$S \cap T$	intersection of sets S and T

DEFINITIONS

Discrete Mathematics

A relation $\Re$ on a set S is
  <u>reflexive</u> if $x \Re x$ for all $x \in S$
  <u>symmetric</u> if $x \Re y \Rightarrow y \Re x$ for all $x, y \in S$
  <u>transitive</u> if $(x \Re y$ and $y \Re z) \Rightarrow x \Re z$ for all $x, y, z \in S$
  <u>antisymmetric</u> if $(x \Re y$ and $y \Re x) \Rightarrow x = y$ for all $x, y \in S$

An <u>equivalence</u> relation is a reflexive, symmetric, and transitive relation.

FORMULAS

Sum

$$\sin(x \pm y) = \sin x \cos y \pm \cos x \sin y$$

$$\cos(x \pm y) = \cos x \cos y \mp \sin x \sin y$$

$$\tan(x \pm y) = \frac{\tan x \pm \tan y}{1 \mp \tan x \tan y}$$

Half-angle (sign depends on the quadrant of $\frac{\theta}{2}$)

$$\sin \frac{\theta}{2} = \pm \sqrt{\frac{1 - \cos \theta}{2}}$$

$$\cos \frac{\theta}{2} = \pm \sqrt{\frac{1 + \cos \theta}{2}}$$

Range of Inverse Trigonometric Functions

$\sin^{-1} x \qquad \left[-\frac{\pi}{2}, \frac{\pi}{2} \right]$

$\cos^{-1} x \qquad [0, \pi]$

$\tan^{-1} x \qquad \left(-\frac{\pi}{2}, \frac{\pi}{2} \right)$

Law of Sines

$$\frac{\sin A}{a} = \frac{\sin B}{b} = \frac{\sin C}{c}$$

Law of Cosines

$$c^2 = a^2 + b^2 - 2ab (\cos C)$$

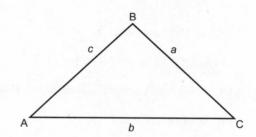

DeMoivre's Theorem

$$(\cos \theta + i \sin \theta)^k = \cos(k\theta) + i \sin (k\theta)$$

Coordinate Transformation

Rectangular (x, y) to polar (r, θ) : $r^2 = x^2 + y^2$; $\tan \theta = \frac{y}{x}$ if $x \neq 0$

Polar (r, θ) to rectangular (x, y): $x = r \cos \theta$; $y = r \sin \theta$

Distance from point (x_1, y_1) to line $Ax + By + C = 0$

$$d = \frac{|Ax_1 + By_1 + C|}{\sqrt{A^2 + B^2}}$$

Volume

Sphere with radius r: $\qquad V = \frac{4}{3}\pi r^3$

Right circular cone with height h and base of radius r: $\qquad V = \frac{1}{3}\pi r^2 h$

Right circular cylinder with height h and base of radius r: $\qquad V = \pi r^2 h$

Pyramid with height h and base of area B: $\qquad V = \frac{1}{3}Bh$

Right prism with height h and base of area B: $\qquad V = Bh$

Surface Area

Sphere with radius r: $\qquad A = 4\pi r^2$

Right circular cone with radius r and slant height s: $\qquad A = \pi rs + \pi r^2$

Differentiation

$(f(x)g(x))' = f'(x)g(x) + f(x)g'(x)$

$(f(g(x)))' = f'(g(x))g'(x)$

$\left(\dfrac{f(x)}{g(x)}\right)' = \dfrac{f'(x)g(x) - f(x)g'(x)}{(g(x))^2}$ if $g(x) \neq 0$

Integration by Parts

$\displaystyle\int u\, dv = uv - \int v\, du$

PRAXIS II: Middle School Mathematics Practice Test 1

TIME: 2 hours
       40 Multiple-choice questions (Part A)
       3 Short constructed-response questions (Part B)

Part A

> **Directions: Read each item and select the best response.**

1. The fraction

$$\dfrac{\dfrac{2}{b^2 a^2}}{\dfrac{1}{b^2 - 2b}}$$

 may be expressed more simply as

 (A) $\dfrac{2a}{b}$.
 (C) $\dfrac{2b - 4}{a^2 b}$.

 (B) $\dfrac{b - 4}{b}$.
 (D) $\dfrac{b - a}{a}$.

2. If there exist positive integers a and b such that $8a + 12b = c$, then c must be divisible by

 (A) 3.
 (C) 18.

 (B) 4.
 (D) 24.

3. For rectangle PQRS, point P is located at $(1, 0)$ and point Q is located at $(8, -3)$. What is the slope of $\overline{QR}$?

 (A) $\dfrac{7}{3}$
 (C) $-\dfrac{1}{3}$

 (B) $\dfrac{1}{3}$
 (D) $-\dfrac{7}{3}$

4. If $27^x = 9$ and $2^{x-y} = 64$, then $y =$

 (A) -5
 (C) $-\dfrac{2}{3}$

 (B) -3
 (D) $-\dfrac{16}{3}$

5. A circular region rotated 360° around its diameter as an axis generates a

 (A) cube.
 (C) cone.

 (B) cylinder.
 (D) sphere.

6. For which one of the following linear equations does the change of $+3$ units for the x value correspond to the change of $+4$ units for the associated y value?

 (A) $3x - 4y = 1$
 (C) $3x + 4y = 7$

 (B) $4x - 3y = 1$
 (D) $4x + 3y = 7$

7. Given the set $\{5, 6, 7, 8, \ldots, 20\}$, how many proper subsets are there?

 (A) 81,917
 (C) 49,152

 (B) 65,535
 (D) 32,768

8. A function is defined as $f(x) = x^2 + 2$. What is the numerical value of $3f(0) + f(-1)f(2)$?

 (A) 6
 (C) 18

 (B) 24
 (D) 36

9. If $f(x) = 3x - 5$ and $g(f(x)) = x$, then $g(x) =$

    (A) $\dfrac{x-5}{3}$.

    (B) $\dfrac{x+5}{3}$.

    (C) $\dfrac{2x+5}{3}$.

    (D) $\dfrac{x+5}{4}$.

10. In a certain geometric sequence, the third term is 8 and the sixth term is 125. What is the first term?

    (A) .064

    (B) .512

    (C) 1.28

    (D) 3.2

11. The graph below shows the relationship between temperature and sales of jackets in $1000 units. Which statement does this graph support?

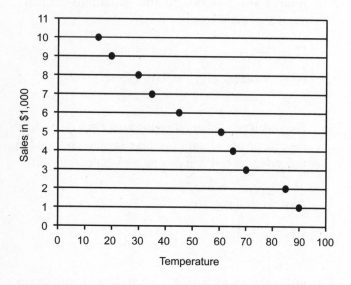

    (A) As temperature decreases, sales of jackets increase.

    (B) The sales of jackets are unchanged by temperature.

    (C) As temperature increases, sales of jackets increase.

    (D) The sales of jackets are unchanged as temperature increases.

12. In a large survey, it was discovered that 1 out of every 5 adults visits Disney World every year. If 30 adults are randomly selected, what is the probability that exactly 7 of them will visit Disney World this year?

    (A) .233

    (B) .167

    (C) .154

    (D) .125

13. A man can do a job in nine days and his son can do the same job in 16 days. They start working together. After four days the son leaves and the father finishes the job alone. How many days did the man take to finish the job alone?

    (A) $2\frac{3}{4}$

    (B) $1\frac{1}{2}$

    (C) $3\frac{3}{4}$

    (D) $2\frac{1}{4}$

14. An AP statistics teacher wants to provide her students with a concrete example of a data set that illustrates the normal curve. Select her best choice from the examples below.

    (A) The shoe sizes of the 15 students in her class.

    (B) The weight of all the 17 year olds in the country.

    (C) The number of times of one hundred that a flipped penny will land on its head.

    (D) The height of the students in the high school.

15. Given the seven numbers 26, 30, 32, 32, 28, 21, 21, which one of the following can be added to this group of numbers so that the median of all eight numbers is 27?

    (A) 23

    (B) 27

    (C) 29

    (D) 31

16. Select the shaded region which graphically represents the conditions $x \geq 0$ and $-3 < y < 3$.

(A)

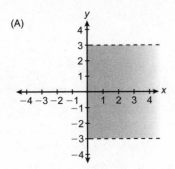

(B)

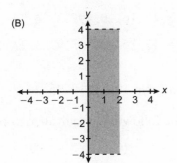

(C)

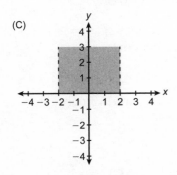

(D)

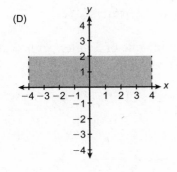

17. The volume of a cone is 72π cubic inches. If the height is 12 inches, what is the length, in inches, of the radius?

  (A) $\sqrt{6}$ (C) $\sqrt{18}$

  (B) $\sqrt{12}$ (D) $\sqrt{24}$

18. Read the graph and answer the question.

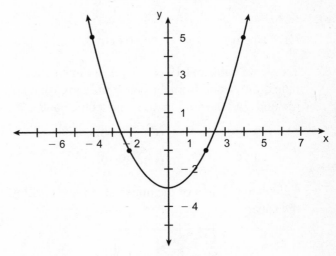

Which equation could be represented by the graph?

  (A) $y = \frac{1}{2}x^2 + 3$ (C) $y = \frac{1}{7}x^2 - 3$

  (B) $y = -\frac{1}{2}x^2 - 3$ (D) $y = -\frac{1}{2}x^2 + 3$

19. The mean of a group of 20 numbers is 9. If one number is removed, the mean of the remaining numbers is 7. What is the value of the removed number?

  (A) 16   (C) 40

  (B) 25   (D) 47

20. Solve the following quadratic equation.

$$2x^2 - 1 = 3x$$

  (A) $\dfrac{3 \pm \sqrt{17}}{2}$ (C) $\dfrac{3 \pm \sqrt{17}}{4}$

  (B) $1, \frac{1}{2}$ (D) $\dfrac{-3 \pm \sqrt{17}}{4}$

21. A rectangle is divided into three squares, as shown in the diagram. If the long side of the rectangle is equal to 12 cm, what is the area of one of the squares?

    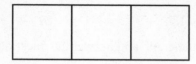

    (A) 8 cm²   (C) 32 cm²

    (B) 16 cm²   (D) 64 cm²

22. Ten white balls and 19 blue balls are in a box. If a man draws a ball from the box at random, what are the odds in favor of him drawing a blue ball?

    (A) 10:29   (C) 19:10

    (B) 19:29   (D) 29:10

23. Calculate the area of the nonshaded region within the square.

    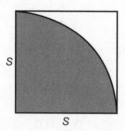

    (A) $s^2 - \pi s^2$ (C) $s^2 - \frac{\pi s^2}{4}$

    (B) $\frac{\pi s^2}{4 - s^2}$ (D) $\frac{\pi s^2}{4}$

24. The sum of the multiplicative inverses of 2 and 3 is equal to the multiplicative inverse of which number?

    (A) $\frac{2}{3}$ (C) $\frac{6}{5}$

    (B) $\frac{5}{6}$ (D) $\frac{3}{2}$

25. Robyn was completing an algebra problem in which she was solving for the variable x. At the last step, she mistakenly subtracted $\frac{1}{2}$ instead of dividing by $\frac{1}{2}$. If her answer was $x = -6$, what was the correct value of x?

    (A) −3   (C) −6.5

    (B) −5.5   (D) −11

26. If $f(x) = 2x + 4$ and $g(x) = x^2 - 2$, then $(f \circ g)(x)$, where $(f \circ g)(x)$ is a composition of functions, is

    (A) $2x^2 - 8$ (C) $2x^2$

    (B) $2x^2 + 8$ (D) $2x^3 + 4x^2 - 4x - 8$

27. Which one of the following groups of data describes the stem-and-leaf plot shown below?

    $$\begin{array}{c|cccccc} 0 & 5 & 3 & 8 & 5 & 1 \\ 1 & 2 & 6 & 9 & 9 & 9 \\ 2 & 4 & 3 & 4 & 3 \end{array}$$

    (A) 1, 3, 5, 8, 12, 16, 19, 23, 23, 24, 24

    (B) 1, 3, 5, 5, 8, 12, 16, 19, 19, 23, 24, 24

    (C) 1, 3, 5, 5, 8, 12, 16, 19, 19, 19, 23, 23, 24, 24

    (D) 1, 3, 5, 8, 12, 16, 19, 19, 19, 23, 24

28. Which one of the following is equivalent to 100^{18}?

    (A) $(100^6)^3$ (C) $100^6 \times 100^3$

    (B) $(10^6)^3$ (D) $10^6 \times 10^3$

29. At what value of x does $f(x) = \frac{x^3}{3} - x^2 - 3x + 5$ have a relative minimum?

    (A) −1 only   (C) +1 only

    (B) −1 and 3   (D) 3 only

30. $\sqrt{108} + 3\sqrt{12} - 7\sqrt{3} =$

    (A) $3 - 3\sqrt{3}$ (C) $4\sqrt{3}$

    (B) 0   (D) $5\sqrt{3}$

31. If Larry walks at the rate of 5 miles per hour, what is his rate in feet per minute?

    (A) 88   (C) 440

    (B) 300   (D) 1048

32. Suppose the length of a rectangle is doubled and the width is tripled. By what percent will the area increase?

    (A) 600%   (C) 400%

    (B) 500%   (D) 300%

33. For which one of the following box plots is the value of the median one-half the sum of the values of the first and third quartiles?

    (A)

    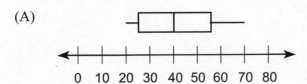

        0 10 20 30 40 50 60 70 80

    (B)

    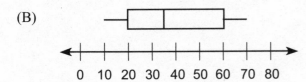

        0 10 20 30 40 50 60 70 80

    (C)

    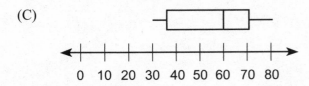

        0 10 20 30 40 50 60 70 80

    (D)

    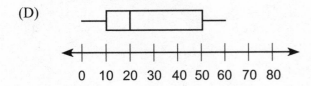

        0 10 20 30 40 50 60 70 80

34. $\int_1^e x \ln x \, dx = ?$

    (A) e   (C) $\frac{e^2+1}{4}$

    (B) $\frac{e^2-1}{2}$ (D) $\frac{e-1}{2}$

35. Consider the function $F(x)$ defined as follows:

$$F(x) = \begin{cases} -x + 3, & \text{if } x < 0 \\ 2x + 3, & \text{if } 0 < x < 3 \\ 3x, & \text{if } x > 3 \end{cases}$$

What is the value of $F(-3) + F(2) - F(4)$?

    (A) 2   (C) -1

    (B) 1   (D) -2

36. $t = -9$ is a root of the equation $t^2 + 4t - 45 = 0$. Which of the following statements is (are) correct for the equation?

    I. $t + 9$ is a factor of the equation.

    II. Division of the equation by $t - 9$ yields the other factor of the quadratic equation.

    III. $t = -5$ is another root of the equation.

    (A) I only.   (C) III only

    (B) II and III only.   (D) I, II, and III.

37. If $f(x) = 2x^2 + 4x + k$, what should the value of k be in order to have the graph of this function intersect the x-axis in only one place?

    (A) -2 (C) 1

    (B) 4   (D) 2

38. The sum of 3 angles of a triangle is 180°. The second angle is 11° less than the first angle. The third angle is twice the measure of the first angle increased by 3. If x represents the number of degrees in the first angle, which equation correctly represents the relationship among the three angles?

    (A) $x + (11 - x) + (2x + 3) = 180$

    (B) $x + (x - 11) + 2(x + 3) = 180$

    (C) $x + (x - 11) + (2x + 3) = 180$

    (D) $x + (x - 11) + (2x - 3) = 180$

39. The mean weight of 20 people in a room is 130 pounds. Bob and Diane are among these 20 people. If both of them leave the room, the mean weight will decrease by 3%. What is the mean weight, in pounds, for Bob and Diane?

    (A) 162   (C) 168

    (B) 165   (D) 171

40. A committee of 5 people is to be selected from a group of 6 men and 9 women. If the selection is made randomly, what is the probability that the committee consists of 3 men and 2 women?

    (A) $\dfrac{1}{3}$ (C) $\dfrac{1}{9}$

    (B) $\dfrac{240}{1001}$ (D) $\dfrac{1260}{3003}$

PRAXIS EXAM Part B: 3 Short Constructed-Response Questions

41. At the ACE Manufacturing Company, each employee has been receiving a 5% increase for each of the last five years. Mike, Linda, and Sandra are employees of this company.

    a.   Last year, Mike was earning an annual salary of $40,000. What is his annual salary this year?

    b.   This year, Linda is earning an annual salary of $48,000. What was her annual salary three years ago? (Round off to the nearest dollar)

    c.   Sandra is a new employee. Two years from now, she would like to earn an annual salary of at least $50,000. If the company can only promise its employees an annual increase of 3% for each of the next two years, what is the minimum annual salary that Sandra will need to earn this year? (Round off to the nearest dollar)

42. The sequence 16, 24, _____, 54, 81, ... is geometric.

    a.   What number belongs in the third position of this sequence?

    b.   What is the 40th term of this sequence? (Nearest integer)

    c.   The number 922.64 is the best approximation of which term of this sequence?

43. The weights, in pounds, of twelve women at the Golden Fitness Club are listed as: 112, 130, 115, 127, 132, 111, 126, 112, 127, 121, 127, 118

    a.   What is the mean weight?

    b.   What is the median weight?

    c.   The interquartile range is the difference between the third quartile and the first quartile. What is the interquartile range for this list of 12 weights?

Practice Test 1 Answer Key

Question Number	Correct Answer	Content Category	Question Number	Correct Answer	Content Category
1.	C	Arithmetic and Basic Algebra	23.	C	Geometry
2.	B	Arithmetic and Basic Algebra	24.	C	Arithmetic and Basic Algebra
3.	A	Geometry	25.	D	Arithmetic and Basic Algebra
4.	D	Arithmetic and Basic Algebra	26.	C	Functions
5.	D	Geometry	27.	C	Data and Statistical Concepts
6.	B	Functions	28.	A	Arithmetic and Basic Algebra
7.	B	Discrete Mathematics	29.	D	Functions
8.	B	Functions	30.	D	Arithmetic and Basic Algebra
9.	B	Functions	31.	C	Arithmetic and Basic Algebra
10.	C	Discrete Mathematics	32.	B	Geometry
11.	A	Data and Statistical Concepts	33.	A	Data and Statistical Concepts
12.	C	Probability	34.	C	Measurement
13.	A	Arithmetic and Basic Algebra	35.	B	Functions
14.	D	Data and Statistical Concepts	36.	A	Arithmetic and Basic Algebra
15.	A	Data and Statistical Concepts	37.	D	Functions
16.	A	Arithmetic and Basic Algebra	38.	C	Geometry
17.	C	Geometry	39.	B	Data and Statistical Concepts
18.	C	Geometry	40.	B	Probability
19.	D	Data and Statistical Concepts	41.	—	Short Constructed Response
20.	C	Arithmetic and Basic Algebra	42.	—	Short Constructed Response
21.	B	Measurement	43.	—	Short Constructed Response
22.	C	Probability			

Practice Test 1
Detailed Explanations of Answers

1. (C)

The fraction is a complex fraction. To simplify, we must multiply both the numerator and denominator by $b^2 - 2b$:

$$\frac{\frac{2}{a^2b^2}}{\frac{1}{b^2-2b}} \times \frac{b^2 - 2b}{b^2 - 2b} = \frac{2(b^2 - 2b)}{a^2b^2}.$$

Multiplying through in the numerator:

$$\frac{2b^2 - 4b}{a^2b^2}$$

The numerator is factored and like terms are cancelled:

$$\frac{b(2b - 4)}{a^2b^2} = \frac{2b - 4}{a^2b}$$

2. (B)

$$8a + 12b = c$$
$$4(2a + 3b) = c$$

Only 4 can be factored out.

3. (A)

The slope of $\overline{PQ} = \frac{-3-0}{8-1} = \frac{-3}{7}$. Since $\overline{QR}$ is perpendicular to $\overline{PQ}$, its slope must be the negative reciprocal of $\frac{-3}{7}$, which is $\frac{7}{3}$.

4. (D)

$$27^x = (3^3)^x = 3^{3x}$$
$$9 = 3^2$$

Thus, we have $3^{3x} = 3^2$, which implies $3x = 2$ or $x = \frac{2}{3}$ because the power function is one-to-one, which means that if

$$a^x{}_1 = a^x{}_2 \text{ then } x_1 = x_2.$$

Now $2^{x-y} = 64 = 2^6$

so $x - y = 6$ or $\frac{2}{3} - y = 6$

Hence, $y = \frac{2}{3} - 6 = -\frac{16}{3}$.

5. (D)

A sphere is formed when a circle is rotated 360° about its diameter.

6. (B)

The slope of any line is represented by the change in y values divided by the corresponding change in x values between any two points on the line. So, we need an equation where the slope of the line is $\frac{4}{3}$. By rewriting $4x - 3y = 1$ as $y = \left(\frac{4}{3}\right)(x) - \frac{1}{3}$, the slope is identified as $\frac{4}{3}$. The slopes for answer choices (A), (C), and (D) are $\frac{3}{4}$, $-\frac{3}{4}$, and $-\frac{4}{3}$, respectively.

7. (B)

The given set has $20 - 5 + 1 = 16$ elements. $2^{16} = 65,536$ total subsets, which includes the set itself. Thus, there are 65,535 proper subsets.

8. (B)

We are given $f(x) = x^2 + 2$. We must find $f(0)$, $f(-1)$, and $f(2)$.

Replacing x with zero, we obtain:

$$f(0) = 0^2 + 2 = 2$$

Similarly:

$$f(-1) = (-1)^2 + 2 = 3$$

Finally:

$$f(2) = (2)^2 + 2 = 6$$

Evaluating:

$$3f(0) + f(-1)f(2) = 3(2) + (3)(6)$$
$$= 6 + 18 = 24$$

9. (B)

$$f(x) = 3x - 5 \text{ and } g(f(x)) = x$$

We want to know what value of x (in terms of x) would cause $g(3x - 5)$ to equal x. To distinguish one x from the other, we can represent the x from $3x - 5$ with a y. This will result in:

$$3y - 5 = x$$
$$3y = x + 5$$
$$y = \frac{x + 5}{3}$$
$$g(y) = g(3x - 5) = \frac{3x - 5 + 5}{3} = x$$

Note: $g(x)$ is the inverse of $f(x)$, since $g(f(x)) = f(g(x)) = x$.

10. (C)

The general formula is $L = (a)(r)^{n-1}$ where L is the nth term, a is the first term, and r is the common ratio be-

tween terms. We can then write $8 = (a)(r)^2$ and $125 = (a)(r)^5$. Dividing the second equation by the first equation, we get $r^3 = 15.625$, so $r = 2.5$ The first term can be found by the equation $8 = (a)(2.5)^2 = 6.25a$. Thus $a = 8/6.25 = 1.28$

11. (A)

Draw a line through the set of data points. Notice that low values of temperature go with high sales, and that high-temperature values go with low sales. Next, evaluate the truth of each possible answer. The graph shows that as temperature decreases, sales of jackets increase.

12. (C)

Use the Binomial Distribution, which states Probability of x successes in n trials $= (_nC_x)(p^x)(1 - p)^{n-x}$. In this formula, $_nC_x =$ the number of combinations of x successes in n trials $= (n)(n - 1)(n - 2)(\ldots)(n - x + 1)/x!$, and $p =$ probability of success on any single trial. Here, $n = 30$, $x = 7$, $p = .2$, and $_{30}C_7 = (30)(29)(28)(\ldots)(24)/7! = 2,035,800$. Thus, the required probability $= (2,035,000)(.2)^7(.8)^{23} \approx .154$.

13. (A)

Let $x =$ the number of days it takes the man to finish the job.

Note that the man actually works $(x + 4)$ days, and the son actually works 4 days.

The relationship used to set up the equation is: Part of job done by man + Part of job done by boy = 1 job

$$\frac{x + 4}{9} + \frac{4}{16} = 1$$
$$16(x + 4) + 4(9) = 144$$
$$x = 2\frac{3}{4} \text{ days}$$

Check:

$$\frac{2\frac{3}{4} + 4}{9} + \frac{4}{16} = 1$$
$$\frac{3}{4} + \frac{1}{4} = 1$$

14. (D)

is correct. The students in the statistics class have a reasonable chance at being able to sample a large enough portion of the students at their high school to get a reasonable estimate of the population and the data collected would produce a normal curve under these circumstances. Therefore the choice is concrete and mathematically correct. Choice (A) is incorrect because there are not enough students and the data being collected is unlikely to yield a normal curve over such a small, homogeneous sample. Choice (B) does not work because there is no way to get the data. An internet source may provide a sample but the problem then becomes abstract — a mind exercise. Choice (C) is incorrect because the data collected would not produce a normal curve.

15. (A)

When 23 is added, the numbers will appear, in ascending order, as follows: 21, 21, 23, 26, 28, 30, 32, 32. The median will equal the mean of the two middle numbers 26 and 28 = 27. Choice (B) is wrong because the median would be 27.5. Choice (C) is wrong because the median would be 28.5. Choice (D) is wrong because the median would be 29.

16. (A)

is the correct response. The inequality $x \geq 0$ identifies the region to the right of the y-axis, eliminating choices (C) and (D). The double inequality of $-3 < y < 3$ represents dotted horizontal lines passing through 3 and -3 on the y-axis with the area between the lines shaded. Of the two remaining choices, (A) is the only one which satisfies this constraint.

17. (C)

The volume of a cone is given by $V = (1/3)(\pi)(R^2)(H)$, where R is the radius and H is the height. By substitution, $72\pi = \frac{1}{3}(\pi)(R^2)(12)$. This simplifies to $R^2 = 18$, so $R = \sqrt{18}$.

18. (C)

The graph passes through the points $(0, -3)$, $(2, -1)$, $(-2, -1)$, $(4, 5)$, and $(-4, 5)$. Also, the graph is a parabola which faces upward and, therefore, the coefficient of the x^2-term must be positive. These conditions are only satisfied by

$$y = \tfrac{1}{2}x^2 - 3$$

and, therefore, answer choices (A), (B), and (D) are incorrect.

19. (D)

The sum of the original group of 20 numbers was $(9)(20) = 180$. The sum of the new group of 19 numbers is $(7)(19) = 133$. The removed number is the difference of 180 and 133, which is 47.

20. (C)

is the correct response. It is necessary to first write the quadratic in standard form: $2x^2 - 3x - 1 = 0$. This quadratic does not factor, so it is necessary to use the quadratic formula to find the solutions. The quadratic formula is as follows:

$$x = \frac{-b \pm \sqrt{b^2 - 4ac}}{2a} \text{ with } a = 2, b = -3, \text{ and } c = -1.$$

$$x = \frac{3 \pm \sqrt{9 - 4(2)(-1)}}{2(2)} = \frac{3 \pm \sqrt{17}}{4}$$

(A), (B), and (D) all contain errors in the use of the formula or with simplifying.

21. (B)

First, you must determine if the three squares are congruent. Because they each have sides, S, equal to the short side of the rectangle, they must be congruent. However, the value of S is not given. We must calculate it by taking the length of the long side of the rectangle, 12 cm, and dividing it into three equal parts:

$$S = \frac{12}{3}\text{cm}$$
$$= 4 \text{ cm}$$

Now that we know that the squares have sides which are 4 cm. long, we can compute the area.

$$\text{Area of one square} = S \times S$$
$$= 4 \times 4$$
$$= 16 \text{ cm}^2$$

The answer is (B).

22. (C)

If an event can happen in p ways and fail to happen in q ways, then, if $p > q$, the odds are p to q in favor of the event happening.

If $p < q$, then the odds are q to p against the event happening. In this case, $p = 19$ and $q = 10$, $p > q$. Thus, the odds in favor of the event of drawing a blue ball are 19:10.

23. (C)

The area of the square is s^2. The shaded section is $\frac{1}{4}$ of a circle with the radius s. The area of this section is $\frac{\pi s^2}{4}$; the nonshaded area is $s^2 - \frac{\pi s^2}{4}$.

24. (C)

The multiplicative inverses of 2 and 3 are $\frac{1}{2}$ and $\frac{1}{3}$, respectively. Their sum is $\frac{3}{6} + \frac{2}{6} = \frac{5}{6}$. This number is the multiplicative inverse of $\frac{6}{5}$.

25. (D)

Robyn's incorrect answer of $x = -6$ must have been derived from a wrong operation on the number -5.5. Since she should have divided -5.5 by $\frac{1}{2}$, the correct answer should be $x = (-5.5)/(\frac{1}{2}) = -11$.

26. (C)

$$(f \circ g)(x) = f(g(x))$$

This is the definition of the composition of functions. For the functions given in this problem we have

$$2(g(x)) + 4 = 2(x^2 - 2) + 4$$
$$= 2x^2 - 4 + 4 = 2x^2.$$

27. (C)

By just reading the values from left to right of the stem-and-leaf shown, we have: 5, 3, 8, 5, 1, 12, 16, 19, 19, 19, 24, 23, 24, 23. This list corresponds to choice (C) when the numbers are arranged in ascending order.

28. (A)

When an expression involving a base and an exponent is raised to an exponent, the base remains unchanged and the exponents are multiplied. Thus, $(100^6)^3 = 100^{18}$.

29. (D)

$$f'(x) = x^2 - 2x - 3 = (x + 1)(x - 3)$$

$(x + 1)(x - 3) = 0 \Rightarrow x = -1$ and 3 are critical values.

The numbers –1 and 3 divide the x-axis into 3 intervals, from $-\infty$ to -1, -1 to 3, and 3 to $-\infty$.

$f(x)$ has a relative minimum value at $x = x_1$, if and only if $f'(x_1) = 0$ and the sign of $f'(x)$ changes from $-$ to $+$ as x increases through x_1.

If $-1 < x < 3$, then $f'(x) = -$

If $x = 3$, then $f'(x) = 0$

If $x > 3$, then $f'(x) = +$

Therefore, $f(3)$ is a relative minimum.

Note that when $x < -1, f'(x) = +$. If $x = -1, f'(x) = 0$. If $-1 < x < 3, f'(x) = -$.

Thus, $f(-1)$ is a relative maximum, not minimum.

30. (D)

$$\sqrt{108} + 3\sqrt{12} - 7\sqrt{3} = \sqrt{(36)(3)} + 3\sqrt{(4)(3)} - 7\sqrt{3}$$
$$= 6\sqrt{3} + 3\left(2\sqrt{3}\right) - 7\sqrt{3}$$
$$= 6\sqrt{3} + 6\sqrt{3} - 7\sqrt{3}$$
$$= 5\sqrt{3}.$$

31. (C)

Five miles per hour is equivalent to $(5)(5280) = 26,400$ feet per hour. To calculate the feet per minute, divide 26,400 by 60. $26,400/60 = 440$.

32. (B)

If L is the original length and W is the original width, the original area is LW. The new length will be $2L$ and the new width will be $3W$, so the new area will be $6LW$. The increase in area is $5LW$. This increase as a percent is $(5LW/LW)(100\%) = 500\%$.

33. (A)

The median is given by the value corresponding to the vertical segment inside the box, which is 40. The left-most vertical segment and the right-most segment of the box represent the first and third quartiles, respectively. For Choice (A), their values are 25 and 55. $40 = (\frac{1}{2})(25+55)$. This relationship is not true for the other answer choices.

34. (C)

Use integration by parts with

$u = \ln x$	$du = \dfrac{1}{x}dx$
$dv = x$	$v = \dfrac{x^2}{2}$

$$\int_1^e x \ln x \, dx = \frac{x^2}{2} \ln x - \int_1^e \frac{x}{2}dx$$
$$= \left(\frac{x^2}{2} \ln x - \frac{x^2}{4}\right)\Bigg|_1^e$$
$$= \frac{e^2 + 1}{4}$$

35. (B)

$F(-3) = - (-3) + 3 = 6$. $F(2) = (2)(2) + 3 = 7$.

$F(4) = (3)(4) = 12$.

$6 + 7 - 12 = 1$.

36. (A)

Since $t = -9$ is a root of the equation

$$t^2 + 4t - 45 = 0$$

then $(t + 9)$ is a factor. Division of the equation by $(t + 9)$ would therefore yield the other factor of the quadratic, which is $(t - 5)$, giving the second root, $t = 5$.

37. (D)

The function given is represented graphically by a parabola. A parabola will intersect the *x*-axis in only one place if both roots are equal, which means *discriminant* = 0.

$$discriminant = b^2 - 4ac = +(4)^2 - 4(2)k = 0$$

$$16 - 8k = 0$$

$$16 = 8k \therefore k = 2$$

38. (C)

x = number of degrees in the first angle. The second angle is 11° less than the **first angle;** so the second angle = $x - 11$, where less than signifies subtraction (switching around), and the first angle (x) is the first term and 11° (11) is the second term.

The third angle is twice **the measure of the first angle** increased by 3; so the third angle = $2x + 3$, where twice represents multiplication by 2 and increased by means addition.

Since the **sum** of the angles of a triangle equals 180°, then

first angle + second angle + third angle = 180°

$\qquad\downarrow\qquad\qquad$ and$\downarrow$

$\quad x \qquad + \quad (x - 11) \quad + \quad (2x + 3) \; = 180°$

Answer choice (A) is wrong because of an error in interpretation of 11 less than x.

$$\angle 2 = (11 - x)$$

Answer choice (B) is wrong because of an error in interpretation of twice x increased by 3.

$$\angle 3 = 2(x + 3)$$

Answer choice (D) is wrong because of an error in interpretation of twice x increased by 3.

$$\angle 3 = (2x - 3)$$

39. (B)

The original total weight of all the people in the room is $(20)(130) = 2600$ pounds. After Bob and Diane leave the room, the mean weight of the remaining 18 people will be $(130)(.97) = 126.1$ pounds. This means that the total weight for these 18 people is $(18)(126.1) \approx 2270$ pounds. Then $2600 - 2270 = 330$ pounds is the total weight for Bob and Diane. Finally, the mean weight for Bob and Diane is $\dfrac{330}{2} = 165$ pounds.

40. (B)

There are 5 members to be selected from a group of 15 people. Therefore the total number of possible ways is

$$\binom{15}{5} = 3003.$$

We have to select 3 men out of 6 men, so the number of possible ways is

$$\binom{6}{3} = 20.$$

Two women have to be selected from 9 women. The total number of possible ways is

$$\binom{9}{2} = 36.$$

Hence the desired probability

$$= \frac{20 \times 36}{3003} = \frac{240}{1001}$$

Calculator: 15 INV nCr 5 = 3003

$\qquad\qquad$ 6 INV nCr 3 = 20

$\qquad\qquad$ 9 INV nCr 2 = 36.

Part B: Solutions

41.

a. Mike's salary this year will be ($40,000) (1.05) = $42,000.

b. To find Linda's salary last year, take her present annual salary and divide by 1.05. Divide the result by 1.05 to find her salary two years ago, and divide that result by 1.05 to determine her salary three years ago.

Thus: $\frac{\$48,000}{1.05} = \$45,714.29$; $\frac{\$45,714.29}{1.05}$ $= \$43,537.42$; $\frac{\$43,537.42}{1.05} = \$41,464$ to the nearest dollar.

c. Take Sandra's desired salary and divide by 1.03; take the result and divide again by 1.03.

Thus: $\frac{\$50,000}{1.03} = \$48,543.69$; $\frac{\$48,543,69}{1.03}$

$= \$47,130$, to the nearest dollar.

42.

a. The common ratio is $\frac{24}{16} = 1.5$ Then (24)(1.5) = 36.

b. The expression for the 40th term is $(16)(1.5)^{39}$ $\approx 117{,}944{,}878$.

c. $922.64 = (16)(1.5)^{n-1}$. Taking the logarithm of both sides of this equation, we get: log 922.64 = log 16 + $(n - 1)$ (log 1.5). Then 2.965 = 1.204 + $(n - 1)$ (0.176), which reduces to: 1.937 = 0.176 n. Thus $n = 11$, and 922.64 is the 11th term of the sequence.

43.

a. The mean is found by adding all the numbers and dividing by 12, which is $\frac{1458}{12} = 121.5$

b. When arranged in ascending order, the sixth number is 121 and the seventh number is 126. The median is the average of these two numbers, which is $\frac{(121 + 126)}{2} = 123.5$

c. The lower quartile Q_1 is that number such that at least 25 percent of the sorted values are less than or equal to Q_1 and at least 75 percent of the values are greater than or equal to Q_1. The upper quartile Q_3 is that number such that at least 25 percent of the values are greater than or equal to Q_3 and 75 percent of the sorted values are less than or equal to Q_3. In this case, the first quartile is the median of the lowest six numbers, which is the average of the 3rd and 4th numbers. Thus, the first quartile is $\frac{(112 + 115)}{2} = 113.5$. Likewise, the third quartile is the median of the highest six numbers, which is the average of the 9th and 10th numbers. This means that the third quartile is $\frac{(127 + 127)}{2} = 127$. Finally, the interquartile range is 127 − 113.5 = 13.5.

Praxis II

Middle School Mathematics Test (0069)

Practice Test 2

This test is also on CD-ROM in our interactive TestWare® for this Praxis II Assessment. We strongly recommend that you first take this exam on computer. You will then have the benefits of enforced time conditions, individual diagnostic analysis, and instant scoring.

Sample Mathematics Definitions and Formulas

NOTATION

(a, b)	$\{x: a < x < b\}$
$[a, b)$	$\{x: a \leq x < b\}$
$(a, b]$	$\{x: a < x \leq b\}$
$[a, b]$	$\{x: a \leq x \leq b\}$
gcd (m, n)	greatest common divisor of two integers m and n
lcm (m, n)	least common multiple of two integers m and n
$[x]$	greatest integer m such that $m \leq x$
$m \equiv k(\text{mod } n)$	m and k are congruent modulo n (m and k have the same remainder when divided by n, or equivalently, $m - k$ is a multiple of n)
f^{-1}	inverse of an invertible function f (not the same as $\dfrac{1}{f}$)
$\displaystyle\lim_{x \to a^+} f(x)$	right-hand limit of $f(x)$; limit of $f(x)$ as x approaches a from the right
$\displaystyle\lim_{x \to a^-} f(x)$	left-hand limit of $f(x)$; limit of $f(x)$ as x approaches a from the left
$\emptyset$	the empty set
$x \in S$	x is an element of set S
$S \subset T$	set S is a proper subset of set T
$S \subseteq T$	either set S is a proper subset of set T or $S = T$
$S \cup T$	union of sets S and T
$S \cap T$	intersection of sets S and T

DEFINITIONS

Discrete Mathematics

A relation $\mathfrak{R}$ on a set S is
> reflexive if $x \mathfrak{R} x$ for all $x \in S$
> symmetric if $x \mathfrak{R} y \Rightarrow y \mathfrak{R} x$ for all $x, y \in S$
> transitive if $(x \mathfrak{R} y$ and $y \mathfrak{R} z) \Rightarrow x \mathfrak{R} z$ for all $x, y, z \in S$
> antisymmetric if $(x \mathfrak{R} y$ and $y \mathfrak{R} x) \Rightarrow x = y$ for all $x, y \in S$

An equivalence relation is a reflexive, symmetric, and transitive relation.

FORMULAS

Sum

$$\sin(x \pm y) = \sin x \cos y \pm \cos x \sin y$$

$$\cos(x \pm y) = \cos x \cos y \mp \sin x \sin y$$

$$\tan(x \pm y) = \frac{\tan x \pm \tan y}{1 \mp \tan x \tan y}$$

Half-angle (sign depends on the quadrant of $\frac{\theta}{2}$)

$$\sin \frac{\theta}{2} = \pm\sqrt{\frac{1 - \cos \theta}{2}}$$

$$\cos \frac{\theta}{2} = \pm\sqrt{\frac{1 + \cos \theta}{2}}$$

Range of Inverse Trigonometric Functions

$\sin^{-1}x \qquad \left[-\frac{\pi}{2}, \frac{\pi}{2}\right]$

$\cos^{-1}x \qquad [0, \pi]$

$\tan^{-1}x \qquad \left(-\frac{\pi}{2}, \frac{\pi}{2}\right)$

Law of Sines

$$\frac{\sin A}{a} = \frac{\sin B}{b} = \frac{\sin C}{c}$$

Law of Cosines

$$c^2 = a^2 + b^2 - 2ab\,(\cos C)$$

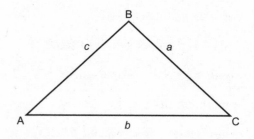

DeMoivre's Theorem

$$(\cos \theta + i \sin \theta)^k = \cos(k\theta) + i \sin(k\theta)$$

Coordinate Transformation

Rectangular (x, y) to polar (r, θ) : $r^2 = x^2 + y^2$; $\tan \theta = \frac{y}{x}$ if $x \neq 0$

Polar (r, θ) to rectangular (x, y): $x = r \cos \theta$; $y = r \sin \theta$

Distance from point (x_1, y_1) to line $Ax + By + C = 0$

$$d = \frac{|Ax_1 + By_1 + C|}{\sqrt{A^2 + B^2}}$$

Volume

Sphere with radius r: $\qquad\qquad\qquad\qquad\qquad\qquad\qquad V = \frac{4}{3}\pi r^3$

Right circular cone with height h and base of radius r: $\qquad V = \frac{1}{3}\pi r^2 h$

Right circular cylinder with height h and base of radius r: $\quad V = \pi r^2 h$

Pyramid with height h and base of area B: $\qquad\qquad\qquad V = \frac{1}{3}Bh$

Right prism with height h and base of area B: $\qquad\qquad\quad V = Bh$

Surface Area

Sphere with radius r: $\qquad\qquad\qquad\qquad\qquad\qquad\qquad A = 4\pi r^2$

Right circular cone with radius r and slant height s: $\qquad A = \pi r s + \pi r^2$

Differentiation

$(f(x)g(x))' = f'(x)g(x) + f(x)g'(x)$

$(f(g(x)))' = f'(g(x))g'(x)$

$\left(\dfrac{f(x)}{g(x)}\right)' = \dfrac{f'(x)g(x) - f(x)g'(x)}{(g(x))^2}$ if $g(x) \neq 0$

Integration by Parts

$\displaystyle\int u\, dv = uv - \int v\, du$

PRAXIS II: Middle School Mathematics Practice Test 2

TIME: 2 hours
40 Multiple-choice questions (Part A)
3 Short constructed-response questions (Part B)

Part A

> **Directions:** Read each item and select the best response.

1. Point A has coordinates $(2, 5)$ and point B has coordinates $(-3, -3)$. What is the distance between point A and point B?

    (A) 5.6

    (B) 9.4

    (C) 8.1

    (D) 2.4

2. The height of an object is given by the equation $z = -16t^2 + 144t$, where z is the distance in feet and t is the time in seconds. After how many seconds will this object reach its maximum height?

    (A) 3

    (B) 4.5

    (C) 7.5

    (D) 9

3. Which one of the following functions has a domain of all real numbers except 2 and -2?

    (A) $\dfrac{x+2}{x-2}$

    (B) $\dfrac{2x}{x^2-4}$

    (C) $\dfrac{x+4}{x+2}$

    (D) $\dfrac{x+4}{2x}$

4. Which one of the following has the same value as $-|-8-(-5)|$?

    (A) $|-8-5|$

    (B) $|-8-(-5)|$

    (C) $-|5-(-8)|$

    (D) $-|-8+5|$

5. Find a, b for the parabola
    $y = ax^2 + bx + 3$
    if the vertex is $(2, 4)$.

    (A) $a = -\frac{1}{4}, b = 1$

    (B) $a = -1, b = -2$

    (C) $a = 1, b = 2$

    (D) $a = -\frac{1}{3}, b = 1$

6. In a shipment of two boxes, Box I has 5 radios and Box II has 4 radios. Box I contains 1 defective radio and Box II contains 2 defective radios. After emptying the contents of both boxes into a bin, a radio is randomly selected. If the selected radio is defective, what is the probability that it came from Box I?

    (A) $\dfrac{1}{2}$

    (B) $\dfrac{2}{5}$

    (C) $\dfrac{1}{3}$

    (D) $\dfrac{2}{7}$

7. Select the geometric figure that possesses all of the following characteristics:

    I.   Quadrilateral

    II. At least one pair of parallel sides

    III. Diagonals are always perpendicular to each other

    (A) Rectangle

    (B) Rhombus

    (C) Trapezoid

    (D) Parallelogram

8. A function is defined as $f(x) = 3x^2 - 1$. What is the numerical value of $2 \cdot f(0) + f(-1) \cdot f(4)$?

   (A) 90

   (B) 92

   (C) 94

   (D) 96

9. A function contains the points $(8, 3)$, $(-1, -3)$, $(-2, 6)$, and $(7, 6)$. Which one of the following <u>must</u> be a point belonging to the inverse of this function?

   (A) $(3, -8)$

   (B) $(1, 3)$

   (C) $(-2, 7)$

   (D) $(6, 7)$

10. A recursive sequence of numbers is defined as follows: $a_1 = 10$, $a_2 = 15$, $a_n = (a_{n-1} - a_{n-2})^2$ for $n > 2$. What is the value of a_5?

    (A) 900

    (B) 3125

    (C) 5625

    (D) 11,250

11. A rectangular box is to be filled with boxes of candy. The rectangular box measures 4 feet long, 3 feet wide, and 2½ feet deep. If a box of candy weighs approximately 3 pounds per cubic foot, what will the weight of the rectangular box be when the box is filled to the top with candy?

    (A) 10 pounds

    (B) 12 pounds

    (C) 36 pounds

    (D) 90 pounds

12. Which of the following can be represented by a graph that has the same vertex as the graph of $f(x) = x^2 + 14x + 51$?

    (A) $f(x) = 3(x + 7)^2 + 2$

    (B) $f(x) = 4(x - 7)^2 + 51$

    (C) $f(x) = 7(x - 14)^2 + 2$

    (D) $f(x) = 6(x + 14)^2 + 51$

13. The equation $x^2 + 2x + 7 = 0$ has

    (A) two complex conjugate roots.

    (B) two real rational roots.

    (C) two real equal roots.

    (D) two real irrational roots.

14. The numbers 4, 2, 7, and 9 occur with frequencies 2, 3, 11, and 4, respectively. Find the arithmetic mean.

    (A) 5

    (B) 6.35

    (C) 7.25

    (D) 6

15. What is (are) the value(s) of x in the following equation?

    $$\sqrt{37 - 3x} = 3 + \sqrt{x + 20}$$

    (A) 10.25 only

    (B) 10.25 and -4

    (C) -4 only

    (D) -10.25 and 4

16. What is the solution for x in the inequality $2x^2 - x - 3 < 0$?

    (A) $-1 < x < 3/2$

    (B) $x > 3/2$ or $x < -1$

    (C) $-3/2 < x < 1$

    (D) $x > 1$ or $x < -3/2$

17.

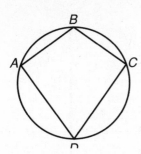

Note: Figure not drawn to scale.

In the figure above, quadrilateral $ABCD$ is inscribed in the circle. If the measure of $\angle B$ is 105° and the measure of $\angle C$ is 95, what is the measure, in degrees, of arc ABC?

(A) 75°   (C) 90°

(B) 80°   (D) 150°

18. In the triangle below, $a = 30$, $b = 50$, $\angle C = 25°$. What is the measure of $\angle B$?

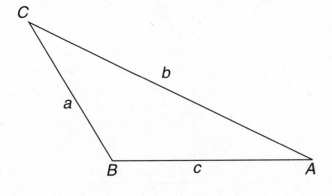

(A) 150°   (C) 220°

(B) 126°   (D) 56°

19. Answer the question based on the following:

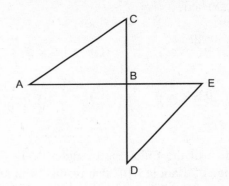

If $\overline{BC} \perp \overline{AE}$, $\overline{DB} \cong \overline{AB}$, and $\angle E = \angle C$, which of the following must be true?

(A) $\overline{AB} = 2\overline{BE}$ (C) $\overline{BC} = \frac{2}{3}\overline{BD}$

(B) $\overline{BC} \cong \overline{AC}$ (D) $\overline{BC} \cong \overline{BE}$

20. The display below shows the cumulative relative frequency histogram of scores from the 20-question math placement examination taken by 40 freshmen upon entering a high school.

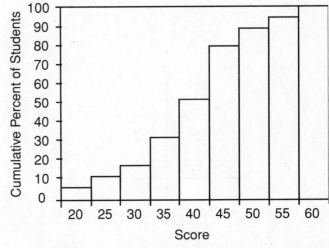

Which of the following is a correct statement based on the information in the display?

(A) The median score is 30.

(B) Most students scored above 50.

(C) No one scored 35 on this test.

(D) There were about equal numbers of students with scores between 50 and 55 as between 55 and 60.

21. What is the range of values for which $|6x - 5| \leq 8$ is satisfied?

(A) $-\dfrac{1}{2} \leq x \leq \dfrac{1}{2}$ (C) $-1 \leq x \leq \dfrac{1}{2}$

(B) $0 \leq x \leq \dfrac{5}{6}$ (D) $-\dfrac{1}{2} \leq x \leq \dfrac{13}{6}$

22. Which of the following triangles A′ B′ C′ is the image of triangle ABC that results from reflecting the triangle ABC across the *y*-axis?

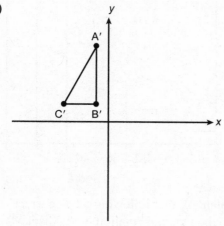

(A)

(B)

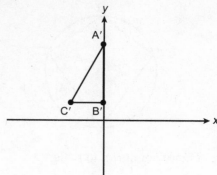

(C)

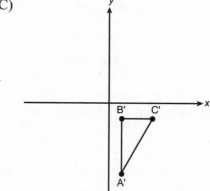

(D)

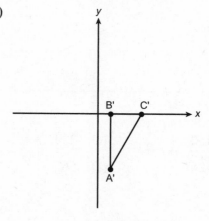

23. If $\log_8 3 = x \log_2 3$ then *x* equals

(A) $\frac{1}{3}$ (C) 3

(B) $\log_4 3$ (D) $\log_8 9$

24. If $f(x) = 3x+2$ and $g(f(x)) = x$, then $g(x) =$

(A) $\dfrac{x-2}{3}$

(B) $\dfrac{x}{3} - 2$

(C) $3x$

(D) $3x - 2$

25. If $x = 3 + 2i$ and $y = 1 + 3i$, where $i^2 = -1$, then $\frac{x}{y} =$

(A) $\dfrac{9}{10} - \dfrac{2}{3}i.$

(B) $\dfrac{9}{10} - \dfrac{7}{10}i.$

(C) $\dfrac{9}{10} + \dfrac{2}{3}i.$

(D) $3 - \dfrac{7}{10}i.$

26. A carpenter is building a big recreation room that is 625 square feet in area, and he must decide how to apportion each section of the room. He has decided to set aside 30% of the room for the Baby Grand Piano and an additional 46.7 square feet for a stage. How much of the room is set aside for the Baby Grand Piano and stage?

(A) 76.7 square feet

(B) 234.2 square feet

(C) 548.3 square feet

(D) 610.99 square feet

27. Which one of the following identities uses both the distributive and commutative properties of numbers?

(A) $(4)(7+9)=(4)(9)+(4)(7)$

(B) $(5)(8+6)=(5)(8)+(5)(6)$

(C) $(6)(2+4)=(2+4)(6)$

(D) $(7)(1+5)=(7)(1)+5$

28. The base of a right prism, shown here, is an equilateral triangle, each of whose sides measure 4 units. The altitude of the prism is 5 units. Find the volume of the prism.

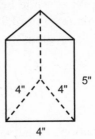

(A) $4\sqrt{3}$

(B) $20\sqrt{3}$

(C) 60

(D) 40

29. Which of the following has the highest value?

(A) The number of distinct ways of arranging nine people in a line

(B) The number of distinct ways of selecting four different letters from the alphabet

(C) The number of distinct committees of five people chosen from a list of 33 people

(D) The number of distinct sequences of heads and tails when an ordinary coin is flipped 18 times

30. If $f(x) = e^{\frac{x^3}{3}-x}$, then $f(x)$

(A) increases in the interval $(-1, 1)$

(B) decreases for $|x| > 1$

(C) increases in the interval $(-1, 1)$ and decreases in the intervals $(-\infty, -1) \cup (1, \infty)$

(D) increases in the intervals $(-\infty, -1) \cup (1, \infty)$ and decreases in the interval $(-1, 1)$

31. What is the range of the function $f(x) = -x^2 - 3x + 4$?

(A) All numbers less than or equal to -1.5

(B) All numbers between -1 and 4, inclusive

(C) All numbers less than or equal to 6.25

(D) All numbers between -4 and 1, inclusive

32. In order to be accepted into a program at West Point, a person must score in the top 2% of a standardized test on general knowledge. Historically, the mean score for this test is 70, with a standard deviation of 3. What would be the <u>minimum</u> integer score on this test in order for a person to be accepted into this program?

    (A) 83   (C) 79

    (B) 81   (D) 77

33. What is the equation of the line which is parallel to $6x + 3y = 4$ and has a y-intercept of -6?

    (A) $y = 2x - 6$ (C) $y = -2x - \frac{4}{3}$

    (B) $y = 2x + \frac{4}{3}$ (D) $y = -2x - 6$

34. If $f(x) = x^2 - x - 3$, $g(x) = \frac{x^2 - 1}{x + 2}$, and $h(x) = f(x) + g(x)$, find $h(2)$.

    (A) $\frac{1}{2}$ (C) $-\frac{1}{4}$

    (B) $-\frac{1}{2}$ (D) 3

35. In calculating the value of $3 + 6^2 \div (7 \cdot 2 - 2) \cdot 4$, which one of the following operations would NOT be used?

    (A) Dividing 36 by 12

    (B) Subtracting 2 from 14

    (C) Multiplying 3 by 4

    (D) Adding 3 to 36

36. A group of n data, where n is an odd number, is arranged in ascending order. The position of the first quartile is given by $\frac{n+1}{4}$, and the position of the third quartile is given by $\frac{3n+3}{4}$. If the 66th number is the third quartile, which number is the first quartile?

    (A) 6th   (C) 22nd

    (B) 11th   (D) 33rd

37. If the second-order difference of terms of a particular sequence is 3, which one of the following could be such a sequence?

    (A) 3, 9, 27, 81, 243, ...

    (B) 3, 6, 9, 12, 15, ...

    (C) 2, 6, 13, 23, 36, ...

    (D) 1, 5, 14, 31, 56, ...

38. A sequence of P values is defined as follows: $P_1 = 1$, $P_2 = 2$, $P_i = (2)(P_{i-1})$ if i is even, and $P_i = P_{i-1} + 1$ if i is odd. What is the value of $P_5 + P_6$?

    (A) 11   (C) 17

    (B) 15   (D) 21

39. If the point $(3, 1)$ is rotated $90°$ counterclockwise on an xy-coordinate plane, what is the point's new coordinates?

    (A) $(-3, 1)$ (C) $(1, 3)$

    (B) $(-3, -1)$ (D) $(-1, 3)$

40.

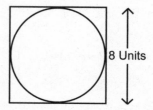

The diagram shown above represents a square dartboard with an inscribed circle. A dart is thrown and lands inside the square. What is the BEST approximation for the probability that this dart lands inside the circle?

    (A) .75   (C) .85

    (B) .80   (D) .90

PRAXIS EXAM Part B: 3 Short Constructed-Response Questions

41. The Floss Mate Dental Insurance Company offers two plans for reimbursement of dental expenses incurred during any calendar year. Melissa and Steve are eligible subscribers, whereby Melissa has chosen Plan A and Steve has chosen Plan B.

    Plan A requires an annual deductible of $250, then the Plan pays 80% of the expenses exceeding $250.

    Plan B requires an annual deductible of $400, then the Plan pays 90% of the expenses exceeding $400.

    a. If Melissa's dental bills totaled $700 during this past year, how much money did she have to pay?

    b. At the end of this past year, Steve discovered that his personal expenses for dental bills was $445. What was the actual total of his dental bills?

    c. For how many dollars of dental bills would a person pay the same amount for Plan A and for Plan B?

42. The Consolidated Juice Company packs its juice in cans that have the shape of a right circular cone. The surface area of a right circular cone where r is the radius of the base and h is the cone's height is given by the formula

    a. The company used to make cans that had a radius of 1 inch and a height of 3 inches. What was the surface area for a can with these dimensions? (Nearest hundredth)

    b. Currently, the cost of the metal used for each can is $0.015 per square inch. To the nearest cent, what is the cost of the metal for a can with a radius of 1.5 inches and a height of 4 inches?

    c. The company has two machines that make these cans. Each machine can make 5 cans per minute. The company does not want to spend more than $1000 per day on the cost of the metal needed for these cans. If the two machines are operating simultaneously, what is the <u>maximum</u> number of allowable minutes per day each machine operates?

43. On the xy-plane, graph the parabola $y = 2(x-3)^2 - 6$.

    a. Use x values of 1, 2, 3, 4, 5. Determine the corresponding y values, plot the five ordered pairs, and draw a smooth curve.

    b. If the curve were extended beyond the five points given in Part A, it would intersect the y-axis. Determine this value of y.

    c. Determine the values of x where the curve intersects the x-axis. Round off your answers to the nearest hundredth.

Practice Test 2 Answer Key

Question Number	Correct Answer	Content Category	Question Number	Correct Answer	Content Category
1.	B	Arithmetic and Basic Algebra	23.	A	Arithmetic and Basic Algebra
2.	B	Arithmetic and Basic Algebra	24.	A	Functions
3.	B	Functions	25.	B	Arithmetic and Basic Algebra
4.	D	Arithmetic and Basic Algebra	26.	B	Measurement
5.	A	Geometry	27.	A	Arithmetic and Basic Algebra
6.	C	Probability	28.	B	Geometry
7.	B	Geometry	29.	A	Discrete Mathematics
8.	B	Functions	30.	D	Functions
9.	D	Functions	31.	C	Functions
10.	C	Discrete Mathematics	32.	D	Data and Statistical Concepts
11.	D	Measurement	33.	D	Arithmetic and Basic Algebra
12.	A	Functions	34.	C	Functions
13.	A	Arithmetic and Basic Algebra	35.	D	Arithmetic and Basic Algebra
14.	B	Data and Statistical Concepts	36.	C	Arithmetic and Basic Algebra
15.	C	Arithmetic and Basic Algebra	37.	C	Discrete Mathematics
16.	A	Arithmetic and Basic Algebra	38.	D	Discrete Mathematics
17.	D	Geometry	39.	D	Geometry
18.	B	Geometry	40.	B	Geometry
19.	D	Geometry	41.	—	Short Constructed Response
20.	D	Data and Statistical Concepts	42.	—	Short Constructed Response
21.	D	Arithmetic and Basic Algebra	43.	—	Short Constructed Response
22.	A	Geometry			

Practice Test 2
Detailed Explanations of Answers

Part A

1. (B)

Distance d between any two points (x_1, y_1), (x_2, x_2) in the two-dimensional coordinate system is

$$d = \sqrt{(x_1 - x_2)^2 + (y_1 - y_2)^2}$$

The problem can be calculated as:

$$d = \sqrt{(2 - (-3))^2 + (5 - (-3))^2} = \sqrt{89} \approx 9.434$$

2. (B)

The maximum height of any parabola given in the form $y = Ax^2 + Bx + C$, where A is negative, is given by the y value of the vertex. In this example, z replaces y, and t replaces x. The x value of the vertex is given by $-B/2A = -144/-32 = 4.5$, and this is the required time in seconds.

3. (B)

For a rational function in the form of $\frac{p(x)}{q(x)}$, where each of $p(x)$ and $q(x)$ are polynomial functions, the domain is found by solving $q(x) = 0$. So, $x^2 - 4 = 0$ becomes $(x - 2)(x + 2) = 0$. This implies that $x = 2$ and $x = -2$.

4. (D)

The value of the item in the stem is $-|-8 + 5| = -|-3| = -3$. Answer choice (D) also has a value of -3. the values of answer choices (A), (B), and (C) are 13, 3, and -13, respectively.

5. (A)

If the vertex is (2, 4) we can substitute this value into the equation of the parabola and obtain:

$$\begin{array}{rl} 4 = & a(2)^2 + b(2) + 3 \\ 4 = & 4a + 2b + 3 \\ \underline{-3 =} & \underline{ - 3} \\ 1 = & 4a + 2b \end{array} \qquad \text{(I)}$$

Also the x-coordinate of the vertex is given by

$$\frac{-b}{2a}$$

so $\qquad 2 = \dfrac{-b}{2a}$ \qquad (II)

From (I) and (II) we obtain

$$4a + 2b = 1 \qquad \text{(I)}$$

$$\frac{-b}{2a} = 2 \qquad \text{(II)}$$

From (II), $b = -4a$ and substituting into (I):

$$4a + 2 \times (-4a) = 1$$
$$4a - 8a = 1$$
$$-4a = 1$$
$$a = -\frac{1}{4}$$
$$b = 1$$

6. (C)

There are a total of nine radios, of which three are defective. Box I contains one defective radio and Box II contains two defective radios. Given that a defective radio has been selected, the probability that it came from Box I is 1/3. An alternative method is to use Bayes' theroem. Let A represent Box I, let B represent Box II, and let D represent a defective radio. Then we need the value of $P(D|A)$.

By Bayes' theorem,

$$P(A|D) = \frac{P(D|A) \cdot P(A)}{P(D|A) \cdot P(A) + P(D|B) \cdot P(D)}.$$

Now, by substitution,

we get $P(A|D) = \dfrac{\left(\dfrac{1}{5}\right)\left(\dfrac{5}{9}\right)}{\left(\dfrac{1}{5}\right)\left(\dfrac{5}{9}\right) + \left(\dfrac{1}{2}\right)\left(\dfrac{4}{9}\right)} = \dfrac{\left(\dfrac{1}{9}\right)}{\left(\dfrac{3}{9}\right)} = \dfrac{1}{3}.$

7. (B)

A rhombus is a quadrilateral, has at least one pair of parallel sides, and its diagonals are always perpendicular to each other.

8. (B)

$f(0) = 3(0)^2 - 1 = -1$, $f(-1) = 3(-1)^2 - 1 = 2$,

and $f(4) = 3(4)^2 - 1 = 47$.

Then $(2)(-1) + (2)(47) = -2 + 94 = 92$.

9. (D)

The inverse of the graph of any function is found by reflecting the graph across the line $y = x$. This means that for any point (x, y) on the original graph, the point (y, x) must be on the inverse graph. The point $(6, 7)$ is a point on the graph of the inverse since $(7, 6)$ is on the graph of the original function.

10. (C)

$a_3 = (15-10)^2 = 5^2 = 25$, $a_4 = (25-15)^2 = 10^2 = 100$, $a_5 = (100-25)^2 = 75^2 = 5625$

11. (D)

The volume of the rectangular box

= (length) (width) (height)

= (4) × (3) × (2 ½)

= (12) × (2 ½)

Writing quantities in fractional form:

$= \dfrac{12}{1} \times \dfrac{5}{2}$

Cancel and multiply numerators:

$= \dfrac{6}{1} \times \dfrac{5}{1} = 30$ cubic feet

If each box of candy weighs approximately 3 pounds per cubic foot and there are 30 cubic feet in the rectangular box, the weight of the rectangular box is

(30) (3 pounds) = 90 pounds

when the box is filled to the top with candy.

Answer (A) is wrong due to an error in computation.

4 ft × 3 ft × $2\dfrac{1}{2}$ ft × $\dfrac{\text{ft}^3}{3}$ pounds = 10 pounds

Answer (B) is wrong because it only considers the length of the box in the computation.

4 ft × 3 pounds/cubic foot = 12 pounds

Answer (C) is wrong because it deletes the height (deepness) from the computation.

4 ft × 3 ft × 3 pounds/cubic foot = 36 pounds

12. (A)

Rewrite the function as $f(x) - (x^2 + 14x + \underline{\quad}) + 51$. To complete the ($\underline{\quad}$) so that it is a perfect square, add 49. (Of course, we must add 49 to the left side as well. Then $f(x) + 49 = (x^2 + 14x + 49) + 51$. This simplifies to $f(x) + 49 = (x + 7)^2 + 51$ and finally to $f(x) = (x + 7)^2 + 2$, which has the same vertex as $f(x) = A(x + 7)^2 + 2$, where A is any real number. Alternate method: For an equation of the form of $f(x) = ax^2 + bx + c$. The vertex is $\left(-\dfrac{b}{2a}, f\left(-\dfrac{b}{2a}\right)\right)$, which is $(-7, 2)$. Recall that if a function $f(x) = A(x - h)^2 = k$, its vertex is located at (h, k). Thus the function in this question has its vertex as $(-7, 2)$. Only answer (A) has its vertex at $(-7, 2)$.

13. (A)

To solve this quadratic equation, we invoke the quadratic formula:

$$x = \frac{-b \pm \sqrt{b^2 - 4ac}}{2a}$$

The equation is $x^2 + 2x + 7 = 0$.

So $a = 1$, $b = 2$, and $c = 7$.

Substituting into the formula:

$$x = \frac{-2 \pm \sqrt{2^2 - 4(1)(7)}}{2(1)}$$

$$= \frac{-2 \pm \sqrt{4 - 28}}{2} = -1 \pm \sqrt{-6}$$

Since $i = \sqrt{-1}$, $x = -1 \pm i\sqrt{6}$.

These roots are complex conjugates of each other.

14. (B)

To find the arithmetic mean, $\bar{x}$, multiply each different number by its associated frequency. Add these products, then divide by the total number of numbers.

$$\bar{x} = [(4)(2)+(2)(3)+(7)(11)+(9)(4)] \div 20$$

$$= (8+6+77+36) \div 20$$

$$= 127 \div 20 = 6.35$$

15. (C)

-4 only

Square each side of the equation to get $37 - 3x = 9 + 6\sqrt{x + 20} + x + 20$. Simplify this to $8 - 4x = 6\sqrt{x + 20}$. Square each side to get $64 - 64x + 16x^2 = 36(x + 20)$. Simplify this to $16x^2 - 100x - 656 = 0$ or reduced to $4x^2 - 25x - 164 = 0$. Using either the Quadratic Formula or by factoring as $(x + 4)(4x - 41) = 0$, the results are $x = -4$ and $x = 10.25$. However, only -4 checks the equation.

16. (A)

Factor the left side of the inequality to get $(2x - 3)(x + 1) < 0$. If $2x - 3 > 0$ and $x + 1 < 0$, we get $x > 3/2$ and $x < -1$, which is impossible. If $2x - 3 < 0$ and $x + 1 > 0$, we have the actual solution of $-1 < x < 3/2$.

17. (D)

As inscribed angles, $\angle B = \dfrac{1}{2}(\overset{\frown}{ADC})$ and $\angle D = \dfrac{1}{2}(\overset{\frown}{ABC})$. If a quadrilateral is inscribed in a circle, then its opposite angles are supplementary. Therefore $B + D = 180°$. The measure of D is $180° - 105° = 75°$. Finally, $75° = \dfrac{1}{2}(\overset{\frown}{ABC})$, so $(\overset{\frown}{ABC}) = 150°$.

18. (B)

Two of the sides of $\triangle ABC$ and their included angle are given. We wish to find the third side, c. Therefore, use the law of cosines to find c.

$$c^2 = a^2 + b^2 - 2ab \cos C$$

$$c^2 = 30^2 + 50^2 - 2(30)(50) \cos 25°$$

$$c^2 = 900 + 2,500 - 2(30)(50)(0.9063)$$

$$c^2 = 681.1$$

$$c \approx 26 \text{ (to two significant digits)}$$

Use the law of sines to find $\angle A$.

$$\frac{\sin A}{30} = \frac{\sin 25°}{26}$$

$$\sin A = \frac{(30)(\sin 25°)}{26} = \frac{(30)(0.4226)}{26}$$

$$\sin A = 0.4876$$

$$\angle A = 29° \text{ (to the nearest degree)}$$

Now $\angle B$ can be found from $\angle A$ and $\angle C$

$$\angle A + \angle B + \angle C = 180°$$

$$\angle B = 180° - \angle A - \angle C$$

$$= 180° - (\angle A + \angle C)$$

$$= 180° - (29° + 25°)$$

$$= 180° - (54°)$$

$$\angle B = 126°$$

19. (D)

If $\overline{BC} \perp \overline{AE}$, then $\angle ABC$ and $\angle DBE$ are both 90°. In addition, if $\angle E = \angle C$, then $\triangle ABC$ is similar to $\triangle DBE$ by the angle-angle correspondence. Therefore, $\angle A = \angle D$. By Angle-Side-Angle, $\triangle CAB \cong \triangle EDB$. Thus, $\overline{BC} \cong \overline{BE}$ since they are corresponding parts of congruent triangles; so, Answer Choice (D) is correct.

Answer choices (A) and (C) do not apply since there are relationships between the line segments in the given triangles besides those relationships resulting from congruent triangles. Answer Choice (B) is wrong since the hypotenuse of a right triangle must be larger than either of its legs.

20. (D)

The change in cumulative percentage from 45 to 50 to 55 to 60 is fairly constant, indicating that about the same number of students scored 50, 55, and 60. Choice A is incorrect. To find the median in a cumulative graph, trace a horizontal line from 50 on the y-axis. We see that here the median is a score of 40. Choice B is incorrect. The height of the bar at score 50 is a cumulative percentage of about 90. This means 90% scored below or at 50. Choice C is wrong. The bars for scores 30 and 35 are not of the same height, so some students must have scored 35.

21. (D)

When given an inequality with an absolute value, recall the definition of absolute value:

$$|x| = \begin{cases} x \text{ if } x \geq 0 \\ -x \text{ if } x < 0 \end{cases}$$

$$6x - 5 \leq 8 \text{ if } 6x - 5 \geq 0.$$

$$-6x + 5 \leq 8 \text{ if } 6x - 5 < 0.$$

$$-6x + 5 \leq 8 \text{ can be written as } 6x - 5 \geq -8.$$

We can set up both of these equations as follows.

$$-8 \leq 6x - 5 \leq 8$$

adding 5: $\quad -3 \leq 6x \leq 13$

dividing by 6: $\quad -\frac{1}{2} \leq x \leq \frac{13}{6}.$

So the values of x which satisfy $|6x - 5| \leq 8$ are $[-\frac{1}{2}, \frac{13}{6}]$.

22. (A)

Find the y-axis. Find the side of the figure closest to the y-axis and measure the distance that this side is from the y-axis. A reflection of the figure will put this side the same distance from the y-axis, but on the other side.

Also, notice the point labelled C. A reflection of this point across the y-axis will also be the same distance from the y-axis, but on the other side.

23. (A)

Let $y = \log_8 3 = x \log_2 3$.

Then $8^y = 3 \Rightarrow 2^{3y} = 3$ (1)

and $y = x\log_2 3 \Rightarrow 2^y = 3^x$ (2)

Substituting the expression for 2^y in (2) into (1) we obtain

$$3 = (2^y)^3 = (3^x)^3 = 3^{3x}.$$

Hence $3x = 1 \Rightarrow x = \dfrac{1}{3}$.

24. (A)

Since $g(f(x)) = x$, $f(x)$ and $g(x)$ must be inverse functions. To find the inverse function for $f(x)$, first solve $f(x) = y = 3x + 2$ for x.

$$x = \frac{y-2}{3}.$$

Then interchange (switch) x and y:

$$y = \frac{x-2}{3}.$$

This is $g(x)$.

25. (B)

$$\frac{x}{y} = \frac{3+2i}{1+3i}$$
$$= \frac{3+2i}{1+3i} \times \frac{1-3i}{1-3i}$$
$$= \frac{3-9i+2i-6i^2}{1^2-3^2i^2}$$
$$= \frac{9-7i}{1+9}$$
$$= \frac{9}{10} - \frac{7}{10}i$$

26. (B)

625 square feet $\times$ .30 room for Baby Grand Piano = 187.5 square feet

187.5 square feet for Baby Grand Piano + 46.7 square feet for stage

= 234.2 square feet

Answer (A) is wrong because addition was incorrectly used.

30 + 46.7 = 76.7 square feet

Answer (C) is wrong because of incorrect usage of a subtraction step.

625 − 30 − 46.7 = 548.3 square feet

Answer (D) is wrong because of incorrect multiplication followed by a subtraction step.

46.7 $\times$ .30 = 14.01

625 − 14.01 = 610.99 square feet

27. (A)

The Distributive Property states that $(a)(b+c) = ab + ac$. The Commutative Property states that m + n = n + m. By substituting 4 for a, 7 for b, and 9 for c, we can see that answer choice (A) satisfies the Distributive Property. Now, by substituting (4)(7) for m and (4)(9) for n, we can see that answer choice (A) also satisfies the Commutative Property. In each case, these properties are satisfied for the operation related to addition. Answer Choice (B) only satisfies the Distributive Property. Answer choice (C) only satisfies the Commutative Property. Answer choice (D) satisfies neither of these two properties, and is actually an incorrect statement.

28. (B)

We imagine the prism as a stack of equilateral triangles, congruent to the base of the prism. Let each of these triangles be one unit of measure thick. We can then calculate the area of the base, B, and multiply it by the number of bases needed to complete the height of the prism, h, to obtain the volume of the prism. Therefore,

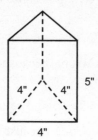

$$V = Bh.$$

All prism volumes can be thought of in this way.

In this particular problem, the base is an equilateral triangle. Therefore

$$B = \frac{s^2\sqrt{3}}{4},$$

where s is the length of a side of the base. By substitution,

$$B = \frac{(4)^2\sqrt{3}}{4} = 4\sqrt{3}.$$

Since the prism is 5 units high,

$$V = Bh = \left(4\sqrt{3}\right)5 = 20\sqrt{3}.$$

Therefore, the volume of the prism is $20\sqrt{3}$ cu. units.

29. (A)

The number of distinct ways of arranging nine people in a line.

The actual numerical value of this answer choice is given by 9 factorial, which equals 362,880. The answers for Answer Choices (B), (C), and (D), respectively are 358,800; 237,336; and 262,144

30. (D)

$$f(x) = e^{\frac{x^3}{3}-x}$$

$$\Rightarrow f'(x) = \left(x^2 - 1\right)e^{\frac{x^3}{3}-x}, \text{ by the chain rule.}$$

We see $f(x) = e^{\frac{x^3}{3}-x} > 0$ for every real number x, and $x^2 - 1 = (x + 1)(x - 1)$

$$\Rightarrow x^2 - 1 < 0 \text{ when } x \in (-1, 1) \text{ and}$$
$$x^2 - 1 > 0 \text{ when } |x| > 1.$$

Hence,

$$f'(x) = (x^2 - 1)e^{\frac{x^3}{3}-x} < 0 \text{ for } x \in (-1, 1) \text{ and}$$

$$f'(x) = (x^2 - 1)e^{\frac{x^3}{3}-x} > 0 \text{ for } |x| > 1.$$

(D) is the answer.

31. (C)

The x-value of the vertex of this parabola is given by $-(-3)/[(2)(-1)] = -1.5$. The corresponding y-value $= -(-1.5)^2 - 3(-1.5) + 4 = 6.25$. Since the coefficient of x^2 is negative, this parabola will have its highest point at the vertex, which is $(-1.5, 6.25)$. Thus, the range will be all numbers less than or equal to the y-value of the vertex, which is 6.25.

32. (D)

Using the Normal Distribution, the critical z value is 2.05. The corresponding raw score is $(3)(2.05) + 70 = 76.15$ Since we need a minimum integer score, the correct answer is 77.

33. (D)

We employ the slope intercept form for the equation to be written, since we are given the y-intercept. Our task is then to determine the slope.

We are given the equation of a line parallel to the line whose equation we wish to find. We know that the slopes of two parallel lines are equal. Hence, by finding the slope of the given line, we will also be finding the unknown slope. To find the slope of the given equation

$$6x + 3y = 4$$

we transform the equation $6x + 3y = 4$ into slope intercept form.

$$6x + 3y = 4$$
$$3y = -6x + 4$$
$$y = -\frac{6}{3}x + \frac{4}{3}$$
$$y = -2x + \frac{4}{3}$$

Therefore, the slope of the line we are looking for is -2. The y-intercept is -6. Applying the slope intercept form,

$$y = mx + b,$$

to the unknown line, we obtain,

$$y = -2x - 6$$

as the equation of the line.

34. (C)

$h(x) = f(x) + g(x)$ and we are told that $f(x) = x^2 - x - 3$ and $g(x) = \frac{x^2 - 1}{x + 2}$.

To find $h(2)$, we replace x by 2 in the above formula for $h(x)$,

$$h(2) = (2^2 - 2 - 3) + \left(\frac{2^2 - 1}{2 + 2}\right)$$

$$= (4 - 2 - 3) + \frac{3}{4}$$

$$= -1 + \frac{3}{4}$$

$$= \frac{1}{4}$$

Thus, $h(2) = -\frac{1}{4}$.

35. (D)

First, calculate $7 \cdot 2 - 2 = 14 - 2 = 12$. Second, calculate $6^2 = 36$. Third, divide 36 by 12 to get 3. Fourth, multiply 3 by 4 to get 12. Finally, add 3 to 12 to get 15. In none of these steps is 3 added to 36.

36. (C)

If the 66th number is the third quartile, $\frac{3n + 3}{4} = 66$. Multiplying both sides by 4, $3n + 3 = 264$. Then $3n = 261$, so $n = 87$. The first quartile's position is given by $\frac{87 + 1}{4} = 22$.

37. (C)

The quickest way to solve this would be to test each sequence. For choice (A), the first-order difference is given by 6, 18, 54, 162, ... , so its second-order difference is given by 12, 36, 108, ... Choice (A) is wrong. For choice (B), the first-order difference is given by 3, 3, 3, 3, ... , so its second-order difference is given by 0, 0 , 0, ... Choice (B) is wrong. For choice (C), the first-order difference is given by 4, 7, 10, 13, ... , so its second-order difference is given by 3, 3, 3, ... Choice (C) is correct. We should also check choice (D). Here, the first-order difference is given by 4, 9, 17, 25, ... , so the second-order difference is given by 5, 8, 8, ... Choice (D) is wrong.

38. (D)

$P_3 = P_2 + 1 = 3$. $P_4 = (2)(P_3) = 6$, $P_5 = P_4 + 1 = 7$, $P_6 = (2)(P_5) = 14$. Then $P_5 + P_6 = 7 + 14 = 21$.

39. (D)

If a point has initial coordinates of (x, y), then after a 90° counterclockwise rotation, its new coordinates will be $(-y, x)$. Thus, the point $(3, 1)$ will become $(-1, 3)$ with this rotation.

40. (B)

The area of the square is $(8)(8) = 64$. Since the diameter of the circle is 8, the radius of the circle is 4. So, the area of the circle is $(\pi)(4)(4) = 16 \pi$. The required probability is $\dfrac{16\pi}{64} \approx .785$, which is approximately .80

Part B: Solutions

41.

a. Since the plan does not pay for the first $250, and pays 80% of the amount that exceeds $250, Melissa paid $250 + (.20)($700−$250) = $250 + $90 = $340.

b. $445 − $400 = $45. Since Plan B covers 90% of the cost above $400, $45 represents 10% of Steve's bills above $400. $45/.10 = $450. Finally, the actual total of his dental bills was $400 + $450 = $850.

c. Let X = total amount for each plan. For Plan A, the individual will pay $250 + (.20)(X − $250). For Plan B, the individual will pay $400 + (.10)(X − $400). Equating these expressions, $250 + (.20)(X−$250) = $400 + (.10)(X − $400). Simplifying, $250 + .20X − $50 = $400 + .10X − $40. Further simplification yields .10X = $160, so X = $1600.

42.

a. Surface Area = $(\pi)(1) \times \sqrt{1^2 + 3^2} + (\pi)(1)^2$

≈ 13.08 square inches.

b. Surface Area = $(\pi)(1.5) \times \sqrt{1.5^2 + 4^2}$

$+ (\pi)(1.5)^2 \approx 27.2$ square inches.

$(27.2)(.015) \approx \$0.41$.

c. The two machines are making a total of 10 cans per minute. (10)($0.41) = $4.10 is the cost of making these 10 cans. $1000/$4.10 ≈ 243.9, which must be rounded <u>down</u> to 243 minutes.

Special Note: If a student uses $0.408 in Part B, then an acceptable answer for Part C is $1000/$4.08 ≈ 245 minutes.

43.

a. The five ordered pairs are (1, 2), (2, −4), (3, −6), (4, −4), and (5, 2). The graph should appear as:

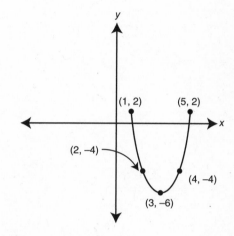

b. Set $x = 0$ and solve for y. $y = 2(0−3)^2 − 6$

$= (2)(9) − 6 = 12$.

c. Set $y = 0$ and solve for x. $0 = 2(x−3)^2 − 6$. Then $6 = 2(x−3)^2$, which becomes $3 = (x − 3)^2$. Simplifying, $x − 3 = \pm\sqrt{3}$. Thus $x = 3 \pm \sqrt{3}$. Rounded off to the nearest hundredth, the answers are 1.27 and 4.73.

Praxis II

Middle School
Mathematics Test (0069)

Practice Test 3

Sample Mathematics Definitions and Formulas

NOTATION

(a, b)	$\{x: a < x < b\}$
$[a, b)$	$\{x: a \leq x < b\}$
$(a, b]$	$\{x: a < x \leq b\}$
$[a, b]$	$\{x: a \leq x \leq b\}$
gcd (m, n)	<u>greatest common divisor</u> of two integers m and n
lcm (m, n)	<u>least common multiple</u> of two integers m and n
$[x]$	<u>greatest integer</u> m such that $m \leq x$
$m \equiv k(\text{mod } n)$	m and k are <u>congruent modulo n</u> (m and k have the same remainder when divided by n, or equivalently, $m - k$ is a multiple of n)
f^{-1}	<u>inverse</u> of an invertible function f (<u>not</u> the same as $\dfrac{1}{f}$)
$\lim\limits_{x \to a^+} f(x)$	<u>right-hand limit</u> of $f(x)$; limit of $f(x)$ as x approaches a from the right
$\lim\limits_{x \to a^-} f(x)$	<u>left-hand limit</u> of $f(x)$; limit of $f(x)$ as x approaches a from the left
$\emptyset$	the empty set
$x \in S$	x is an element of set S
$S \subset T$	set S is a proper subset of set T
$S \subseteq T$	either set S is a proper subset of set T or $S = T$
$S \cup T$	union of sets S and T
$S \cap T$	intersection of sets S and T

DEFINITIONS

Discrete Mathematics

A relation $\Re$ on a set S is
> reflexive if $x \Re x$ for all $x \in S$
> symmetric if $x \Re y \Rightarrow y \Re x$ for all $x, y \in S$
> transitive if $(x \Re y$ and $y \Re z) \Rightarrow x \Re z$ for all $x, y, z \in S$
> antisymmetric if $(x \Re y$ and $y \Re x) \Rightarrow x = y$ for all $x, y \in S$

An equivalence relation is a reflexive, symmetric, and transitive relation.

FORMULAS

Sum

$\sin(x \pm y) = \sin x \cos y \pm \cos x \sin y$

$\cos(x \pm y) = \cos x \cos y \mp \sin x \sin y$

$\tan(x \pm y) = \dfrac{\tan x \pm \tan y}{1 \mp \tan x \tan y}$

Half-angle (sign depends on the quadrant of $\dfrac{\theta}{2}$)

$\sin \dfrac{\theta}{2} = \pm \sqrt{\dfrac{1 - \cos \theta}{2}}$

$\cos \dfrac{\theta}{2} = \pm \sqrt{\dfrac{1 + \cos \theta}{2}}$

Range of Inverse Trigonometric Functions

$\sin^{-1} x \qquad \left[-\dfrac{\pi}{2}, \dfrac{\pi}{2} \right]$

$\cos^{-1} x \qquad [0, \pi]$

$\tan^{-1} x \qquad \left(-\dfrac{\pi}{2}, \dfrac{\pi}{2} \right)$

Law of Sines

$\dfrac{\sin A}{a} = \dfrac{\sin B}{b} = \dfrac{\sin C}{c}$

Law of Cosines

$c^2 = a^2 + b^2 - 2ab (\cos C)$

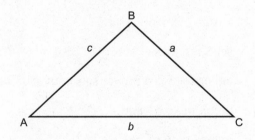

DeMoivre's Theorem

$(\cos \theta + i \sin \theta)^k = \cos(k\theta) + i \sin(k\theta)$

Coordinate Transformation

Rectangular (x, y) to polar (r, θ) : $r^2 = x^2 + y^2$; $\tan \theta = \dfrac{y}{x}$ if $x \neq 0$

Polar (r, θ) to rectangular (x, y): $x = r \cos \theta$; $y = r \sin \theta$

Distance from point (x_1, y_1) to line $Ax + By + C = 0$

$$d = \frac{|Ax_1 + By_1 + C|}{\sqrt{A^2 + B^2}}$$

Volume

Sphere with radius r: $\quad\quad\quad\quad\quad\quad\quad\quad\quad\quad\quad V = \frac{4}{3}\pi r^3$

Right circular cone with height h and base of radius r: $\quad V = \frac{1}{3}\pi r^2 h$

Right circular cylinder with height h and base of radius r: $\quad V = \pi r^2 h$

Pyramid with height h and base of area B: $\quad\quad\quad\quad\quad V = \frac{1}{3}Bh$

Right prism with height h and base of area B: $\quad\quad\quad\quad V = Bh$

Surface Area

Sphere with radius r: $\quad\quad\quad\quad\quad\quad\quad\quad\quad\quad\quad A = 4\pi r^2$

Right circular cone with radius r and slant height s: $\quad\quad A = \pi rs + \pi r^2$

Differentiation

$(f(x)g(x))' = f'(x)g(x) + f(x)g'(x)$

$(f(g(x)))' = f'(g(x))g'(x)$

$\left(\dfrac{f(x)}{g(x)}\right)' = \dfrac{f'(x)g(x) - f(x)g'(x)}{(g(x))^2}$ if $g(x) \neq 0$

Integration by Parts

$\displaystyle\int u\, dv = uv - \int v\, du$

PRAXIS II: Middle School Mathematics Practice Test 3

TIME: 2 hours
40 Multiple-choice questions (Part A)
3 Short constructed-response questions (Part B)

Part A

> **Directions:** Read each item and select the best response.

1. Use this graph to answer the question.

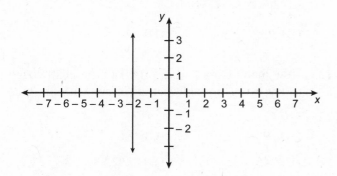

Which equation is represented above?

(A) $x = 2$ (C) $y = 2$

(B) $x = -2$ (D) $y = -2$

2. Which is a factor of $6x^2 + 2x - 4$?

(A) $(3x - 4)$ (C) $(x - 1)$

(B) $(6x - 1)$ (D) $(3x - 2)$

3. In an apartment building there are 9 apartments having terraces for every 16 apartments. If the apartment building has a total of 144 apartments, how many apartments have terraces?

(A) 137   (C) 63

(B) 81   (D) 102

4. If $m \overset{\frown}{ABC}$ is $\frac{3}{2}\pi$ radians, then y is equal to

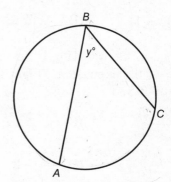

(A) 90°.   (C) 45°.

(B) 72°.   (D) 36°.

5. The best representation to highlight periodic behaviour is a

(A) line graph.

(B) paragraph describing the amplitude.

(C) trigonometric equation.

(D) diagram of the unit circle.

6. From the following choices, select a good definition for the mathematics term *slope*

   (A) Rise over run.

   (B) The ratio of the change in the dependent variable to the change in the independent variable.

   (C) *m*

   (D) How steep something is compared to another thing that is not steep.

7. If $f(x) = 7x^2 + 3$ and $g(x) = 2x - 9$, then $g(f(2)) =$

   (A) 53.   (C) 28.

   (B) 31.   (D) 19.

8. What is the domain of the function defined by

$$y = f(x) = \sqrt{-x + 1} + 5?$$

   (A) $\{x \mid x \geq 0\}$ (C) $\{x \mid 0 \leq x \leq 1\}$

   (B) $\{x \mid x \leq 1\}$ (D) $\{x \mid x \geq -1\}$

9. Which one of the following is the correct representation of the expression, "Eight less than the quotient of 50 and 5"?

   (A) $\dfrac{(50-8)}{5}$ (C) $\dfrac{(8-50)}{5}$

   (B) $8 - \dfrac{50}{5}$ (D) $\dfrac{50}{5} - 8$

10. Choose the correct solution set for the system of linear equations.

$$4x + 2y = -1$$
$$5x - 3y = 7$$

   (A) $\{(2, 1)\}$

   (B) $\{(\frac{1}{2}, -\frac{3}{2})\}$

   (C) $\{(x, y) \mid 4x + 2y = -1\}$

   (D) The empty set

11.

In the above figure, if *B* is the midpoint of segment *AD*, then the length of segment *AC* is

   (A) $3\dfrac{1}{2}$ (C) 4

   (B) $3\dfrac{3}{4}$ (D) $4\dfrac{1}{4}$

12. How many games would it take a baseball coach to try every possible batting order with his nine players?

   (A) 9   (C) 81

   (B) 45   (D) 362,880

13. Find the median of the following sample data: 6, 20, 7, 3, 18, 4, 8, 14.

   (A) 7.5   (C) 10

   (B) 8   (D) 80

14. The following plot represents an individual's shoe size and height.

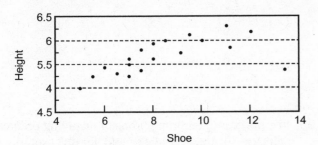

Which of the following best describes the relationship between shoe size and height?

(A) There appears to be no relationship between shoe size and height.

(B) An increase in height causes an increase in shoe size.

(C) There appears to be a negative relationship between shoe size and height.

(D) There appears to be a positive relationship between shoe size and height.

15. Solve for x.

$$5x + 2y = -5$$
$$-3x + y = 3$$

(A) 0   (C) 1

(B) $-\dfrac{1}{11}$ (D) −1

16. Multiply.

$$(5x^2 + 2)(4x^2 - 7)$$

(A) $20x^4 - 27x^2 - 14$

(B) $20x^4 + 43x^2 - 14$

(C) $20x^4 - 14$

(D) $20x^4 - 35x^2 - 14$

17. Which function(s) below is(are) symmetric with respect to the origin?

I. $f(x) = x^3 - x$

II. $f(x) = 2x + x^5$

III. $f(x) = 2x + 4$

(A) I and II.   (C) I and III.

(B) I only.   (D) II and III.

18. If two fair dice are thrown, what is the probability that the sum of the number of dots on the top faces will be 7?

(A) $\dfrac{1}{2}$ (C) $\dfrac{1}{9}$

(B) $\dfrac{1}{6}$ (D) $\dfrac{1}{12}$

19. If a function is defined as $f(x) = |2 - 5x| < 3$, then the interval which does not contain any solution for x is

(A) $0 < x < 1$.   (C) $-\dfrac{1}{25} < x < 0$.

(B) $0 < x < 2$.   (D) $-\dfrac{3}{5} < x < -\dfrac{1}{2}$.

20. Of a freshman class, half of the students are enrolled in 15 class hours, and most of the remaining freshmen are taking 12 hours with a few students taking 18 hours. Select the statement which is true about this distribution.

(A) The mode is the same as the mean.

(B) The median is less than the mean.

(C) The mean is greater than the mode.

(D) The mean is less than the median.

21.

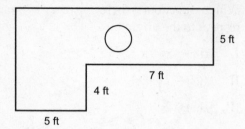

The ceiling of George's bedroom must be painted. The diagram above represents his bedroom and includes a circular light fixture with a diameter of 2 feet. A gallon of paint covers 16 square feet and costs $8.95. How much will George have to spend on paint to cover the entire ceiling except for the light fixture? Assume that paint **cannot** be purchased in fractions of a gallon.

(A) $44.75

(C) $35.80

(B) $50.20

(D) $42.99

22. What is the range of values for which $|2x + 1| \geq 5$ is satisfied?

(A) $x \leq -3$ or $x \geq -2$ (C) $x \leq -2$ or $x \geq 3$

(B) $x \leq 2$ or $x \geq 3$ (D) $x \leq -3$ or $x \geq 2$

23. A certain arc of a circle has a measure of π radians. The ratio between the measure of the arc and the diameter is approximately

(A) 3.14

(C) 2

(B) 6.28

(D) 1.57

24. Representatives to a student group are being selected to fill vacancies. Two of five freshmen will be selected and three of four sophomores will be selected. In how many different ways can these students be selected?

(A) 480

(C) 80

(B) 120

(D) 40

25. If $x = 4 + i$ and $y = 2 - i$, where $i^2 = -1$, then $\frac{x}{y} =$

(A) $\frac{5}{7} + \frac{5}{6}i$

(C) $\frac{5}{6} + \frac{5}{7}i$

(B) $\frac{7}{5} + \frac{6}{5}i$

(D) $\frac{6}{5} + \frac{7}{5}i$

26. In a linear programming problem involving ordered pairs (x, y), the restraints yield feasible solutions in a region where the corner points are $(0, 0)$, $(0, 10)$, $(16, 8)$, and $(40, 0)$. Which one of the following objective functions would <u>not</u> have a unique point on this region that corresponds to a maximum P value?

(A) $P = 20x + 70y$ (C) $P = 40x + 100y$

(B) $P = 30x + 90y$ (D) $P = 30x + 350y$

27. If the probability of a certain team winning is ¾, what is the probability that this team will win its first 3 games and lose the fourth?

(A) $\frac{3}{256}$

(C) $\frac{27}{256}$

(B) $\frac{9}{256}$

(D) $\frac{81}{256}$

28.

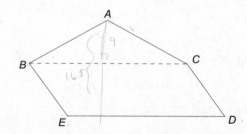

NOTE: Figure not drawn to scale

In the figure above, BCDE is a parallelogram. The distance from point A to $\overline{BC}$ is 9 and the distance from point A to $\overline{DE}$ is 16.5. If the area of ABCDE is 136.8, what is the length of $\overline{DE}$?

(A) 16.55

(C) 8.45

(B) 11.40

(D) 6.50

29. What is the range of values for which $|3x - 4| \leq 8$ is satisfied?

   (A) $-4 \leq x \leq -\dfrac{4}{3}$ (C) $\dfrac{4}{3} \leq x \leq 4$

   (B) $-4 \leq x \leq \dfrac{4}{3}$ (D) $-\dfrac{4}{3} \leq x \leq 4$

30. What type of triangle is $\triangle ABC$?

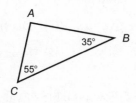

   (A) Right triangle

   (B) Equilateral triangle

   (C) Isosceles triangle

   (D) Obtuse triangle

31. The position of a particle moving along a straight line at any time t is given by $s(t) = 2t^3 - 4t^2 + 2t - 1$. The least velocity during the time interval $[0, 2]$ is

   (A) 4.25   (C) -0.67

   (B) 0.5   (D) -1.5

32. The scatter plot below shows the relationship between grade level and hours of reading each week. Which statement describes this relationship?

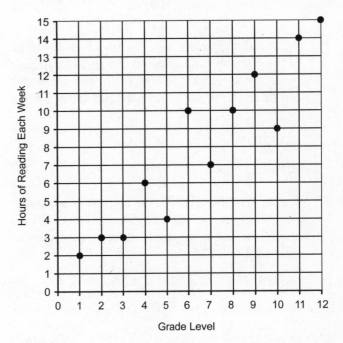

   (A) As grade level goes down, the number of reading hours goes up.

   (B) As grade level goes up, the number of reading hours goes down.

   (C) As grade level goes up, the number of reading hours goes up.

   (D) Grade level and reading hours are unrelated.

33. If $f(x) = x^3 - x - 1$, then the set of all c for which $f(c) = f(-c)$ is

   (A) {all real numbers}.

   (B) {0}.

   (C) {0, 1}.

   (D) {−1, 0, 1}.

34. If $f'(c) = 0$ for $f(x) = 3x^2 - 12x + 9$, where $0 \leq x \leq 4$, then $c =$

    (A) 2   (C) 0

    (B) 3   (D) 1

35. A zoo has eight elephants. On any given day three of the elephants are selected and lined up to give rides to the visitors. In how many different ways can three elephants be selected and arranged in a line?

    (A) 21   (C) 336

    (B) 24   (D) 6

36. For the rhombus ABCD, the point A is located at $(-1, 5)$ and the point B is located at $(5, 3)$. Which one of the following could represent the coordinates of point C?

    (A) $(3, -4)$ (C) $(7, -3)$

    (B) $(5, -1)$ (D) $(9, -2)$

37. In calculating the value of $5 + 7^2 \div (9 - 3)$, which order of operations should be performed *last*?

    (A) Subtraction   (C) Addition

    (B) Squaring   (D) Division

38. Which of the following groups of data has two modes?

    (A) 2, 2, 3, 3, 4, 4, 5, 6, 7

    (B) 2, 2, 2, 3, 3, 4, 4, 4, 5

    (C) 2, 3, 3, 4, 4, 4, 5, 5, 6

    (D) 2, 3, 3, 3, 3, 4, 5, 6, 6

39. $(7)(3 + 2) = (3 + 2)(7)$ is an example of which property of numbers?

    (A) Associative   (C) Distributive

    (B) Commutative   (D) Inverse

40. Look at the following table of values:

x	0	3	a	9	12
y	7	1	-5	b	-17

    If there is a linear relationship between x and y, what is the value of ab?

    (A) -66 (C) -12

    (B) -30 (D) -4

PRAXIS EXAM Part B: 3 Short Constructed-Response Questions

41. Let A represent the event that it will rain tomorrow in Seattle. Let B represent the event that it will be sunny tomorrow in Tampa. Assume that these two events are independent. The probability of A occurring is 0.80, and the probability of B occurring is 0.30

    a. What is the probability that it will <u>not</u> rain tomorrow in Seattle and that it will <u>not</u> be sunny in Tampa tomorrow?

    b. What is the probability that at least one of these two events will occur?

    c. What is the probability that exactly one of these two events will occur?

42. In a class of 50 students, 23 of them like vanilla ice cream, 22 like chocolate ice cream, and 16 like strawberry ice cream. Also, 7 like both vanilla and chocolate ice cream, 6 like both chocolate and strawberry ice cream, 11 like both vanilla and strawberry ice cream, and 4 students like all three flavors.

    a. Draw a complete Venn Diagram, showing all three circles that will represent each ice cream flavor. Include the cardinality of each of the 8 regions. (One region lies outside all three circles, but within the Universal Set of 50 students).

    b. How many students like exactly one of these flavors?

    c. How many students like neither chocolate nor strawberry ice cream?

43. a. On the xy-plane, graph the ellipse given by the equation $\dfrac{x^2}{36} + \dfrac{y^2}{16} = 1$. Identify the coordinates of the center and label the coordinates of the four intercepts.

    b. What are the coordinates of the foci?

    c. Determine which points on the ellipse satisfy the condition that the x and y values are equal. (Round off the answers to the nearest hundredth).

Practice Test 3 Answer Key

Question Number	Correct Answer	Content Category	Question Number	Correct Answer	Content Category
1.	B	Arithmetic and Basic Algebra	23.	D	Geometry
2.	D	Arithmetic and Basic Algebra	24.	D	Discrete Mathematics
3.	B	Arithmetic and Basic Algebra	25.	B	Arithmetic and Basic Algebra
4.	C	Geometry	26.	B	Discrete Mathematics
5.	A	Discrete Mathematics	27.	C	Probability
6.	B	Arithmetic and Basic Algebra	28.	B	Geometry
7.	A	Functions	29.	D	Arithmetic and Basic Algebra
8.	B	Functions	30.	A	Geometry
9.	D	Arithmetic and Basic Algebra	31.	C	Functions
10.	B	Arithmetic and Basic Algebra	32.	C	Data and Statistical Concepts
11.	C	Measurement	33.	D	Functions
12.	D	Discrete Mathematics	34.	A	Functions
13.	A	Data and Statistical Concepts	35.	C	Discrete Mathematics
14.	D	Data and Statistical Concepts	36.	C	Geometry
15.	D	Arithmetic and Basic Algebra	37.	C	Arithmetic and Basic Algebra
16.	A	Arithmetic and Basic Algebra	38.	B	Data and Statistical Concepts
17.	A	Functions	39.	B	Arithmetic and Basic Algebra
18.	B	Probability	40.	A	Arithmetic and Basic Algebra
19.	D	Functions	41.	—	Short Constructed Response
20.	D	Data and Statistical Concepts	42.	—	Short Constructed Response
21.	A	Geometry	43.	—	Short Constructed Response
22.	D	Arithmetic and Basic Algebra			

Practice Test 3

Detailed Explanations of Answers

Part A

1. (B)

The graphs of the equations represented by the other choices are as follows.

Answer choice (A): $x = 2$

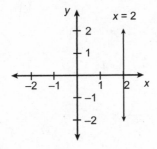

Answer choice (C): $y = 2$

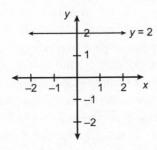

Answer choice (D): $y = -2$

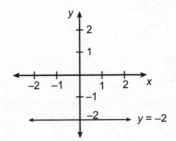

The graph of $x = -2$ is parallel to the y-axis and passes through the point $(-2, 0)$.

2. (D)

$$6x^2 + 2x - 4 = 2(3x^2 + x - 2),$$

factoring out a 2 from each term. The $(3x^2 + x - 2)$ is further factored by finding the terms which multiply to $3x^2$, namely, $3x$ and x; and by finding the terms which multiply to -2, namely, -2 and 1 or $+2$ and -1. Here are the possibilities. Check the product of the inner terms and the product of the outer terms for each factor. We are looking for the middle term of $3x^2 + x - 2$, i.e., $+1x$.

$$3x^2 + x - 2 =$$

$$
\begin{array}{cc}
\overset{-3x}{(3\overbrace{x + 2)(x}-1)} & \overset{+3x}{(3\overbrace{x - 2)(x}+1)} \\
\underline{+2x} & \underline{-2x} \\
-1x & +1x
\end{array}
$$

$$-6x$$
$$(3\,x+1)(x-2)$$
$$+1x$$
$$-5x$$

$$+6x$$
$$(3\,x-1)(x-2)$$
$$-1x$$
$$+5x$$

This says

$$3x^2 + x - 2 = (3x - 2)(x + 1).$$

Therefore,

$$6x^2 + 2x - 4 = 2(3x - 2)(x + 1),$$

and the factor which appears as one of the choices is $(3x - 2)$.

Answer choice (A) is incorrect because of a wrong use of the distributive law.

$$6x^2 + 2x - 4$$
$$2(3x^2 + x - 2) = 2(3x - 2)(x + 1)$$
$$2(3x - 2) = 3x - 4$$

Answer choice (B) is incorrect because of improper factoring out using the "F.O.I.L." method.

$$6x^2 + 2x - 4 = (6x - 1)(x + 4)$$

Answer choice (C) is also incorrect because of a change in sign.

$$6x^2 + 2x - 4 = 2(3x - 2)(x + 1), (x + 1)$$
$$= (x - 1)$$

3. (B)

$$\frac{9 \text{ apartments with terraces}}{16 \text{ apartments}} = \frac{?}{144 \text{ apartments}}$$

Solving this proportion for the "?"

$$? = \frac{9 \text{ apartments} \times 144 \text{ apartments}}{16 \text{ apartments}}$$

$$= \frac{1296 \text{ apartments}}{16 \text{ apartments}} = 81 \text{ apartments}$$

Answer (A) is incorrect because the apartments were subtracted.

$$144 - (16 - 9) = 144 - 7 = 137 \text{ apartments}$$

Answer (C) is incorrect because the number of apartments with terraces is 9 not $16 - 9$.

$$(144 \div 16) \times (16 - 9) = 9 \times 7 = 63$$

Answer (D) is incorrect due to a multiplication factor guess of 6.

$$144 - [(16 - 9) \times 6] = 102$$

4. (C)

From a theorem we know that the measure of an inscribed angle is equal to $\frac{1}{2}$ the intercepted arc.

We are told that $m \stackrel{\frown}{ABC}$ is $\frac{3}{2}\pi$ radians. There are 2π radians in a circle. Therefore, the intercepted arc is the remaining $\frac{\pi}{2}$ radians.

Converting to degrees:

$$\left(\frac{\pi}{2}\right)\left(\frac{180}{\pi}\right) = 90°$$

The angle y is half of this:

$$y = \frac{90°}{2} = 45°.$$

5. (A)

Choice (A) is the correct answer. A line graph allows the user to see trends in the data and to explore those trends. Choice (B) is incomplete in that it includes only a discussion of the amplitude of the periodic behavior. As well, written words would not provide the visual evidence and impact that is supplied by a graph. Choice (C) may provide a clue to the periodic nature of the behavior to someone that is already very comfortable with trigonometric functions and their graphs. However, the user that can see this behavior by looking at an equation is actually translating the information from the equation to the graph in their mind. To display the nature of periodicity a graph is essential. Choice (D) is not correct for the same reasons as Choice (C).

6. (B)

The answer is (B). It is the mathematical definition of slope. The comparison shows how one variable changes with respect to change in another variable. Choice (A) is incorrect because although it is a common mnemonic device to remember the formula for slope it provides very little information about what the slope actually is and requires the user to remember the definitions of rise and run. Choice (C) is simply a letter, perhaps a variable, but without any other reference the reader does not know if it is the 'm' from the equation for a linear function. Choice (D) is an explanation that a student with cursory understanding might provide. There is insufficient detail and lack of clarity.

7. (A)

$$f(x) = 7x^2 + 3, g(x) = 2x - 9$$

Substituting 2 into $f(x)$:

$$f(2) = 7(2)^2 + 3 = 31.$$

So $g(f(2)) = g(31)$.

Substituting and solving:

$$g(31) = 2(31) - 9 = 53$$

8. (B)

The only restriction for the domain is that $-x + 1$ must be greater than or equal to zero.

$$-x + 1 \geq 0$$
$$\Rightarrow x \leq 1$$

9. (D)

The quotient of 50 and 5 means to divide 50 by 5, written as $\dfrac{50}{5}$. Eight less than this amount means to subtract 8, which leads to $\dfrac{50}{5} - 8$.

10. (B)

Multiply the first equation by 3 and the second equation by 2. Then add them together.

$$\begin{array}{r} 3(4x + 2y = -1) \\ 2(5x - 3y = 7) \\ \hline 12x + 6y = -3 \\ 10x - 6y = 14 \\ \hline 22x = 11 \\ x = \dfrac{1}{2} \end{array}$$

Take this value of x and put it into either original equations, and solve for y.

$$4x + 2y = -1$$
$$4\left(\dfrac{1}{2}\right) + 2y = -1$$
$$2 + 2y = -1$$
$$2y = -3$$
$$y = -\dfrac{3}{2}$$

The answers are $x = \dfrac{1}{2}$ and $y = -\dfrac{3}{2}$ or $\left(\dfrac{1}{2}, -\dfrac{3}{2}\right)$

11. (C)

$$\begin{aligned} AC &= AD - CD \\ &= 2AB - CD \qquad \text{(as } AD = 2AB) \\ &= 2 \times 2\dfrac{3}{4} - 1 - \dfrac{1}{2} \\ &= \dfrac{22}{4} - \dfrac{6}{4} \\ &= \dfrac{16}{4} \\ &= 4 \end{aligned}$$

12. (D)

This is the number of possible permutations of nine items which is $n!$ (n-factorial). Most scientific calculators have a $x!$ button. Otherwise, the factorial formula is $9 \times 8 \times 7 \times 6 \times 5 \times 4 \times 3 \times 2 \times 1 = 362,880$.

13. (A)

Choice (A) is the correct answer. The median is the middle number of a data set in numerical order. First arrange the set in order: 3, 4, 6, 7, 8, 14, 18, 20. Then locate the middle term. In this case the middle term would fall midway between 7 and 8, so the median is 7.5. (B) is from incorrectly rounding the median. (C) is the mean, and (D) is the sum total of the data set.

14. (D)

is the correct solution. We can see from the figure that as shoe size increases so does height, so there is a positive relationship which rules out (A) and (C). The problem with (B) is that neither variable causes a change in the other variable.

15. (D)

$$5x + 2y = -5$$
$$-3x + y = 3$$

Multiply the bottom equation by -2 so that the terms in the y-column will cancel as follows (in this way if the y-terms cancel you will be solving for x).

$$
\begin{array}{ll}
5x + 2y = -5 & 5x + 2y = -5 \\
-2(-3x + y) = -2(3) \Rightarrow & 6x - 2y = -6 \\
\hline
& \dfrac{11x}{11} = \dfrac{-11}{11} \\
& x = -1
\end{array}
$$

Add the coefficients/terms in the x-column and the constants on the right side. Then divide both sides by 11, the coefficient of the x-term.

Answer choice (A) is incorrect because it solved for the variable y.

$$
\begin{array}{l}
3(5x + 2y = -5) = 15x + 6y = -15 \\
5(-3x + y = 3) = -15x + 5y = 15 \\
\hline
\qquad\qquad\qquad 11y = 0 \\
\qquad\qquad\qquad\ y = 0
\end{array}
$$

Answer choice (B) is incorrect because of an error in adding 2 negative numbers.

$$
\begin{array}{l}
5x + 2y = -5 \\
6x - 2y = -6 \\
\hline
11x \quad\ = -1, \ x = -\dfrac{1}{11}
\end{array}
$$

Answer choice (C) is incorrect because of an error in signs.

$$
\begin{array}{l}
5x + 2y = -5 \\
-6x - 2y = -6 \\
\hline
x \quad\ = 1
\end{array}
$$

16. (A)

Multiplication of binomials assumes that for

$$(5x^2 + 2)(4x^2 - 7) =$$

with labels *last*, *inner*, *first*, *outer*.

we multiply the first terms $(5x^2)\,(4x^2)$ in the parentheses; then we multiply the outer terms $(5x^2)\,(-7)$ in the parentheses; then we multiply the inner terms $(2)\,(4x^2)$ in the parentheses; and then we multiply the last terms $(2)\,(-7)$ in the parentheses.

This means

$$(5x^2 + 2)(4x^2 - 7) =$$
$$\underbrace{(5x^2)(4x^2)}_{20x^4} + \underbrace{(5x^2)(-7)}_{-35x^2} + \underbrace{(2)(4x^2)}_{+8x^2} + \underbrace{(2)(-7)}_{-14} =$$

$\left\{\begin{array}{l}\text{multiplying each}\\ \text{pair of terms and}\\ \text{adding exponents}\\ \text{in the first term}\end{array}\right.$

Combine the like terms $-35x^2 + 8x^2$ and we get

$$20x^4 - 27x^2 - 14$$

Answer (B) is incorrect due to an error in multiplying by a negative number.

$$
\begin{aligned}
(5x^2 + 2)&(4x^2 - 7) \\
&= (5x^2)(4x^2) + (2)(4x^2) + (5x^2)(-7) + (2)(-7) \\
&= 20x^4 + 8x^2 + (-35x^2) - 14 \\
&= 20x^4 + 8x^2 + 35x^2 - 14 \\
&= 20x^4 + 43x^2 - 14
\end{aligned}
$$

Answer (C) is incorrect because the product of inner and outer terms were not added.

$$
\begin{aligned}
(5x^2 + 2)(4x^2 - 7) &= (5x^2)(4x^2) + (2)(-7) \\
&= 20x^4 - 14
\end{aligned}
$$

Answer (D) is also incorrect because the inner product was not added to the outer product.

$$
\begin{aligned}
(5x^2 + 2)(4x^2 - 7) &= (5x^2)(4x^2) + \\
&\quad (5x^2)(-7) + (2)(-7) \\
&= 20x^4 - 35x^2 - 14
\end{aligned}
$$

17. (A)

A function is symmetric with respect to the origin if replacing x by $-x$ and y by $-y$ produces an equivalent function.

(I) $y = f(x) = x^3 - x$

$(-y) = (-x)^3 - (-x)$

$-y = -x^3 + x$

$y = x^3 - x$

(I) is symmetric.

(II) $y = f(x) = 2x + x^5$

$-y = 2(-x) + (-x)^5$

$-y = -2x - x^5$

$y = 2x + x^5$

(II) is symmetric.

(III) $y = f(x) = 2x + 4$

$-y = 2(-x) + 4$

$-y = -2x + 4$

$y = 2x - 4$

(III) is not symmetric.

18. (B)

There are 36 possible outcomes. Six of these produce the number 7:

$(1, 6), (2, 5), (3, 4), (4, 3), (5, 2),$ and $(6, 1).$

Hence the probability is

$$\frac{6}{36} = \frac{1}{6}.$$

19. (D)

The inequality $|2 - 5x| < 3$ may be rewritten as

$-3 < 2 - 5x < 3.$

Subtracting 2 from each side, we obtain:

$-5 < -5x < 1$

Dividing by -5 gives:

$-\frac{1}{5} < x < 1$

This is the interval over which all solutions lie. We are looking for an interval which does not contain any solutions to the inequality. The only interval given in the choices that satisfies this criterion is

$$-\frac{3}{5} < x < -\frac{1}{2}.$$

20. (D)

is the correct choice. From the information given, the mode and median would be 15, and the mean would be less than 15. So, the mean is less than the median. (A) is incorrect because the mode is not the same as the mean. (B) is incorrect because the median is greater than the mean. (C) is incorrect because the mean is less than the mode.

21. (A)

In order to solve this problem, we must determine the area of the ceiling. This is accomplished by drawing a line that creates two rectangles as shown in the accompanying figure.

Determine the area of both rectangles using the formula

$A = \text{length} \times \text{width}$

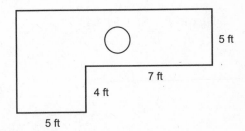

The smaller rectangle will have an area of 5×4 or 20 sq. ft.

To find the length of the larger rectangle, use the information provided on the diagram. The lengths given on the bottom of the diagram are 7 and 5 which add up to 12.

Use the area formula and multiply 12 by 5 which yields 60 sq. ft.

Add the two areas together to obtain $60 + 20 = 80$.

Do not forget about the area of the light fixture. George does not want to paint over the fixture, so we must subtract the area of the light fixture from the total area of the ceiling.

The area of a circle is determined by the formula π times the radius squared.

We are given the diameter of the circle, 2 feet. The radius is half of the diameter, so our radius is 1 foot. Squaring this number leaves us with 1 still. So our formula is now π times 1. This will give us π which is equivalent to about 3.14.

Subtract the area of the light from the total area.

$$80 - 3.14 = 76.86$$

Next, determine how many times 16 (the number of square feet one gallon of paint covers) divides into 76.86.

$$76.86 \div 16 = 4.8.$$

To determine the cost of the project, multiply the number of gallons it will take to paint the ceiling by the price per gallon, $8.95.

Since the number of gallons did not come out to an even number, we must round this number up because you cannot buy 8/10 of a gallon.

4.8 rounds up to 5.

$$5 \text{ gallons} \times \$8.95 = \$44.75$$

22. (D)

When given an inequality with an absolute value, recall the definition of absolute value:

$$|x| = \begin{cases} x \text{ if } x \geq 0 \\ -x \text{ if } x < 0 \end{cases}$$

If $2x + 1 \geq 5$, then $2x \geq 4$, which implies that $x \geq 2$.

If $-2x - 1 \geq 5$, then $-2x \geq 6$, which implies that $x \leq -3$.

So the values of x that satisfy $|2x + 1| \geq 5$ are $x \leq -3$ or $x \geq 2$.

23. (D)

Call the arc AB. $AB = \pi r$ (given). If we multiply both sides by 2 we obtain:

$$2AB = 2\pi r = \pi d, \ AB = \frac{\pi}{2}d$$

$$\frac{AB}{d} = \frac{\pi}{2} \approx \frac{3.14}{2} = 1.57$$

Calculator: $\pi \div 2 = 1.57$

24. (D)

is the correct response. In how many ways can two of five freshmen be selected:

$$_5C_2 \text{ or } \frac{5!}{2!3!} = \frac{5 \times 4 \times 3 \times 2 \times 1}{2 \times 1 \times 3 \times 2 \times 1} = 10$$

Three of four sophomores can be selected in the same manner.

$$_4C_3 \text{ or } \frac{4!}{3!1!} = \frac{4 \times 3 \times 2 \times 1}{3 \times 2 \times 1 \times 1} = 4$$

Since the two events are independent, the values are multiplied (10 × 4 or 40) to determine the number of different ways these students can be selected. (A), (B), and (C) result from the use of inappropriate formulas.

25. (B)

$$\frac{x}{y} = \frac{4+i}{2-1}$$

$$= \frac{4+i}{2-i} \times \frac{2+i}{2+i}$$

$$= \frac{8+6i+i^2}{4-i^2}$$

$$= \frac{7+6i}{5}$$

$$= \frac{7}{5} + \frac{6}{5}i$$

26. (B)

In order for an objective function not to have a unique point that corresponds to a maximum P value, the slope of this function must be the same as one of the lines that form the boundary of this region. The slope of the x-axis is zero and that of the y-axis is undefined. The slope of the line containing (0, 10) and (16, 8) is $-\frac{1}{8}$; the slope of the line containing (40, 0) and (16, 8) is $-\frac{1}{3}$. The only objective function among these four answer choices with any of these slope values is $P = 30x + 90y$. This objective function has a slope of $\frac{-30}{90} = \frac{-1}{3}$.

27. (C)

Let's call the event winning A and not winning $\overline{A}$. We want the probability P given by the expression below:

$$P = P(A) \times P(A) \times P(A) \times P(\overline{A})$$
$$= \frac{3}{4} \times \frac{3}{4} \times \frac{3}{4} \times \frac{1}{4} = \frac{27}{256}$$

28. (B)

The height of parallelogram BCDE is 16.5 − 9 = 7.5. If x is the length of DE, then the area of parallelogram BCDE can be represented by 7.5x. Likewise, the area of $\triangle ABC$ can be represented by $\left(\frac{1}{2}\right)(x)(9) = 4.5x$. Then, 7.5$x$ + 4.5x = 136.8. Solving, $x = \frac{136.8}{12} = 11.40$

29. (D)

When given an inequality with an absolute value, recall the definition of absolute value:

$$|x| = \begin{cases} x \text{ if } x \geq 0 \\ -x \text{ if } x < 0 \end{cases}$$

If $3x - 4 \leq 8$, then $3x \leq 12$, which implies that $x \leq 4$.

If $-3x + 4 \leq 8$, then $-3x \leq 4$, which implies that $x \geq -\frac{4}{3}$.

30. (A)

is the correct answer. The two given angles sum to 90°. Since the angles of a triangle sum to 180°, this leaves 90° for $\angle A$. Since $\angle A$ is 90°, this makes $\triangle ABC$ a right triangle. There is no angle greater than 90°, so $\triangle ABC$ is not an obtuse triangle. Since the angles of $\triangle ABC$ are all different, the sides all have different measures which eliminates (B) and (C).

31. (C)

The rate of movement of the particle is the velocity $s'(t)$. Use your graphic calculator to draw both $s(t)$ and $s'(t)$.

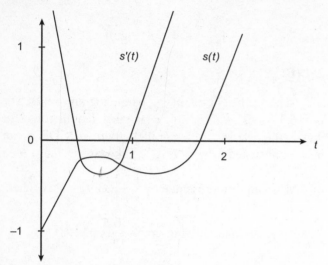

The velocity is given by $v(t) = 6t^2 - 8t + 2$.

The acceleration $a(t) = 12t - 8$ vanishes at $t = \frac{2}{3}$; at this time the velocity has reached its minimum. This occurs during the interval $[0, 2]$.

Therefore, the minimum velocity of $v = -\frac{2}{3}$ occurs at $t = \frac{2}{3}$.

32. (C)

Draw a line through the set of data points. Notice that low grade levels go with low hours of reading, and that high grade levels go with high hours of reading. Next, evaluate the truth of each possible answer. The graph shows that as the grade level goes up, the number of reading hours goes up.

33. (D)

$$f(c) = c^3 - c - 1, f(-c) = -c^3 + c - 1$$
$$c^3 - c - 1 = -c^3 + c - 1$$
$$c^3 = c$$
$$\therefore c = -1, 0, \text{ or } 1$$

34. (A)

$$f'(x) = 6x - 12$$
$$f'(c) = 0$$
$$6c - 12 = 0$$
$$c = 2$$

35. (C)

is the correct response. Eight elephants are available to be selected for the first position. Given that the first elephant has been selected, only 7 elephants are left to be selected for the second position. The first and second positions have been selected, leaving 6 for the third position. Thus $8 \times 7 \times 6 = 336$. (A), (B), and (D) are incorrect because they do not illustrate the fundamental counting principle for this example.

36. (C)

The distance of $\overline{AB} = \sqrt{[(5 - (-1)]^2 + (3 - 5)^2}$ $= \sqrt{36 + 4} = \sqrt{40}$. Point C must be at a location such that the distance of $\overline{BC}$ is also $\sqrt{40}$. Note that for answer choice C, the distance of $\overline{BC} = \sqrt{(7 - 5)^2 + (-3 - 3)^2} = \sqrt{4 + 36} = \sqrt{40}$. For answer choice (A), the distance would be $\sqrt{53}$. For answer choice (B), the distance would be $\sqrt{16}$. For answer choice (D), the distance would be $\sqrt{41}$.

37. (C)

The sequence of steps is: subtract 3 from 9 to get 6, square 7 to get 49, divide 49 by 6 to get, $8\frac{1}{6}$, then finally to add 5 to $8\frac{1}{6}$ to get $13\frac{1}{6}$.

38. (B)

$$2, 2, 2, 3, 3, 4, 4, 4, 5$$

The two modes are 2 and 4. Answer Choice (A) is wrong since it has three modes. Answer Choice (C) is wrong since 4 is the only mode. Answer Choice (D) is wrong since 3 is the only mode.

39. (B)

The commutative property of numbers states that $a + b = b + a$ and that $(a)(b) = (b)(a)$. Using the latter equation, 7 replaces a and $3 + 2$ replaces b.

40. (A)

Using the ordered pairs $(0, 7)$ and $(3, 1)$, the slope of the line containing these points is $(1 - 7)/(3 - 0) = -2$. Using the point-slope formula with the point $(0, 7)$, we have $y - 7 = -2(x - 0)$, which simplifies to $y = -2x + 7$. To find the value of a, substitute -5 for y. So, $-5 = -2x + 7$. Simplifying, $-12 = -2x$, and so $x = 6$. Likewise, substitute 9 for x to find the value of b. $y = (-2)(9) + 7 = -11$. Finally, $(6)(-11) = -66$.

Part B: Solutions

41.

a. Let $P(A)$ represent the probability of event A occurring. $P(B)$ represent the probability of event B occurring, $P(\overline{A})$ represent the probability of event A not occurring, and $P(\overline{B})$ represent the probability of event B not occurring. $P(\overline{A}) = 1 - 0.80 = 0.20$ and $P(\overline{B}) = 1 - 0.30 = 0.70$. Then $P(\overline{A} \text{ and } \overline{B}) = P(\overline{A}) \cap P(\overline{B}) = (0.20)(0.70) = 0.14$

b. The probability of at least one of these two events occurring is given by the formula $P(A \cup B) = P(A) + P(B) - P(A \cap B)$. Since these events are independent, $P(A \cap B) = P(A) \cdot P(B)$. Thus, $P(A \cup B) = 0.80 + 0.30 - (0.80)(0.30) = 0.86$

c. The probability of exactly one of A and B occurring is given by $P(A) \cdot P(\overline{B}) + P(\overline{A}) \cdot P(B) = (0.80)(0.70) + (0.20)(0.30) = 0.62$

42.

a.

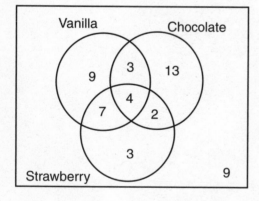

b. $9 + 13 + 3 = 25$ students like exactly one of these flavors.

c. Using the 9 inside the circle representing vanilla and the 9 outside the circles, there are $9 + 9 = 18$ students who like neither chocolate nor strawberry.

43.

a.

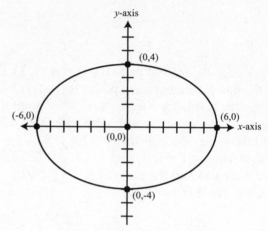

The center should be labeled (0, 0). The length of the major axis is $2 \times \sqrt{36} = 12$, so each x-intercept is 6 units from (0, 0). The x-intercepts are (-6, 0) and (6, 0). The length of the minor axis is $2 \times \sqrt{16} = 8$, so each y-intercept is 4 units from (0, 0). The y-intercepts are (0, -4) and (0, 4).

b. Let $(-c, 0)$ and $(c, 0)$ represent the coordinates of the foci, since the foci must be located on the major axis.

For the ellipse,

$$\frac{x^2}{a^2} + \frac{y^2}{b^2} = 1, \; c = \sqrt{a^2 - b^2} = \sqrt{6^2 - 4^2} = \sqrt{20}$$

Thus, the foci are located at $\left(\sqrt{20}, 0\right)$ and $\left(-\sqrt{20}, 0\right)$.

c. If $x = y$, the original equation can be written as $\frac{x^2}{36} + \frac{x^2}{16} = 1$. Multiplying by 144, the equation becomes $4x^2 + 9x^2 = 144$. Solving, $x^2 = \frac{144}{13}$, so $x \approx \pm 3.33$. The two points are (-3.33, -3.33) and (3.33, 3.33).

Praxis II

Middle School
Mathematics Test (0069)

Answer Sheets

Practice Test 1 Answer Sheet

1. Ⓐ Ⓑ Ⓒ Ⓓ
2. Ⓐ Ⓑ Ⓒ Ⓓ
3. Ⓐ Ⓑ Ⓒ Ⓓ
4. Ⓐ Ⓑ Ⓒ Ⓓ
5. Ⓐ Ⓑ Ⓒ Ⓓ
6. Ⓐ Ⓑ Ⓒ Ⓓ
7. Ⓐ Ⓑ Ⓒ Ⓓ
8. Ⓐ Ⓑ Ⓒ Ⓓ
9. Ⓐ Ⓑ Ⓒ Ⓓ
10. Ⓐ Ⓑ Ⓒ Ⓓ
11. Ⓐ Ⓑ Ⓒ Ⓓ
12. Ⓐ Ⓑ Ⓒ Ⓓ
13. Ⓐ Ⓑ Ⓒ Ⓓ
14. Ⓐ Ⓑ Ⓒ Ⓓ
15. Ⓐ Ⓑ Ⓒ Ⓓ

16. Ⓐ Ⓑ Ⓒ Ⓓ
17. Ⓐ Ⓑ Ⓒ Ⓓ
18. Ⓐ Ⓑ Ⓒ Ⓓ
19. Ⓐ Ⓑ Ⓒ Ⓓ
20. Ⓐ Ⓑ Ⓒ Ⓓ
21. Ⓐ Ⓑ Ⓒ Ⓓ
22. Ⓐ Ⓑ Ⓒ Ⓓ
23. Ⓐ Ⓑ Ⓒ Ⓓ
24. Ⓐ Ⓑ Ⓒ Ⓓ
25. Ⓐ Ⓑ Ⓒ Ⓓ
26. Ⓐ Ⓑ Ⓒ Ⓓ
27. Ⓐ Ⓑ Ⓒ Ⓓ
28. Ⓐ Ⓑ Ⓒ Ⓓ
29. Ⓐ Ⓑ Ⓒ Ⓓ
30. Ⓐ Ⓑ Ⓒ Ⓓ

31. Ⓐ Ⓑ Ⓒ Ⓓ
32. Ⓐ Ⓑ Ⓒ Ⓓ
33. Ⓐ Ⓑ Ⓒ Ⓓ
34. Ⓐ Ⓑ Ⓒ Ⓓ
35. Ⓐ Ⓑ Ⓒ Ⓓ
36. Ⓐ Ⓑ Ⓒ Ⓓ
37. Ⓐ Ⓑ Ⓒ Ⓓ
38. Ⓐ Ⓑ Ⓒ Ⓓ
39. Ⓐ Ⓑ Ⓒ Ⓓ
40. Ⓐ Ⓑ Ⓒ Ⓓ

Short Constructed-Response Answer Sheets

Begin your work on this page. If necessary, continue on the next page.

Continue on the next page if necessary.

Continuation of your work from previous page, if necessary.

Continuation of your work from previous page, if necessary.

Practice Test 2 Answer Sheet

1. Ⓐ Ⓑ Ⓒ Ⓓ   16. Ⓐ Ⓑ Ⓒ Ⓓ   31. Ⓐ Ⓑ Ⓒ Ⓓ

2. Ⓐ Ⓑ Ⓒ Ⓓ   17. Ⓐ Ⓑ Ⓒ Ⓓ   32. Ⓐ Ⓑ Ⓒ Ⓓ

3. Ⓐ Ⓑ Ⓒ Ⓓ   18. Ⓐ Ⓑ Ⓒ Ⓓ   33. Ⓐ Ⓑ Ⓒ Ⓓ

4. Ⓐ Ⓑ Ⓒ Ⓓ   19. Ⓐ Ⓑ Ⓒ Ⓓ   34. Ⓐ Ⓑ Ⓒ Ⓓ

5. Ⓐ Ⓑ Ⓒ Ⓓ   20. Ⓐ Ⓑ Ⓒ Ⓓ   35. Ⓐ Ⓑ Ⓒ Ⓓ

6. Ⓐ Ⓑ Ⓒ Ⓓ   21. Ⓐ Ⓑ Ⓒ Ⓓ   36. Ⓐ Ⓑ Ⓒ Ⓓ

7. Ⓐ Ⓑ Ⓒ Ⓓ   22. Ⓐ Ⓑ Ⓒ Ⓓ   37. Ⓐ Ⓑ Ⓒ Ⓓ

8. Ⓐ Ⓑ Ⓒ Ⓓ   23. Ⓐ Ⓑ Ⓒ Ⓓ   38. Ⓐ Ⓑ Ⓒ Ⓓ

9. Ⓐ Ⓑ Ⓒ Ⓓ   24. Ⓐ Ⓑ Ⓒ Ⓓ   39. Ⓐ Ⓑ Ⓒ Ⓓ

10. Ⓐ Ⓑ Ⓒ Ⓓ   25. Ⓐ Ⓑ Ⓒ Ⓓ   40. Ⓐ Ⓑ Ⓒ Ⓓ

11. Ⓐ Ⓑ Ⓒ Ⓓ   26. Ⓐ Ⓑ Ⓒ Ⓓ

12. Ⓐ Ⓑ Ⓒ Ⓓ   27. Ⓐ Ⓑ Ⓒ Ⓓ

13. Ⓐ Ⓑ Ⓒ Ⓓ   28. Ⓐ Ⓑ Ⓒ Ⓓ

14. Ⓐ Ⓑ Ⓒ Ⓓ   29. Ⓐ Ⓑ Ⓒ Ⓓ

15. Ⓐ Ⓑ Ⓒ Ⓓ   30. Ⓐ Ⓑ Ⓒ Ⓓ

Short Constructed-Response Answer Sheets

Begin your essay on this page. If necessary, continue on the next page.

Continue on the next page if necessary.

Continuation of your essay from previous page, if necessary.

Continuation of your essay from previous page, if necessary.

Practice Test 3 Answer Sheet

1. Ⓐ Ⓑ Ⓒ Ⓓ   16. Ⓐ Ⓑ Ⓒ Ⓓ   31. Ⓐ Ⓑ Ⓒ Ⓓ

2. Ⓐ Ⓑ Ⓒ Ⓓ   17. Ⓐ Ⓑ Ⓒ Ⓓ   32. Ⓐ Ⓑ Ⓒ Ⓓ

3. Ⓐ Ⓑ Ⓒ Ⓓ   18. Ⓐ Ⓑ Ⓒ Ⓓ   33. Ⓐ Ⓑ Ⓒ Ⓓ

4. Ⓐ Ⓑ Ⓒ Ⓓ   19. Ⓐ Ⓑ Ⓒ Ⓓ   34. Ⓐ Ⓑ Ⓒ Ⓓ

5. Ⓐ Ⓑ Ⓒ Ⓓ   20. Ⓐ Ⓑ Ⓒ Ⓓ   35. Ⓐ Ⓑ Ⓒ Ⓓ

6. Ⓐ Ⓑ Ⓒ Ⓓ   21. Ⓐ Ⓑ Ⓒ Ⓓ   36. Ⓐ Ⓑ Ⓒ Ⓓ

7. Ⓐ Ⓑ Ⓒ Ⓓ   22. Ⓐ Ⓑ Ⓒ Ⓓ   37. Ⓐ Ⓑ Ⓒ Ⓓ

8. Ⓐ Ⓑ Ⓒ Ⓓ   23. Ⓐ Ⓑ Ⓒ Ⓓ   38. Ⓐ Ⓑ Ⓒ Ⓓ

9. Ⓐ Ⓑ Ⓒ Ⓓ   24. Ⓐ Ⓑ Ⓒ Ⓓ   39. Ⓐ Ⓑ Ⓒ Ⓓ

10. Ⓐ Ⓑ Ⓒ Ⓓ   25. Ⓐ Ⓑ Ⓒ Ⓓ   40. Ⓐ Ⓑ Ⓒ Ⓓ

11. Ⓐ Ⓑ Ⓒ Ⓓ   26. Ⓐ Ⓑ Ⓒ Ⓓ

12. Ⓐ Ⓑ Ⓒ Ⓓ   27. Ⓐ Ⓑ Ⓒ Ⓓ

13. Ⓐ Ⓑ Ⓒ Ⓓ   28. Ⓐ Ⓑ Ⓒ Ⓓ

14. Ⓐ Ⓑ Ⓒ Ⓓ   29. Ⓐ Ⓑ Ⓒ Ⓓ

15. Ⓐ Ⓑ Ⓒ Ⓓ   30. Ⓐ Ⓑ Ⓒ Ⓓ

Short Constructed-Response Answer Sheets

Begin your essay on this page. If necessary, continue on the next page.

Continue on the next page if necessary.

Continuation of your essay from previous page, if necessary.

Continuation of your essay from previous page, if necessary.

Installing REA's TestWare®

SYSTEM REQUIREMENTS

Pentium 75 MHz (300 MHz recommended) or a higher or compatible processor; Microsoft Windows 98 or later; 64 MB available RAM; Internet Explorer 5.5 or higher.

INSTALLATION

1. Insert the PRAXIS Middle School Mathematics 0069 CD-ROM into the CD-ROM drive.

2. If the installation doesn't begin automatically, from the Start Menu choose the RUN command. When the RUN dialog box appears, type d:\setup (where d is the letter of your CD-ROM drive) at the prompt and click OK.

3. The installation process will begin. A dialog box proposing the directory "C:\Program Files\REA\Praxis_0069\" will appear. If the name and location are suitable, click OK. If you wish to specify a different name or location, type it in and click OK.

4. Start the PRAXIS Middle School Mathematics TestWare® application by double-clicking on the icon.

REA's PRAXIS Middle School Mathematics TestWare® is **EASY** to **LEARN AND USE**. To achieve maximum benefits, we recommend that you take a few minutes to go through the on-screen tutorial on your computer. The "screen buttons" are also explained here to familiarize you with the program.

SSD ACCOMMODATIONS FOR STUDENTS WITH DISABILITIES

Many students qualify for extra time to take the PRAXIS Middle School Mathematics 0069 exam, and our TestWare® can be adapted to accommodate your time extension. This allows you to practice under the same extended-time accommodations that you will receive on the actual test day. To customize your TestWare® to suit the most common extensions, visit our website at www.rea.com/ssd.

TECHNICAL SUPPORT

REA's TestWare® is backed by customer and technical support. For questions about **installation or operation of your software**, contact us at:

> **Research & Education Association**
> **Phone: (732) 819-8880 (9 a.m. to 5 p.m. ET, Monday–Friday)**
> **Fax: (732) 819-8808**
> **Website: *www.rea.com***
> **E-mail: info@rea.com**

Note to Windows XP Users: In order for the TestWare® to function properly, please install and run the application under the same computer administrator-level user account. Installing the TestWare® as one user and running it as another could cause file-access path conflicts.